Mayer, Egon, 1944—

Love & tradition

DATE DUE

APR 6 1995			
APR 1 1 1995			

LOVE & TRADITION

Marriage between Jews and Christians

LOVE & TRADITION

Marriage between Jews and Christians

EGON MAYER

PLENUM PRESS • NEW YORK AND LONDON

Library of Congress Cataloging in Publication Data

Mayer, Egon, 1944–
  Love and tradition.

  Bibliography: p.
  Includes index.
  1. Marriage, Mixed—United States. 2. Marriage—Religious aspects—Judaism. 3.
Jews—United States—Social conditions. I. Title.
HQ1031.M379   1985   306.8'43   85-6588
ISBN 0-306-42043-0

Plenum Press is a Division of Plenum Publishing Corporation
233 Spring Street, New York, N.Y. 10013

Printed in the United States of America

To My Parents
Eugene and Hedy Mayer,
who have imparted tradition with love
to their children
and grandchildren.

PREFACE

This book is about a particular kind of marriage: intermarriage. The kind of marriage that occurs when a Jew marries a Christian or an Italian marries a Greek, or even when a Mormon from Utah marries a WASP from New England. In all such marriages, men and women are moved by their love for one another to cross significant social boundaries. Their desires for personal happiness frequently place them at odds with the time-honored norms of their ethnic or religious heritage.

The primary focus of the book is on the intermarriage of Jews and Christians because that form of marriage has been resisted by both groups longer and more vigorously than any other, at least in the Western World. Yet despite powerfully entrenched resistance to such intermarriages for at least the past 2,000 years, the rate at which young Jews have been marrying Christians in the past several decades has risen dramatically. Not more than two in one hundred young Jews married Christians in America as late as in the 1920s. By the early 1980s nearly four out of ten did. As late as the 1940s, more than 60 percent of the American public at large disapproved of marriages between Jews and Christians, when asked in public opinion surveys. By 1980, nearly 80 percent approved of them. In short, the last half of the twentieth century has witnessed a shift in the balance of the forces of tradition and those of love and personal preference in the process of mate selection.

The rapid growth of intermarriage has created extraordinary new family circumstances for hundreds of thousands of families—Jews and Christians alike. From cuisine to child rearing to the celebration of holidays and personal life cycle events, families are being challenged to deal emotionally as well as interpersonally with the cross-pressures of divergent (and, at times, antagonistic) cultural traditions.

To some, intermarriage represents the fulfillment of the American dream emblazoned on our national coinage, *E Pluribus Unum* (from many, one). It is the ultimate embodiment of the melting pot. To others, it represents the inevitable curse of equality; the price that all minority groups must be willing to pay in the coinage of their own valued traditions for living peaceably in a free and pluralistic society.

Those who live in such marriage know, of course, that living with intermarriage generally does not generate any grand ideological conclusions. Rather, it constitutes an often delicate balancing of the pulls and tugs of love and tradition; a balancing between the loyalties to individuals and loyalties to ancestral memories; attachments to the compelling present and affinities to a lingering past.

Parents of intermarriers are often puzzled and hurt by what they see in their children's marriage as a rejection of their own values and traditions. They frequently sense that they have failed somehow as parents in conveying the importance of their heritage to their children. Guilt, then, mingles with resentment and feeble attempts to control the lives of young (and, at times, not so young) adults. The result is often a strained relationship between the newlyweds and their parents. Ultimately, the strains can undermine both the peace of mind and the relationships of all concerned, and contribute further to the erosion of family traditions.

Children of intermarriages face unique problems not of their own making. In an effort to prevent confusion or inner conflict, their parents often keep from them the symbolic and normative diversity of their mixed cultural heritage. They expect their children to "make their own decision" about "what they want to be" ethnically or religiously—as if it were possible to make such choices without an understanding of particular heritages from early childhood on. What kinds of choices such children make, and how they relate to the heritages and communities of their choice, is the growing concern of religious educators and communal leaders, particularly in the Jewish community. The identity choices of these children promise to have a powerful effect on the size and the characteristics of the Jewish community in America, on the values and life-styles that have been customarily associated with American Jewry. They are also a vivid reflection of the kind of person who is molded in the "melting pot."

The object of this book is to place the modern Jewish intermarriage experience in the broader context of the evolution of the modern American family and the parallel development of Jewish identity. It is hoped that doing so will not only illuminate that experience for all those who are most directly concerned with it, but will also shed new light on the complex relationships of group heritage, personal identity, and family life.

In the introduction to his seminal work, *The Uprooted* (1951), the great American historian Oscar Handlin wrote, "Once I thought to write the history of immigrants in America. Then I discovered that the immigrants *were* American history."[1] Somewhat analogously, I might say that in trying to discover the nature of intermarriage, one inevitably comes to the realization that at its core we are looking at the dynamics of modern marriage itself. In some fundamental respects, there is little that separates marriage and intermarriage. At best (or worst), the latter is but a subset of the former.

All of us come from somewhat divergent heritages even if we have highly similar backgrounds, and rare is the husband and wife—even if they have virtually identical ethnic and religious group backgrounds—who continue to feel the same way about their heritage throughout their lives together. Therefore, in many ways, the study of intermarriage ultimately leads to general insights into the ways in which married couples reconcile their feelings for one another with their feelings about ethnic and religious group identification.

As of 1980, there were about 5½ million Jews living in the United States. Of these, about 350 thousand are married (or have been married) to partners who were not born Jews. Some, of course, have become Jews. It is also estimated that these marriages have produced between 4 to 6 hundred thousand children. All told, there are nearly 1 million individuals who are directly involved in intermarriages between Jews and non-Jews. If one considers that these nuclear families are each connected to in-laws, grandparents, siblings, and wider kinship networks, it is readily apparent that these intermarriages touch on the lives of literally millions of Jews and Christians. In the Jewish community, one will hardly find a single family, except perhaps among the most traditional, whose lives have not been touched by intermarriage.

Life experience has made experts of many men and women about intermarriage but, in spite of this, the subject arouses strong feelings and challenges deeply held convictions. Many Jews and Christians are troubled by the prospect of their children "marrying out," even when they themselves are not particularly religious. Many are troubled without really being able to explain to themselves or to others, and especially to their children, why they feel this way. When sober discussion would be most in order, the subject frequently generates more heat than light. The ambivalence that many feel about their own commitments to human brotherhood, to the primacy of the love relationship, and to individualism, on the one hand, and the strong desire to pass on certain traditions of one's ethnic and religious group, on the other, often leads to intense friction between parents and their adult children, among couples who are contemplating (or are already in) an intermarriage, and throughout the wider ethnic and religious community. If this book sheds a little cool light in the places where there is now intense heat, it will have accomplished much of its purpose.

Given the nature of this book, a confessional word is also in order right at the start. I am not intermarried; at least not in the sense of having crossed any ethnic or religious line. My wife and I shared Orthodox Jewish-Hungarian ancestors as far back as we can tell, yet this incidental biographical detail glosses over the fact that we had profoundly different conceptions about how our shared ancestral heritage ought to be integrated into our everyday lives. We struggled with the issue of how to reconcile love and tradition, almost as a matter of course. The shared terms of the struggle, I suspect, made it easier for us to understand the passions and antipathies of the other intuitively. Much does not have to be spoken because if you can understand another's words, you can also understand another's silences. With all that, our struggles have not been harmoniously resolved.

The shared universe of discourse that underlaid our own struggle with love and tradition is far less clear for couples who draw their identities from different cultural wellsprings. I have no doubt, therefore, that my life experience is not a sufficient basis for expertise.

The expertise that informs this book is the life experience of others. For background, it draws on a decade of extensive reading in the social science literature of marriage and family life, generally, and in the literature dealing with intermarriage, specifically. But most importantly, it draws on a body of survey data, and personal interviews with intermarried families since 1975. It was in that year that the American Jewish Committee undertook the sponsorship of a series of investigations into the causes and consequences of intermarriage between Jews and non-Jews. In a venerable tradition of commitment to dispassionate social science research in matters concerning human relations in general, and Jewish family life in particular, the Committee commissioned me, in my capacity as a sociologist, to carry out these investigations. Between 1977 and 1979 we conducted a nationwide survey of some 450 intermarried couples in communities from coast to coast, including communities in Los Angeles, New York, Cleveland, and Dallas.[2] Nearly one-quarter of the couples we interviewed were couples in which the partner who was not born Jewish had converted either just before the marriage or after it. For the sake of conceptual precision, I will refer to the marriages of these couples as "conversionary" in subsequent discussions, in order to distinguish them from those of couples in which neither spouse converted to the religion of the other; these I shall refer to as "mixed marriages." I will continue to use the term "intermarriage" as a generic term to cover both types.

Between 1981 and 1983 we conducted a follow-up survey of the children of the couples who were studied earlier in order to gauge the impact of intermarriage upon the lives of the generation that is raised in a familial melting pot, so to speak.[3]

In the course of doing these two studies, and speaking about them afterward to literally thousands of people, I have had the unique opportunity to be granted glimpses into the lives of couples as they come to grips with the dynamic forces of love and tradition. It is their life experiences that constitutes the real base of expertise for this book.

Although the book makes continuous reference to Jews and Christians, it will be clear that in a great many instances the non-Jewish person in the intermarriage is not a Christian. In fact, the marriage with which the book opens is between a Jew and a Buddhist. Also, in a great many instances, even if the non-Jewish marriage partner were born a Catholic or a Protestant, he or she has stopped identifying with his or her religion of birth. Therefore, many intermarriages are not, strictly speaking, between people who continue to identify with different religions. However, the central theme of this book is that all people are carriers of at least some of the elements of a religion-based tradition. To the extent that the overwhelming majority of Americans have a Christian background, intermarriages between Jews and non-Jews invariably include a person of Christian ancestry. Therefore, it is appropriate to think of most intermarriages in which Jews are involved as marriages between Jews and Christians.

ACKNOWLEDGMENTS

This book is the result of a decade of research, and a unique relationship. It was in the spring of 1975 that Yehuda Rosenman, Director of the Jewish Communal Affairs Department of the American Jewish Committee, convened a "brainstorming" luncheon of scholars to discuss the broad range of issues concerning intermarriage and its impact on Jewish family life. There were many talented colleagues present. Perhaps, I simply spoke up the most. But, out of that intellectually stormy session grew a personal and professional relationship between us that led to two pioneering studies of intermarried couples and their children.

Yehuda's grasp of the deep anxieties at the heart of the Jewish community and the Jewish family has inspired and charted the course of these studies from the beginning. His Old-World personal charm and his masterful ability to generate institutional support for what he believed to be vital studies of real-life concerns were the indispensable elements that sustained these studies. My gratitude for his avuncular personal encouragement can only be acknowledged, not sufficiently repaid. It was he who mustered the support of his august organization, the American Jewish Committee, on behalf of these studies, and he who continued to rally the interest and enthusiasm of both its professional staff and lay leaders in their progress.

Milton Himmelfarb, Director of Research, and Irving Levine, Director of the National Affairs Department, both of the AJC, stimulated my thinking early on about the historical and

15

cross-cultural dimensions of intermarriage. Sonya F. Kaufer, Director of Publications at the AJC, and her able associate, Francine Etlinger, provided strong and invaluable guidance in the presentation of social science information for non-professional readers. They have taught me to respect the English language *sans* jargon. I hope their lessons have not been forgotten in the pages that follow. Morton Yarmon, Director of the AJC's Public Relations Department, proved to be an indispensable guide to the strange and wondrous ways of the mass media, without which even the most brilliant studies remain hidden from public view in the ivory towers of academia. Gladys Rosen, Program Specialist in the Jewish Communal Affairs Department, has been a steadfast friend and sounding board who helped nurture me in my struggles with the larger and smaller issues surrounding my studies. Larry Grossman, David Singer, and Ann Bloom have all taken turns helping to sharpen my understanding of some of the facets of intermarriage by their intelligent and witty reluctance to be easily impressed with the findings of sociologists.

In addition to its professional staff, some of the lay leaders of the American Jewish Committee also played a significant role in helping to carry my intermarriage studies to fruition. E. Robert Goodkind, Robert Rifkind, and Ruth Septee played major roles in the development and execution of the intermarriage studies, as did the lay and technical advisory committees of the Charles and Elaine Petschek National Jewish Family Center.

Colleagues who have become good friends over the years, particularly through our mutual ties to the Association for the Sociological Study of Jewry, such as Alvin Chenkin, Steven M. Cohen, Harold Himmelfarb, Rela Geffen Monson, Esther Fleischman, Paul Ritterband, and Chaim I. Waxman have helped to deepen as well as broaden my understanding of Jewish sociology and its relevance to intermarriage. Other friendships that have helped my understanding of the subject include those with Paul and Rachel Cowan, Lydia Kukoff, David and Lena Romanoff, and Frank and Diane Roma.

At my academic home, the Department of Sociology in Brooklyn College, I have been both sustained and challenged by the intellectual companionship of Sidney Aronson, Paul Charosh, Oscar Glantz, Laura Kitch, Marvin Koenigsberg, Roberta Satow, and Mervin Verbit. I am also deeply grateful for the personal support of Dr. Robert Hess, President of Brooklyn College. Other members of the Brooklyn College staff whose support is gratefully acknowledged include Marilyn Rubenstein and Anne Lane, our departmental secretaries, the late Dr. James Wang of the Brooklyn College Computer Center, and Julio Berger, David Pasternak, and Wong Chi of the Computer Center. The research assistance of my students, Heidi Altman, Bart Bashist, James Creamer, Donna McKeon, and Ibrahim Nigri is also gratefully acknowledged.

Since I began my studies of intermarriage, I have had the privilege of being invited to speak about my findings to literally hundreds of community groups from coast to coast. Wherever I have spoken, I have had my knowledge and experience deepened by the questions and comments of the men and women who came to listen and ended up sharing their own life experiences with me.

Perhaps, the most important contributors to this book will have to remain unnamed. They are the hundreds of couples and their children who gave generously of their time and their thoughts by participating in my surveys. The pledge of confidentiality does not permit naming them personally. But I hope that they will recognize themselves through the pseudonyms in the pages that follow, as well as the deep sense of gratitude with which their confidences were accepted.

Where would an author be without a typist and an editor? Tom Robinson has brought a degree of professionalism to the typing of research questionnaires as well as to the final manu-

script of this book that is grievously understated by the appella-
tion "typist." Linda Greenspan Regan, of Plenum Publishing
Corporation, is gratefully acknowledged for urging and encour-
aging the writing of this book from its inception on. Marshall
Sklare, the *eminence gris* of modern Jewish sociology, played the
role of the matchmaker in bringing me and Plenum together in
the first place. For that we shall all remain in his debt.

Finally, some personal words of gratitude: to my dear
friend, Dr. Joseph Marbach, my "shabbes friend," as my
daughter calls him, for the many hours of thought and talk in
which I've learned some of life's most important lessons about
the dialectic of work, thought, friendship, and the Sabbath. I
pray that we both have many more fruitful years of that kind of
learning together. And, to my daughter, Daphne. At the age of
eight years she has been hard put to understand all my "No's"
to her entreaties of "Daddy, come and play something with me"
on evenings and weekends. I only hope that in the years ahead,
when she will be old enough to understand the contents of
these pages, she will realize that I had been planting intellectual
seeds for her garden all along. And, to Susan for eighteen years
of marriage in which she impelled me to grow through confrontation with many of the issues that follow in this book.

CONTENTS

Chapter One

TWO CAN MAKE A REVOLUTION

Two Can Make a
Revolution

Paul's grandmother, Ba Thi Tu, had been cooking for the Bar
Mitzvah for days alongside her daughter, Josephine Tu Steinman. The menu included veal with black mushroom sauce, Vietnamese meatballs, beef chow fun, chicken and cashew nuts, rice
noodles, and other Oriental delicacies. A dish calling for pork
had to be eliminated, along with shellfish dishes, because they
were not kosher.

This was no ordinary Bar Mitzvah fare: no chopped herring,
stuffed derma, or matzoh ball soup here. This was the home-
catered Bar Mitzvah feast of Paul Steinman—the son of Ron
Steinman, an executive at NBC–TV News—and Josephine
Steinman, formerly Ngoc Suong Tu, a Vietnamese Buddhist
who converted to Judaism after she came to the United States
with her husband.

That *The New York Times* chose to report on the "Bar Mitzvah with a Vietnamese Flavor" (June 29, 1983) is ample indication, of course, that such ceremonies are far from common.
Indeed, such families are far from common. Jews and Vietnamese are generally not found together in large enough numbers to produce more than one or two intermarriages. But the
story highlights what have become increasingly common facts
of family life for Jews, as well as other minorities, since the early
part of the twentieth century. America is blending, and out of its
cultural caldron are emerging life-styles and new customs that
defy age-old distinctions. When it comes to mate selection and
the family forms that follow from it, love triumphs over tradition; inclinations triumph over timeless customs; and even re-

ligious rituals are transfigured to meet private needs and desires.

In that simple human interest story in *The Times*, which focused on the menu rather than on the ironies of the occasion, one can see reflected centuries of tension, and the fermenting of cultural forces and contending human drives coming to fruition.

Paul's Hebrew teacher was *kvelling* (rejoicing) at what appeared to her to be the fulfillment of the American dream. "A blending of two ancient cultures have met here today," Ms. Saletsky said. One is almost moved to the clichéd exultation "Love Conquers All." But as we shall see, such simple generalizations are defied by the complex realities of intermarriages.

Here, and in most other cases, too, love is no blind conqueror. It does not vanquish all other bonds or loyalties. Ron Steinman's Jewishness was important enough for him to have Ngoc Suong convert; important enough to have his children raised as Jews and educated in a Hebrew school; and important enough to have his firstborn son go through the traditional Jewish rite of passage. In subsequent personal conversation with Ron and Josephine, it became apparent that those same Jewish sentiments were not a salient consideration in Ron's mind when he chose to marry the then Ngoc Suong. Moreover, Josephine observed that one of her deeply felt reasons for wanting to become Jewish was her Vietnamese heritage that obliges a married woman to join her fate entirely to her husband and his family. Thus, for her, conversion to Judaism was a traditional wifely obligation. At the same time, for Ron, marriage to a Vietnamese woman was very much a break from his Brooklyn Jewish family tradition. For both, albeit for different reasons and in different ways, love and marriage entailed not following the customary path of their respective families, at least as far as mate selection was concerned.

The modern vocabulary of motives for marriage emphasizes love, compatibility, and mutual fulfillment. It leaves but little room for such considerations as duty, respect for tradition, and responsibility to one's ancestors and parents. Individualism, personalism, and privatism form the cornerstones of contemporary family relationships—at least that is the conventional wisdom. In the light of that wisdom, the very concept—intermarriage—is an anachronism. What should it matter, as the question is often asked, what a person's religious, ethnic, racial, etc., background is? Only one man and one woman are united in a marriage. Ron and Ngoc Suong no doubt underwent such questioning before their marriage; at least in their own minds, if not with one another and their respective parents.

Yet their very life as a modern Reform Jewish family is a testimonial to the persistence of tradition, albeit in modern garb. The fact that she became Jewish, an American, and changed her name to Josephine is an indication of just how important it was for both of them to bridge the cultural and religious differences that many think should not matter any more to modern men and women living in the age of hi-tech.

The brief story of Paul's Bar Mitzah points to a multitude of insights about what it means to be a Jew in modern America; about what it means to be a member of a religious or ethnic minority in a liberal, pluralistic society; about what it means to be a family today; and, indeed, about the very nature of identity in modern society.

The story symbolizes the simultaneous drive of individuals to pursue their own individual happiness under circumstances that are made unpredictable by the impersonal forces of history (e.g., war). At the same time, the story also symbolizes the deeply rooted tenacity of traditions and the capacity of free individuals to blend and connect the most time-honored traditions in the most unconventional ways. In a sense, the story of Paul's Bar Mitzvah epitomizes the irony of Jewish survival.

The image of love emerging out of the ashes of war has always been one of profound irony. That an American-Jewish bureau chief for NBC, covering the war in Vietnam, should return to the United States with a Buddhist wife who becomes a

Jew, and that they should, in turn, raise Jewish children, is truly newsworthy. At least one of the sources of the irony is war itself. That love should emerge from it is somewhat understandable, but that it should leave intact two people's attachments to their heritage, despite their experience of the war and despite their love across vastly different heritages, is remarkable. To be sure, the Steinmans' experience is virtually unique, and hardly generalizable. Yet it recalls for me my own first encounter with Jewish intermarriage as a child, in the person of one of our closest family friends—Allen Feher, or Sándor bácsi, as I called him—in my childhood in Budapest.

Sándor had been one of my father's closest friends, ever since they were teenagers in Komárom (a small town in southwestern Czechoslovakia). They had attended yeshiva together, both being from Orthodox Jewish families. Sándor had married a few years before World War II and lived a traditional Orthodox Jewish life as a small merchant. When the Nazis entered Hungary in 1944 he happened to be away from home on business. His wife and two children were deported and never returned from the concentration camp. Sándor had gone into hiding in Budapest in the apartment of a Christian friend. There he was befriended by Irene, the daughter of a high-ranking officer in the Hungarian military, naturally, a Christian.

At the end of the war, Sándor and Irene married and had a child. Sándor abandoned his Orthodoxy and even joined the Communist Party—at least for appearance's sake. It helped him advance in the nationalized shop in which he worked. Yet, he continued to cling to a lifelong desire to go to Israel. In Communist Hungary in the late 1940s and early 1950s, that was—for all intents and purposes—a Messianic hope. But Irene, using her family contacts in the government, was able to obtain an exit visa for the three of them. In 1953 (at the close of the Stalinist era), Sándor—an intermarried Jew with a Catholic wife and daughter—immigrated to Israel, the land of his Jewish dreams. Irene never converted. She felt that she had returned to the land of Jesus and continued to live her life as an Israeli Catholic, as did her daughter.

A different war, a different continent and, surely, different personalities, yet one cannot help but feel that the same forces were working their curious chemistry in the lives of the Steinman and the Feher families. Ron and Sándor drew from the same well of tradition. And, for some as yet mysterious reason, Ngoc Suong and Irene both found it to be their desire to link their lives and fates to the ways in which their men would come to grips with their heritages. Ngoc Suong joined Ron Steinman's religion; Irene joined Allen Feher's nation.

Surely neither couple sought to make a social revolution of any kind and would probably be surprised to see themselves spoken of as "revolutionaries." Yet their relationships, along with the multitude of other similar relationships, continue to exert transformative pressures on the ancient culture of the Jewish people, as well as on the laws of a modern nation-state, Israel.

Allen and Irene's daughter, for example, has remained a Christian, but as a young, dynamic woman, she has also served in the Israeli army. Naturally, she met and socialized with Israeli young men, virtually all of whom were Jews. For her, it was hardly a break with any social convention to fall in love with a Jewish man. But marriage for the two of them in Israel was out of the question, since matrimonial law in Israel is determined by Jewish religious regulations that prohibit such marriages. Ironically, they had to "elope" to Cyprus to marry in a Greek civil ceremony so as to be able to live as a legitimately married couple in Israel. Their case, along with untold others, remains a source of festering tension in Israeli political life.

Bar Mitzvahs like that of the Steinmans' also stretches the meaning of the ancient Jewish ritual. According to the *halacha* (the body of Jewish law made up by the commandments in the *Five Books of Moses* and their rabbinic interpretations in the Talmud and subsequent exigetical texts), Bar Mitzvah refers to the ancient legal status of adulthood at which point an adolescent is obligated to abide by the laws. The term applied only to young men who were regarded as having reached their Bar Mitzvah at the age of thirteen. There had been no comparable status for Jewish women, nor a celebration thereof, until the Conservative movement institutionalized the Bat Mitzvah in the 1920s.

Interestingly enough, the Bar Mitzvah was one of the many observances the Reform movement abandoned in the nineteenth century. The Reform movement, born out of the spirit of the enlightenment and German nationalism at the end of the eighteenth century, sought to do away with all those Jewish religious customs that could not be rendered plausible in the light of modern reason and contemporary life-style. The notion that a pubescent young man at the tender age of thirteen should somehow be regarded as a legal adult responsible for his actions was one of those implausible customs in the eyes of the Reform movement.

Consequently, some of the oldest and most respectable Reform temples in America would not permit Bar Mitzvahs to be performed as late as the 1950s, nor were Bat Mitzvahs permitted.

But ancient traditions die hard, and sometimes not at all. The need on the part of Jewish families to signify to themselves and their communities that their children are part of the Jewish fold through some kind of joyous public ceremony could not be eradicated by rational philosophy. The Bar Mitzvah has gradually made its return into the Reform movement since the 1950s. In fact, with the increasing incidence of marriages between Jews and non-Jews, particularly in the Reform community, the Bar Mitzvah has emerged as the signal Jewish ceremony by which an intermarried family publicly proclaims that their child is being raised as a Jew.

In a twist of modern Jewish family history, the Steinmans, as Reform Jews, were celebrating the Bar Mitzvah, which had lost its apparent meaningfulness for Reform Jews earlier. It now

serves a highly potent social and psychological function precisely as a result of intermarriage. To be sure, not all children of
intermarriages go through a Bar or a Bat Mitzvah ceremony.
Indeed, most do not. My own studies have shown that in those
intermarried families in which the non-Jewish spouse does not
convert to Judaism, only about 15 percent of the children will go
through that symbolic Jewish life cycle ceremony. In what we
call conversionary families, in which the formerly non-Jewish
spouse converts to Judaism, as in the case of the Steinmans,
nearly 75 percent of the children go through the ceremony; it
apparently does not take many to stimulate cultural reforms.

The Steinmans' Bar Mitzvah menu also hints at an unfold-
ing cultural revolution. Although most of America's Jews have
relinquished the ethnic distinctiveness of their daily diet over
the past few generations (hardly anyone really lives on chopped
herring, *gefilte* fish, or *chulent* any more), such Jewish ceremonial
occasions as weddings and Bar Mitzvahs are still marked by
highly traditional food. For most modern American Jews, that is
probably one of the salient features of these occasions: the opportunity to recollect the flavors and images of the past through
their palates. But because most typical Jewish homes no longer
prepare traditional Jewish foods as part of their normal diet,
professional Jewish catering has emerged as an industry in its
own right. Ostensibly, the function of the industry is to provide
food and style consistent with the middle-class consumer values
of American Jews. However, its more subtle, latent function is
to serve up a feast of traditions through culinary inventiveness:
to blend the taste of the immigrant with the style of the successful American.

In "olden days," it was not the caterer, but rather the wom-
en of the family who prepared the food for days and weeks
before a Bar Mitzvah or a wedding. One of the objects of the
ceremony was to exhibit before the larger invited community
the mastery of the family of shared food values. "Look at my
kugel," or *strudel*, or *gefilte* fish, the proud mother of a Bar

Mitzvah boy would exclaim to her friends. And recipes, memories of mothers, and culinary techniques would be exchanged.
But who asks a caterer for a recipe or memories of his mother?

Not surprisingly, it was Paul Steinman's Vietnamese grandmother and mother who spent their days cooking in preparation
for the Bar Mitzvah. After all, where do you get a kosher caterer
who cooks Vietnamese style? And the arousal of sensory memories through food is evidently no less important to the Vietnamese than it is to Jews—even if it is at a Bar Mitzvah. But the
irony is this: Given the obvious importance attached to the
memories of the palate by both Jews and Vietnamese, and probably all other ethnic Americans as well, what kind of memories
are being built into young Paul's palate, and what kind of a Bar
Mitzvah feast will he lay out for his own son?

The old adage that an army marches on its stomach may be
true, but, at least from the brief account of Paul Steinman's Bar
Mitzvah feast, it may also be surmised that cultural revolutions
can be instigated in the kitchen.

The ironies of Paul's Bar Mitzvah and the late Sándor bácsi's
marriage to Irene and immigration to Israel all point to the historical tension between love and tradition; between the drive of
the individual for self-expression and fulfillment and his affinity
for the norms and values of his heritage. This tension, of course,
is not unique to intermarriages. It is endemic to all modern
marriages. It is therefore appropriate and necessary to turn our
attention briefly to the role of love and tradition in the making of
modern family life.

Modern marriages, generally, and intermarriages, most
particularly, are based on the feeling that two people share by
being in love. In a brilliantly argued essay, Franceso Alberoni,
the Italian sociologist, has suggested that the experience of falling in love is very much akin to the birth of a social movement; it
is the moment that signals the birth of a new collective "we."

> In an existing social structure, the movement divides whoever
> was united and unites whoever was divided to form a new collec-

tive subject, a "we" which, in the case of falling in love, is formed
by the lover–beloved couple.[1]

"No experience of falling in love exists without the transgres-
sion of a difference," writes Alberoni, and therefore, "falling in
love challenges institutions on the level of their fundamental
values."[2] The potential of two individuals to make a revolution
is realized through love.

But love, like any other revolutionary force, can only trans-
form people or social institutions if it is harnessed in some kind
of ongoing collective enterprise such as marriage. Perhaps for
this reason, love had not been allowed to play a significant role
in mate selection in most societies until the last 200 years.

In a collection of essays with the title *Romanticism: Definition, Explanation and Evaluation* (1965), the historian John B.
Halsted informs us that "the term Romanticism came into currency at the very beginning of the nineteenth century" and referred primarily to the works of poets and writers, later artists
and composers, who gave primacy in their works to moods,
feelings, passions, and enthusiasms.[3] They saw themselves as
rebelling against the strictures of Classicism and Rationalism.
Historians of the modern family, such as Edward Shorter and
Ellen K. Rothman, have shown that at more or less the same
time that Romanticism was emerging as a thematic force in the
world of the arts, romance—the primacy of empathy and spontaneity as well as sexuality between men and women—was
emerging as an ideology on the basis of which couples would
seek to form marriages and families.[4] It is in its latter, more
layman's sense that we will use the terms *romance* and *romantic*.

Whereas love unites, tradition divides. The feelings of love
burst through walls and spill over boundaries of conventionality. The feelings toward a tradition are quite different. No
matter how passionately one may be committed to it, the sentiments inspired by tradition can be expressed only in forms and
rituals that were established by others long ago. Tradition inspires conformity, just as surely as love inspires inventiveness.

Tradition makes careful distinctions in time, in space and, most importantly, between categories of people. Love is oblivious to all that.

In point of fact, modern marriages are not merely based on love. More importantly, they are based on a belief; an ideology of romance that regards the deep psychological and sexual attachments that are experienced as love as socially legitimate and desirable; an adequate basis for the making of a complex relationship called marriage. A related tenet of this ideology of romance is that the social identity or group background of the beloved has no place in the emotional calculus of the loving relationship, nor should it have a role to play in the organization and quality of the marriage that ensues from loving.

But as we shall see in this, as well as in subsequent chapters, the heritages, traditions, cultural memories, and group identities of individuals who fall in love and marry do continue to play a significant role in the individuals' self-concepts and also in the life-styles of their families.

Thus, love is only the spark that may start a revolution. But real social transformation occurs precisely when the energy of love is harnessed and integrated in the flux of established situations: the family, religion, the state, and the community. That the love of two should have such far-reaching consequences, that is a real revolution.

For all these reasons, love and tradition have never lived comfortably with one another. Tracing the history of love in the West since the time of the ancient Greeks, Morton Hunt—a historian—shows vividly, and with some sense of both its drama and its humor, that the "joining of romantic passion, sensuous enjoyment, friendship and marriage" took nearly 2,000 years to evolve to its modern form.[5]

The general lovelessness of ancient marriages is captured in a somewhat cruel Greek adage of the sixth century before the Christian era: "Marriage brings a man only two happy days: the day he takes his bride to his bed, and the day he lays her in her grave."[6] But as late as our own twentieth century, the fictional Goldie, wife of Sholom Aleichem's *Tevyeh, The Milkman* (popularized in America as *Fiddler on the Roof*), is perplexed when her husband asks her, "Do you love me?" She replies:

> For twenty-five years I've washed your clothes, cooked your meals, cleaned your house, given you children, and milked the cow. After twenty-five years, why talk about love right now?[7]

Goldie's words are virtually a mirror image of the ancient Greek view of matrimony attributed by Morton Hunt to the famous orator Demosthenes: "Mistresses we keep for pleasure, concubines for daily attendance upon our needs, and wives to bear us legitimate children and to be our housekeepers."[8]

Undoubtedly, many more wives and husbands probably loved one another, before, as well as during the course of their married life, than one finds recorded in the annals of history. But it is also true, and far more widely established historically, that love has been but rarely considered an acceptable reason, much less an expected forerunner, of matrimony. If love was to be found at all, it was most often to be found briefly before, and frequently outside of, marriage, generally in forbidden relationships.

Marriage, however, was a moral duty and a social responsibility particularly incumbent upon men. It was through marriage that a family name, the family heritage, and property would be passed, unto posterity. Singlehood was as much frowned upon in the ancient Jewish tradition as it was in the ancient Greek and Roman traditions. Indeed, even in colonial America, bachelors were highly suspect and, in most colonies, were burdened with special taxes and generally kept under the watchful eyes of their neighbors. In Connecticut, William Kephart reports, "every kind of obstacle was put in the way of a bachelor keeping his own house. . . . Unless a bachelor had authority to live alone he was fined one pound (£) a week."[9]

But although marriage was a duty almost universally honored by most adults since ancient times, who actually married whom was not left to the individual. Such decisions were too important to be left in private hands, subject to personal whim or fancy. Given its strong social, moral, and religious objectives, marriages were arranged throughout most of history, in both the East and West, by parents, older siblings, and other guardians of family tradition. They made certain that the marriage partners who were chosen for their young ones were consistent with the needs and values of the family and the larger community. Naturally, under such a controlled mate selection system, marriages between Jews and Christians were virtually out of the question on both sides; only social deviants would intermarry.

To be sure, even under such a system, a son or daughter might be granted veto power by a permissive parent over a particular choice. But it is highly unlikely that more than a rare few ever had the freedom to choose a mate based entirely on their private emotional preference and without due regard to the broad conventional preferences of their families and communities. Those who violated the imperatives of custom or clan, the Romeos and Juliets of history, most often paid the price. In short, for much of our history, the dictates of tradition clearly dominated the inclinations of the heart when it came to marriage. It is more than likely that the ancestors of Ron Steinman— as well as those of his wife, Ngoc Suong Tu—were married off in their early teen years to mates chosen by their parents.

It took several far-reaching revolutions, and about two centuries, to dismantle traditional constraints upon mate selection and to replace them with romantic idealism. By the end of the eighteenth century, writes Edward Shorter, "young people began paying much more attention to inner feelings than to outward considerations, such as property and parental wishes, in choosing marriage partners."[10]

The onset of the Industrial Revolution in the latter half of the seventeenth century began to unsettle the closely bunched lives of people in villages and farms, forcing increasing numbers to leave their highly traditional rural enclaves for larger towns and cities.

The feudal West was beginning to stir, shaking the age-old foundations of family organization. Of course, for most Jews, those early stirrings were barely noticed. They would continue to live in restricted isolation from their Christian neighbors for yet another two centuries. But a few famous "court Jews" were beginning to enter intimate political and economic arrangements with dukes and princes in Germany, which, in due time, would lead to even greater intimacies between their children and grandchildren, as one can see among the illustrious Rothschilds. Selma Stern's colorful account of the adventurous lives of the seventeenth-century court Jews amply hints at the advance of the industrial age that was beginning to pave the way for a growing intimacy between Jews and non-Jews.[11] But whether that intimacy would lead to love and marriage would depend on the relative power of tradition and love in the prevailing social norms.

With the benefit of hindsight, we now know that romanticism followed closely on the heels of the American and French revolutions, the two epoch-making revolutions at the end of the eighteenth century that ushered in the modern era. As Edward Shorter put it, in the years after 1750, "the libido unfroze in the blast of the wish to be free." Gradually the idea gained currency that marriage should be much more than a joining of hands, of fortunes, and of families—that it should be a joining of hearts.

At least as it applies to the making of marriages, the romanticism that followed in the wake of two great political revolutions probably advanced much further in the United States than elsewhere in the West. In a delicately drawn history of courtship in America, Ellen Rothman shows that parents increasingly allowed and expected their children to freely choose their own marriage partners.[12] In turn, young men and women recognized that in order to find a mate, they must first find love. Perhaps Thomas Jefferson himself might be credited (or blamed) for the ascendancy of love. After all, it was he who changed the famous slogan of liberty attributed to John Locke ("Life, Liberty, and Property") to "Life, Liberty, and the Pursuit of Happiness."

In a profound analysis of that Jeffersonian turn of phrase, Jan Lewis, a historian, has shown that the freedom to pursue personal happiness soon became a moral as well as a psychological imperative, with wide-ranging effects on both family life and religion.[13] Put succinctly, "in the decades after the Revolution, the head fell victim to the heart." Marriage was now to grow out of passionate desire and was to lead to mutual emotional fulfillment and inner peace, and not simply to outer stability and respectability.

In their *Manifesto of the Communist Party*, Karl Marx and Friedrich Engels argued that the purely economic forces of capitalism that they saw all around them in the Europe of 1848 were sweeping away age-old customs that had governed religion, family life, and social relations in general. However, a closer look at the surge of Romanticism in that era—be it in the form of sublime poetry read in the drawing rooms of the bourgeoisie or in the form of the unbridled sexuality of the lower classes— suggests that it was not the power of capital alone (or even primarily) that was transforming social norms. Rather, it was the revolutionary new idea that each individual had the right to pursue his or her own personal happiness: that society could be so ordered that people might find true happiness in their choice of mates, and that they might try to exploit their own talents to their best possible advantage.

Today, the unconditional value of conjugal love as both the basis for and the proper object of marriage is so thoroughly taken for granted that it is difficult to imagine that it was ever otherwise, or that any alternate view of that tender emotion might be equally valid. But if such social historians as the Frenchman, Philippe Aries; or the Canadian, Edward Shorter; or the American, Morton M. Hunt, are correct, the popular infatuation with romantic love and its close connection in the popular mind with marriage is a relatively recent phenomenon. For most of history, men and women were joined in matrimony out of more practical considerations, such as the demands of social conventionality or the needs for security.

Looking back upon traditional patterns of courtship, Shorter writes,

> All situations in which boys and girls met for the first time were monitored by some larger group. . . . Young women simply did not encounter young men without other people around.[14]

The opportunity for the spontaneous involvement of members of the opposite sex with one another was rigorously controlled so as to prevent undesirable amorous entanglements. The "other people around" were most often parents, older siblings, or even peers who could safeguard the individual against "stepping out" of the bounds of social propriety—emotionally or otherwise. Arranged marriages, which often took place among well-to-do families in Europe, be they Jews or Christians, were the surest way to prevent romance from intruding into the all-important process of family formation. Continuing his backward glance, Shorter continues,

> The most important change in the nineteenth- and twentieth-century courtship has been the surge of sentiment. . . . People started to place affection and personal compatibility at the top of the list of criteria in choosing marriage partners. These new standards became articulated as romantic love. And secondly, even those who continued to use the traditional criteria of prudence and wealth in selecting partners began to behave romantically within these limits.[15]

Like stardust in the trail of a comet, the romantic revolution followed in the wake of twin social revolutions of the eighteenth and nineteenth centuries: the industrial and the democratic.

In the United States, love and the pursuit of happiness had yet another major role in transforming the society. It was to be the flame under the melting pot.

What, then, is the American, this new man? He is neither a
European, nor the descendant of a European; hence that strange
mixture of blood, which you will find in no other country. I could
point out to you a family whose grandfather was an Englishman,
whose wife was Dutch, whose son married a French woman, and
whose present four sons have now four wives of different
nations.[16]

This often-quoted passage, from the pen of French-Ameri-
can Jean De Crevocouer in his *Letters from an American Farmer*
(1782), presaged by some 120 years the theme if not the title of
the Jewish-American Israel Zangwill's play, *The Melting Pot*
(1908).[17] As some critics of the period observed, Zangwill captured in a phrase the spirit of the nation.

The Melting Pot was a drama about a romance, a thinly
veiled imitation of Shakespeare's *Romeo and Juliet*, only with a
happy ending—at least for the couple. David Quixano, a Russian-born Jewish immigrant, falls in love with Vera Revendal, a
Russian-born Christian; both work on the Lower East Side of
New York—that quintessential immigrant ghetto of the turn of
the century. For some reason, Zangwill chose the most un-Rus-
sian last names for his principal characters. Perhaps he thought
that they would blend better if they were not burdened with
more distinctive names. Be that as it may, the young lovers were
determined to marry, despite the turbulance of their emotions
and opposition of their relatives. They put off their marriage
only when it was learned that Vera's father, a colonel in the
Tsar's army, was personally responsible for the killing of
David's family in the Kishinev *pogrom* of 1903.

However, by the end of the play love prevails over all the
sorrow, bitterness, and prejudice. To paraphrase Zangwill, the
shadows of Kishinev melt away in the American crucible. The
young lovers walk hand in hand into the sunset against the
skyline of lower Manhattan, to the background strains of "My
Country 'Tis of Thee."

The play opened at the Columbia Theater in Washington, D. C. with President Theodore Roosevelt in attendance. In fact, the play was dedicated to Roosevelt. When the final curtain fell, Arthur Mann, the historian, writes, the President shouted from his box, "That's a great play, Mr. Zangwill! That's a great play!" *The Melting Pot* went on to become a huge popular success, continues Mann.

> After showing in the nation's capital, it ran for six months in Chicago, and then for 136 performances in New York City. Thereafter, for close to a decade, it played in dozens of cities across America. In 1914 it was produced in London, again before full houses and admiring audiences.[18]

The play became a text in high schools and colleges; it was produced by amateur theatrical groups frequently, and its publisher, Macmillan, reprinted it at least once a year until 1917.

One does not need a great deal of historical insight to understand why that play should have become so popular and, particularly, so highly praised by the official champions of American culture. Between 1870 and 1924 (when the Johnson Act finally stemmed the tide of mass immigration), the population of America more than doubled from about 45 million to about 110 million.[19] The growth was fueled by the entry of about 25 million immigrants, overwhelmingly from southern, eastern, and middle Europe: Jews, Slavs, Poles, Italians, Serbs, Croats, etc. In some of the larger American cities, nearly 40 percent of the population was comprised of the foreign-born and recently arrived immigrants: "The tired, the poor, the wretched refuse of the earth," as Emma Lazarus described them on the base of the Statue of Liberty.

Lincoln Steffens voiced the central question of the period in a title of an article, "What Are We Going to Do with Our Immigrants?"[20] Perforce, the answer had to be assimilation. The pervasive and troubling division between blacks and whites, which continues as the single most salient social division in America,

inevitably drew all immigrants into the general society and
made their gradual assimilation a popular social goal. Ralph
Waldo Emerson gave poetic voice to this sentiment.

> As in the old burning of the Temple at Corinth, by the melting
> and intermixture of silver and gold and other metals a new com-
> pound more precious than any, called Corinthian brass, was
> formed, so in this continent—asylum of all nations—the energy
> of the Irish, Germans, Swedes, Poles, Cossacks, and all the Euro-
> pean tribes—of the Africans, and the Polynesians—will construct
> a new race, a new religion, a new state, a new literature, which
> will be as vigorous as the new Europe which came out of the
> smelting pot of the Dark Ages.[21]

Although social scientists make useful distinctions between
such concepts as assimilation, amalgamation, and pluralism, it
is clear from all the studies of the great immigration of that
period that the process of Americanization was to involve both
the relinquishing of many old-world traditions and the acquisi-
tion of many new ones.

How rapidly the process would occur in the lives of particular individuals, and in the collective history of one ethnic group
or another, was to vary according to biographical and social
circumstances. The peddler who found himself in the hinterlands of Pennsylvania was surely Americanized more rapidly
than his cousin who manned a pushcart on New York's Lower
East Side. But what would ultimately make America a true amalgam—an embodiment of the ideal printed on her coinage, *E
Pluribus Unum*—was to be a universal human emotion: love.

Zangwill's play owed its popularity to the fact that it held
out a promise that both the masses of immigrants yearning to
become full-fledged Americans and the guardians of American
culture, trying to cope with the massive influx of foreign multi-
tudes, dearly wished to believe. The fire that was to heat the
melting pot was none other than love—not the love of nation or
folk, nor the love of abstract ideas, but the entirely private kind
of love between a man and a woman.

It was expected that contact between different ethnic groups would lead to acculturation: borrowing a custom here and there, sharing recipes, and the like. The practical necessity of working and living in America would lead to assimilation in such matters as language, education, and political and economic aspirations. But what would forge the blended American, as Roosevelt, Emerson, or Steffens envisioned him, would be none other than marriage—the union of diverse groups through the power of romantic love.

In Jewish communities, the social revolutions of the nineteenth century socially emancipated the individual Jew, thus enabling him to become an equal citizen. As the German historian Heinrich Graetz put it,

> The hour of freedom for the European Jews dawned in the revolutions of February and March, 1848, in Paris, Vienna, Berlin, in Italy, and other countries. An intoxicating desire for liberty came over the nations of Europe, more overpowering and marvelous than the movement of 1830. With imperious demands the people confronted their princes and rulers. Among the demands was the emancipation of the Jews. In all popular assemblies and proclamations, the despised Jews of yesterday were admitted into the bond of "Liberty, Equality, and Fraternity" (the slogan of the French Revolution of 1789).[22]

As a result of those revolutions, Jews streamed from confined settlements in backward towns and villages into the capitals of Europe; from narrowly restricted occupations into the full range of modern pursuits that were being opened up by the Industrial Revolution; and into a new kind of relationship with Christians—one that, at least in principle if not in fact, was based on a doctrine of social equality.

Intermarriages between free-thinking Jews and Christians followed on the heels of emancipation in an inexorable sequence. Historians surmise that the salons in the homes of Jewish bankers in Berlin and Vienna offered the first common meeting places for liberated Jews and Christians, and it was from these sociable acquaintanceships that the first intermarriages resulted. First the privilege of only the well-to-do Jews, intermarriage between Jews and Christians gradually became an available option for the broad masses of urban middle-class Jews.

Although statistics on the rate of Jewish intermarriage at the beginning of the modern era are spotty and imprecise, there are some available that clearly buttress the general impressions. In a study of marriage records right after the American Revolution, the historian Malcolm H. Stern found that in 699 marriages of Jews, 201, or about 29 percent, were intermarriage between a Jew and a Christian.[23] Similar patterns are reported by others elsewhere in the Western World.

Citing the work of such early students of Jewish social life as Drachsler, Engelman, Fishberg, and Ruppin, Milton L. Barron reports, for instance, that the percentage of intermarriages as a proportion of all marriages in which Jews were involved increased in Switzerland from 5 percent in 1888 to about 12 percent by 1920; in Hungary, the rate increased from about 5 percent in 1895 to about 24 percent by 1935; and in Germany, the rate increased from about 15 percent in 1901 to about 44 percent by 1933, on the eve of the Nazi rise to power and the passage of the draconian Nurenberg Laws that forbade marriage between Jews and Christians.[24]

Citing the work of the French demographer E. Schnurmann, Moshe Davis similarly reports that in Strasbourg, the rate of intermarriage between Jews and Christians increased from an undetermined "very low rate" to over one-third of all marriages of Jews between 1880 and 1909. The French city of Strasbourg had a substantial Jewish population at the time, so the increase in intermarriage could not be attributed to a dearth of eligible Jewish marriage partners.[25]

Jews were apparently eager to enter the mainstream of modern society through the portals of romance and matrimony with their Christian neighbors, and they were also being more readily accepted in their host societies. The separation of church and state following the revolutions in America and France, and the availability of civil marriage—there as well as in much of the rest of the Western World—further hastened the incidence of intermarriages that would not have been legal in earlier generations.

Although the statistics are spotty, as we have seen, and not as precise as most social scientists would prefer, their message is unmistakable. Jews were choosing Christian mates (most often a Jewish man choosing a Christian woman), as well as being chosen by them, in ever-increasing number. They were breaking sharply with one of the oldest and most deeply held norms of Jewish life: the norm of endogamy—the *halachic* requirement (based on biblical injunctions) that Jews only marry other Jews.

The one sleeping-giant exception to this trend at the turn of the twentieth century was the Jew of Eastern Europe, about half of the world's approximately 8 to 9 million Jews at the time. They lived in the infamous Pale of Jewish Settlement, a territory about the size of Texas on the periphery of Russia and Poland.[26] In these small, isolated, economically backward and politically enfeebled villages, they were barely touched by the great revolutions of the previous two centuries. Whereas the lives of Western Jews had undergone significant transformations since the end of the seventeenth century, particularly rapidly from the mid-eighteenth century, the lives of Eastern European Jews in the 1880s did not differ much from what they might have been in the Middle Ages. Indeed, some might say that they were probably better off in the Middle Ages than they were in the last decades of the nineteenth century.

As described by many writers, in varying hues of pain, humor, and bitterness, as well as some nostalgia, Eastern European Jewry lived a cloistered, virtually medieval existence until the first decades of the twentieth century.

Their language, Yiddish; their religious life, a highly ritualized and fundamentalist form of Orthodox Judaism laced with the mysticism of the Hasidic Jews; their economy, pre-industrial

and progressively rendered impoverished by anti-Semitic de-
crees; their host culture, Polish and Russian peasantry wantonly
anti-Semitic and given to periodic orgies of organized violence
against Jews; their self-image, a moral kingdom of priests and
philosophers who were destined to attain a loftier existence
someday. All these features of their life served to erect an almost
impregnable barrier between Jews and Christians who lived as
neighbors in the villages (or *shtetlach*, as they were called in
Yiddish). Social intimacy at the level of friendship was almost
non-existent between them. Therefore, the possibility of intermarriage was virtually unthinkable.

And yet, if the story of *Tevyeh, the Milkman* is any indication
of social realities, despite those great barriers some Jews and
Catholics or Russian Orthodox peasants did fall in love; did go
against the prevailing social norms and did marry, although
often they did so by eloping to the West. Clearly the inclination
of the individual to pursue his or her own personal happiness,
even in the face of powerful opposing social norms, could not be
entirely suppressed.

Nevertheless, the central point remains—marriages between Jews and Christians were far less common in the ghettoized areas of Eastern Europe than they were for Western Jewry. Arthur Ruppin one of the early sociologists of world Jewry,
has amply documented that, for instance, the proportion of intermarriages in one hundred Jewish marriages was less than 1
percent in Galicia as late as 1929. By contrast, the rate in places
like Germany was 23 percent, and it was 13 to 27 percent in
Budapest and Vienna. Elsewhere in Eastern Europe—in Latvia,
Lithuania, White Russia, and the Ukraine—mixed marriages
rarely occurred.[27] Moreover, it stands to reason that they were
not any more frequent at the end of the nineteenth century than
they were in the first decades of the twentieth.

However, it must be recalled that between the 1880s and
the 1920s, about half of the approximately 5 million Jews who
lived in Eastern Europe immigrated to the United States. Begin-

ning with the pogroms of 1881, masses of *shtetl* Jews were quite literally chased into the modern world by the whips and swords of Russian Cossacks. Rather than try to bear it stoically, dying martyrs' deaths as their ancestors might have done, millions of Jews from the Pale chose the path of migration to the West, specifically to the United States.

Between 1881 and 1923, approximately 2.8 million Jews entered through Ellis Island, the "golden door" to America. They quickly overwhelmed the 250,000 Jews, mostly of German descent, who had comprised American Jewry up to that time. As is well known from Irving Howe's popular *World of Our Fathers*, the first generation of Eastern European immigrants settled in such densely Jewish ghettos as the Lower East Side in New York, Maxwell Street in Chicgao, and similar enclaves in Philadelphia, Baltimore, and Washington, D. C.[28]

Their settlement patterns, their economic circumstances, their dependence on *mameloschen* (mother tongue, i.e., Yiddish), and the rising tide of anti-Semitism in America soon resulted in the re-establishment of the kind of ghettoized mode of social life that they had all just recently left behind in the Old World. The convergence of all these social factors resulted in a dramatic decline in the overall rate of mixed marriages for American Jews.

In contrast to the approximately 30 percent rate of Jewish mixed marriages discovered by Malcolm Stern among American Jews in the Federal period (when there were no more than 100 thousand Jews in the country, representing about one-quarter of 1 percent of the total population), the proportion of intermarriages among Jews in the first decades of this century (when they were about 3.5 percent of the total U. S. population) was less than 2 percent.[29]

At the very historical moment when Israel Zangwill was rhapsodizing about the power of love, and intermarriage in particular, and as the great emotional fire flamed under the "melting pot," more of his own people were huddling together—as were immigrant Italians, Poles, Irish, Greeks, and

Chinese—than they might have been a half century earlier. The
tough realities of immigrant life, and the traditions of the Old-
World culture that most immigrants brought with them, placed
a powerful check on the romanticism of the nineteenth century;
but not for long.

In a popular compilation of letters to the editor of the *Jewish
Daily Forward*, the preeminent Yiddish newspaper in America
since 1890, we find that from the earliest times their readers
were writing to the illustrious editor of the paper about problems having to do with marriage, particularly between Jews and
non-Jews. Isaac Metzker, who published the popular compilation in 1971 under the title *A Bintle Brief* (a bundle of letters),
gives us a vivid flavor of some of their concerns.

> 1908
>
> Worthy Editor:
>   I have been in America almost three years. I came from Rus-
> sia where I studied in yeshiva. . . . At the age of twenty I had to
> go to America. Before I left I gave my father my word that I would
> walk the righteous path and be good and pious. But America
> makes one forget everything.
>   Here I became a (machine) operator, and at night I went to
> school. In a few months I entered a preparatory school, where for
> two subjects I had a gentile girl as teacher. . . . Soon I realized
> that her lessons with me were not ordinary . . . she wanted to
> teach me without pay. . . . I began to feel at home in her house
> . . . also her parents welcomed me warmly. . . . Then she spoke
> frankly of her love for me and her hope that I would love her.
>   I was confused and I couldn't answer her immediately. . . . I
> do agree with her that we are first human beings, and she is a
> human being in the fullest sense of the word. She is pretty,
> educated, intelligent, and has a good character. But I am in de-
> spair when I think of my parents. I go around confused and yet I
> am drawn to her. I must see her every day, but when I am there I
> think of my parents and I am torn by doubt.
>   Respectfully,
>   Skeptic from Philadelphia[30]

Reading this poignant letter nearly 80 years after it was
written, and with the hindsight of history, one wonders what

the nameless correspondent was skeptical about. Was it about his faith, about the wisdom of his parents, or the wisdom of his attachment to them? Was it about his love for the girl or her love for him, or was it perhaps about love itself?

Another correspondent, writing to the editor just about a year later, had other problems, but seemed to be unperturbed by any skepticism.

1909

Dear Editor:

I come from a small town in Russia. I was brought up by decent parents and got a good education. I am now twenty years old and am a custom-peddler in a Southern city. Since my customers here are Colored people, I became acquainted with a young Negro girl, twenty-two years of age, who buys merchandise from me. . . . She is a teacher, a graduate of a Negro college, and I think she is an honorable person.

I fell in love with the girl but I couldn't go around with her openly because I am White and she is Colored. However, whenever I deliver her order, I visit with her for awhile.

In time she went away to another city to teach, and I corresponded with her. When she came home for Christmas, I told her I loved her and I intended to marry her and take her North to live. But she refused me and gave me no reason. Perhaps it was because I am a White man.

I spoke about my love for her to my friends, who are supposedly decent people, and they wanted to spit in my face. To them it appeared that I was about to commit a crime.

Therefore I would like to hear your answer as to whether I should be condemned for falling in love with a Negro woman and wanting to marry her. And if you can, explain to me also her reason for refusing me.

Respectfully,
Z.B.[31]

One wonders how many young Jewish peddlers, machine operators, and night school students who had recently come to America were having their first taste of the bittersweet pulls and pinches of romance with Italians, Irish, WASPs, and blacks. One wonders, and wishes for more data. But even in the absence of such data, it is safe to say that there were many more such matches, resulting in marriages (and even occasional conversions to Judaism), than there had been in Eastern Europe.

Writing in 1920, Julius Drachsler reported that the rate of intermarriage for Jews in New York City was 2.27 percent between 1908 and 1912. However, the trend was clearly upward as one looked past the immigrant generations and outside the ghettoized areas of Jewish Settlements.[32]

The trend became most clearly defined for American Jews only as recently as 1971. It was in that year that the Council of Jewish Federations and Welfare released its landmark study of the U. S. Jewish population known as the National Jewish Population Study, or NJPS. The table below succinctly presents the key finding of that study with regard to the intermarriage trend. Although there is some scholarly debate about the precise, most current intermarriage rate, there is no debate about the direction of the trend.

It took about sixty years, or roughly three generations, for

Percentage of Jewish Persons
Marrying Someone Who Was
Not Born Jewish, out of All
Jews Who Married at Given
Time Periods

Time period	Jews marrying non-Jews
1900–1920	2.0
1921–1930	3.2
1931–1940	3.0
1941–1950	6.7
1951–1955	6.4
1956–1960	5.9
1961–1965	17.4
1966–1971	31.7

the descendants of the Eastern European immigrants (who constitute approximately 75 to 80 percent of the total American Jewish population) to catch up in their rate of mixed marriage with those of their brethren in America and Western Europe who had been modernized in the eighteenth and nineteenth centuries.

The magnitude of the most recent rates, and the speed with which they had increased, rang out like a thunderclap in the Jewish community. In a seminal work, *Assimilation in American Life* (1964), Milton Gordon had argued that "if marital assimilation . . . takes place fully, the minority group loses its ethnic identity in the larger host or core society."[33] The findings of NJPS rang a powerful alarm in the minds of those concerned with Jewish group survival.

The convergence of Gordon's sociological insights and the statistical patterns discovered by the NJPS led many learned observers to a foreboding conclusion. American Jewry might become an "extinct species" as a result of marital assimilation. At the very least, so it was feared, the size and significance of an already small minority in the American mosaic might be further reduced to ultimate insignificance as a result of intermarriage. In a carefully calculated analysis, Harvard demographer Elihu Bergman cautioned in 1977 that the net effect of the increased rate of intermarriage projected out over a century would be to reduce the size of the American-Jewish population from the approximately 5.7 million in 1976 to as few as about 10 thousand by the time of the American tricentennial, in the year 2076.[34]

Nor have the concerns been based upon Jewish facts alone. In the wake of Vatican Council II, the *Decree on Ecumenism* (1966) proposed that the Catholic Church mitigate its historically rigorous opposition to mixed marriages. By 1970, the Church no longer required in such marriages that the non-Catholic partner promise to raise the children as Catholics—much less to convert to Catholicism. The result of the liberalizing trend in the Church was to see a steady increase in Catholic intermarriages and a corresponding decline in conversions to Catholicism. Indeed, as Andrew Greeley has shown in his *Crisis in the Church* (1979), "by far the largest numbers of those who have disidentified from the Roman Catholic Church have done so in connection with a mixed marriage."[35]

If religious tradition was steadily losing its grip on cupid's arrows, the once restraining influence of ethnic traditions was faring even worse. In an influential article in the *American Sociological Review*,[36] Richard Alba showed that marriage across ethnic lines among Catholics had increased significantly with the coming of age of successive generations of the descendents of immigrants. Ethnic in-group marriage among the immigrant generations of English, Irish, German, Polish, French, and Italian Catholics quickly yielded to ethnic mixing among the second and third generations, according to Alba's deft analysis.

Among Jews, too, the breaching of the previous generations' ethnic divisions was nearly total by the end of the 1950s. As recently as the 1910s, Konrad Bercovici reports, intermarriage between a Sephardic Jew and a Russian Jew was as rare, if not rarer (and more frowned upon), as marriage between a Jew and a non-Jew.[37] Indeed, Bavarian Jews even hesitated to marry German Jews who came from nearer the Polish border, derisively referring to them with the ethnic slur "Pollacks." In turn, the Russian Jews looked down upon the Polish Jews as well as upon the Galicians and would not permit their children to marry them, reports Milton Barron. But by mid-century the inter-ethnic aversions had largely disappeared in the Jewish community, in much the same way as they had among Catholics.

In retrospect, it would seem that the wholesale crossing of ethnic boundaries *within* religious groups paved the way for the crossing of religious boundaries. The walls of tradition were being battered down by sentiment and emotional attachments, one cultural building block at a time. If those trends would continue unabated for even a few successive generations, Israel

Zangwill's play about the melting pot would prove to be pro-
phetic. The romantic ideology of the eighteenth and the nineteenth centuries would indeed sweep away the last vestiges of
traditional constraint on the individual's choice of a mate. Such
a fundamental change in the making of family life would prove a
more profound point as well. It would prove that happiness—
and, indeed, identity itself—is quite possible in the modern
world without any significant rootedness in a shared tradition.

However, alongside the increasing rates of intermarriage
for Jews and others, mid-century modernity was marked by
other cultural trends as well. Perhaps none is more notable than
the Americans' search for their diverse heritages. The period
saw a spate of publications, both in the social sciences and popular literature, extolling the virtues of ethnicity and tradition.
Opposing Zangwill, Michael Novak heralded *The Rise of the Unmeltable Ethnic* (1972) and the age of "White ethnicity."[38] Earlier,
Herbert Gans and Michael Parenti had also seen the signs
amidst the suburban and urban transitions of the 1950s and
1960s.[39] Ethnic group ties continued to play a powerful role in
shaping the residential as well as friendship preferences of people long after ethnicity had been declared irrelevant in American
life by the conventional wisdom.

In popular literature, the enthusiasm for nearly lost heritages reached its crescendo with the publication and subsequent
serialization on TV of Alex Haley's *Roots*. It is particularly ironic
that Haley dedicated his book to America's bicentennial, since it
was published in 1976. The "nation of many nations," in which
the culture was to blend and render indistinguishable the diversity of cultures that it comprised, was being greeted, on its bicentennial, with a massive outpouring of interest in ethnic distinctiveness and family heritage. The interest in "roots"
spawned a virtual cottage industry in geneology as a family
pastime for several years. It was being fed by such books as Bill
R. Linder's *How to Trace Your Family History* (1978) and, for Jews,
Arthur Kurzweil's popular *Tracing Your Jewish Roots*.[40] As re-

cently as 1984, no less a personage than the President of the United States, Ronald Reagan, created a significant "media event" by visiting the village in Ireland from whence his ancestors emigrated to the United States in the 1840s.

The "Bar Mitzvah with the Vietnamese flavor" with which this chapter began, now points to an even deeper irony. It purports to blend two cultures, Jewish and Vietnamese, very much in keeping with the American ideal of the melting pot. But it simultaneously speaks to the persistence of an unalloyed attachment to the traditions of those cultures. It particularly speaks to the persistence of Jewish identity and ritual in the lives of people—some born Jewish, some newly so—who, at least on the basis of their choice of marriage partners, would seem to have agreed that love is more important than tradition.

The Steinman Bar Mitzvah underscores the emergence of two apparently contradictory trends among modern American Jews, in particular, and perhaps among all modern ethnic Americans, in general. One is the trend described by Shorter, by Lewis, by Rothman, and by other students of the romanticization of the modern family: the triumph of the heart over the head, of love over tradition in matters of mate selection. The other is the trend of resurgent ethnicity described by Novak, by Parenti, by Glazer and Moynihan, and by others since the 1960s. These two contradictory trends have been made even more puzzling since the mid-1970s with the resurgence of religious emotionalism and fundamentalism among those very segments of society—the young, professional, educated, and middle class—who had been thought to be immune to spiritual matters because of their modern consciousness and life-style.

As do all profound contradictions, these contradictory trends raise several compelling questions that strike at the very core of the meaning of intermarriage. Why do people choose to celebrate particular symbols or rituals of a larger tradition whose main tenets they have rejected? For example, why did Josephine Steinman want her son's Bar Mitzvah to have a "Vietnamese flavor" when she had converted to Judaism and presumably now sees herself as part of the Jewish people? Why did Ron Steinman want his wife to become Jewish, as do tens of thousands of other young Jews who marry Christians, when his sense of equality was such that he was able to fall in love with a woman who was a Buddhist? Why do the hundreds of thousands of Jews and Christians, who marry one another in defiance of their age-old ethnic and religious traditions, persist in memorializing many of those very same traditions in their holiday celebrations, in the way they rear their children, in what they read and what they eat, and in their very concept of themselves as human beings? Particularly among American Jews who have experienced such a great and rapid increase in intermarriages, why has the trend toward intermarriage *not* been accompanied by a comparable trend of disidentification from the Jewish people?

Perhaps Josephine Steinman herself was answering some of those deep questions in her own mind when she commented on the unique Bar Mitzvah menu to *The Times'* reporter, "It was a desire to put on a party in one's own image. That became particularly important with the kind of family we have. After all, there aren't many Vietnamese-Jewish families."

Of course, Mrs. Steinman is right. There aren't many Vietnamese-Jewish families, but, until the 1950s, it is not likely that one would have found culturally blended Jewish families of even less exotic mixture, such as Italian-Jewish or Irish-Jewish, which are far more common. It is not that such marriages did not occur. Of course, they did. Jews have been marrying non-Jews since biblical times. But the social stigma attached to such marriages usually compelled intermarried couples to become more or less socially invisible—at least in the eyes of the Jewish community and often in the eyes of the Christian community as well.

What stands out as remarkable about the Steinman's Bar Mitzvah is that this family has no desire or need to "pass" as either exclusively Jewish or Vietnamese, or exclusively anything else. They can create a party in their own image, indeed an entire social identity in their own image. Moreover, they can find a Reform Jewish congregation (of which they are members) that seems not only to accept but also to actually delight in this family's ability to express their Jewishness in their own unique idiom.

Rose Epstein, an old friend of the family, is quoted as commenting on the celebration, "It's a new world, isn't it? I can't get over how nice it is when people accept." Her comment is almost liturgical. It recalls the well-known Hebrew song "Hine Ma Tov U'Manaim, Shevet Achim Gam Yachad" (Behold, how good and pleasant it is when brethren dwell in unity).[41] One almost has to pinch one's self to realize that the unity of brethren rhapsodized by the Hebrew poet certainly did not envision the celebration of Bar Mitzvahs with Vietnamese cousins or chicken with cashew nuts.

Some might say that the desire, as Josephine put it, to "put on a party in one's own image" proclaims nothing more profound than the contemporary consumerist values of modern upper-middle-class Americans—young, professional urbanites—whose numbers are legion in New York City and other major metropolitan areas. Perhaps they merely reflect the narcissism of the postwar baby-boomers coming of age and expressing their passionate individualism in a traditional idiom. Perhaps tradition here is nothing more than yet another vehicle for their highly personal "ego trip." Perhaps.

But, in fact, Ron and Josephine Steinman went through a long period of searching within themselves, as well as through various Jewish institutions on two continents, before they could arrive at a form of religious identification and affiliation that was harmonious with their view of life. Josephine was searching for the compassion and respect for life she had learned as a child. Ron wanted to belong to a community that reflected tolerance and social responsibility. Their personal outlooks, although drawn from vastly different cultures, were surprisingly similar. What the two wanted was to be able to link their inner felt similarity to a single tradition; in this instance, the Jewish tradition—to link the personal feelings shared by two to a tradition shared by many. The particular resolutions they have made in dealing with their dual family heritage have come at the cost of great effort and, at times, the suffering of callousness and intolerance from those closest to them.

Their search, and particular resolution, reflects an apparent need on the part of many intermarried couples to not dismiss their heritages, but, rather, to integrate them into some kind of harmonious whole. Who has such needs and why is an issue that will be explored in subsequent chapters. Suffice it to say, here, that the Steinmans are not alone, even if their particular cultural blend is a bit more unusual than that of others.

Amidst the general alarm among American Jews over the increasing rate of intermarriage throughout the 1970s, relatively little attention was paid to the fact that unprecedented numbers of non-Jews were becoming Jewish by choice. The National Jewish Population Study had found that about one-third of the contemporary intermarriages involved the conversion of the non-Jewish partner. My own study of intermarried couples, conducted on behalf of the American Jewish Committee (1976–1977), confirmed those figures and also found that in about 20 percent of the intermarriages in which no conversion to Judaism had taken place, the non-Jewish spouse had more or less "assimilated" into the Jewish community through the Jewishness of the family.

Other demographic studies of Jewish communities, such as those of Floyd Fowler in Boston (1975), of Albert Mayer in Kansas City (1977), of Bruce Phillips in Denver (1982), and of Steve Cohen and Paul Ritterband in New York (1983), all show that the rate of conversion into Judaism has increased along with the increase in intermarriage.[42] In fact, the percentage of conversions from among the intermarriers has tended to run ahead of the rate of intermarriage itself. Taken together, these studies show that the rate of conversion into Judaism during the past thirty years has increased by about 300 percent.

In 1954, Rabbi David Eichhorn published a report estimating that the Reform and Conservative movements were producing between 1,500 to 1,750 "new Jews" each year through conversions.[43] In 1984, Rabbi Sanford Seltzer of the Reform Union of American Hebrew Congregations estimated, in a personal conversation, that his movement was producing between 7,000 to 8,000 "new Jews" each year. Although increases among the Conservative and Orthodox have not been as great, knowledgeable observers in those movements also point to significant increases in their conversion activities—all this, by the way, without any direct efforts by any of the movements thus far to seek out converts actively.

As will be shown, in the great majority of such conversionary families, a high value is placed on the maintenance of Jewish traditions, as in the Steinman family. But there appears also to be an inclination to express those values in a life-style and cultural idiom that reflects the non-Jewish heritage of the family as well, at least in some respects. In those intermarried families in which no conversion has taken place, considerably less value is placed on the maintenance of Jewish traditions, as one might expect. Yet even in those families, there is a tendency in a great many cases to include certain Jewish traditions in the life-style of the home, along with such non-Jewish traditions as the celebration of Christmas with Christian relatives, and possibily other Christian holidays and life-cycle events.

One Jewish-Catholic couple—the husband had actually studied for the priesthood before he became an agnostic social worker—used the occasion of their honeymoon to travel to some of the small villages of southern Italy to try to trace the husband's ancestors. Yet this couple's son had a Bar Mitzvah thirteen years later. At the time of our meeting in 1980, their home offered a comfortable display of Italian-Catholic memorabilia; reproductions of Gothic portraits of saints alongside Diane's menorah, a reproduction of Chagall's famous fiddler on the roof picture, and Danny's Hebrew books from which he was studying for his Bar Mitzvah. And Frank—who is a master of Italian cuisine—also did much of the cooking for his son's Bar Mitzvah. Apparently the Leone family also wanted a party in their own image, a Bar Mitzvah with an Italian flavor.

Perhaps one has to be a bit narcissistic to make such casual use of divergent cultural symbols to satisfy one's own sense of the good fit between traditional and personal life-style. But such an invidious psychological label as narcissism is hardly adequate to account for the lingering attachments of contemporary intermarrieds to greater or lesser fragments of their ancestral traditions. Nor are the other explanations of intermarriage as helpful as they once might have been. The proverbial power of love, which popularly accounts for the incidence of intermarriage itself, should have rendered all previous tribal loyalties for naught. Or as Zangwill put it, the melting pot should have so alloyed the couple's traditions that the new amalgam would not betray traces of its origins.

Finally, any understanding of how intermarrieds merge their ancestral traditions with their contemporary life-style must encompass the ways in which modern families, Jewish families especially, incorporate tradition into their lives. After all, the life-styles of all ethnic groups have been greatly influenced by one another, as well as by the general patterns of American culture. Just as "you don't have to be Jewish to love Levy's real Jewish rye bread,"[44] so, too, you don't have to be intermarried to have a Jamaican calypso band at a Jewish wedding or to have kosher Chinese food at a Bar Mitzvah.

At the heart of the matter lies the cardinal principle of modern consciousness: that, in American society as in most other modern societies, the individual enjoys simultaneous membership in a great variety of groups and cliques—from work to community to leisure—and yet is freer from the constraints of any of those memberships than at any previous time in history. But that very freedom impels many to seek linkages with the timeless traditions of their ancestors.

Chapter Two

MARRIAGE AND CONSCIOUSNESS

Marriage and Consciousness

The questions of intermarriage ultimately come down to the question of the relationship between modern consciousness and marriage.

Perhaps none have addressed that question more thoughtfully than Peter Berger and Hansfried Kellner in an article in *Diogenes* (1954) called "Marriage and the Construction of Reality." Their analysis merits careful consideration in any attempt at understanding the contemporary intermarriage phenomenon. Reflecting upon the timeless functions of marriage and family life in human societies throughout history, Berger and Kellner point out that

> marriage and the family used to be firmly embedded in a matrix of wider community relationships, serving as extensions and particularizations of the latter's social controls. There were few separating barriers between the world of the individual family and the wider community, a fact even to be seen in the physical conditions under which the family lived before the industrial revolution. The same social life pulsated through the house, the street, and the community.[1]

The ancient Jewish Talmud probably had this very point in mind, without the benefit of the language of social science, when it referred to the family as a *mikdash m'at* (a sanctuary in the microcosm). In other words, the traditional family was an extension of the total community, its sacred and secular institutions reaching directly into the personal lives of its members. The traditional family was no haven of privacy or retreat from the norms, influences, or expectations of the wider community.

On the contrary, it was the institution par excellence in which the individual was trained, groomed, and tested for correct conduct by neighbors, friends, and even strangers.

Among the ancient Israelites, the *bet ha mikdash* (literally, house of sanctification or temple) was the central sanctuary in which the key ceremonies of Jewish religious life were celebrated publicly. Private rituals and celebrations that also followed the meticulous requirements of religious law were performed primarily in the home, hence the description of the home as a *mikdash m'at*. Thus, life in the home was as circumscribed by law and custom as was life in the temple. There was virtually no separation between the private domain of the family and the public domain of the community. This connectedness of the private and public domain is precisely the view of the traditional family presented by Berger and Kellner, and it is substantiated by virtually all historians of the family.

The physical arrangements of homes in the villages of premodern societies generally denied privacy to the family as much as they did to the individual. Consequently, the individual was no freer in the environment of his or her home than in any other institutional setting. In fact, the individual probably could experience more freedom from institutional constraint and social control along the hidden byways on the edge of the village than within the home.

As a result, traditional men and women rarely were able to separate in their own minds their sense of corporate or group identity (e.g., "I am a Jew," "I am the eldest daughter of so and so," or "I am from the village of Vitebsk") from their personhood as individuals. The French sociologist Emile Durkheim coined the term *collective consciousness* to capture the essence of this mode of thought.[2] In this mind set, there is but the dimmest awareness of personality and virtually no legitimacy attached to any individual desire that would go against the norms of the group.

Thus, the family is truly not a private institution, and it is barely distinguishable from such other institutions as the temple or church. Its primary function is to transmit the shared values of the community and to monitor their fulfillment in the everyday lives of its members.

In light of this view of the traditional family, it is no surprise that love and sentimentality would have had such a small role to play in the making of families. Love and sentimentality have a tendency to produce spontaneity, to disrupt routine social arrangements. Therefore, they could not serve as a useful basis for the making of a traditional home. How could men control their women and women their men? How could the proper balance be maintained between parents and children if their relationships were subject to unpredictable emotions? The function of the traditional home was to provide sustenance, safety, social standing in the community, and patrimony from one generation to the next. None of those functions would be much advanced by allowing love to play a salient role in the making of family relationships. As Edward Shorter demonstrated with dogged historical scholarship, "the traditional family was much more a productive and reproductive unit than an emotional unit . . . lineage was important, being together at the dinner table was not."[3]

The critical moment in the modernization of the family occurred when work, and later religion and political life, were substantially separated from the physical locale of family life. When factory or shop or marketplace are places to "go out to" and where one is away from the family for some extended period of time, a split between what social scientists call the "private sphere" and the "public sphere" occurs. The family gradually crystallized in the wake of the Industrial Revolution as the "private sphere," along with such other voluntary associations as cliques, clubs, and leisure time groups (leisure itself is a late product of the Industrial Revolution). Thus, the home slowly emerged as the place to which one could retreat from the pressures and controls of the larger society.

The emergence of a capitalistic form of economy, particularly in the Western World, since the late seventeenth century, also pushed the multitude of individuals to make their livelihoods independently of their traditional relationships with kin or ancestral community. Consequently, from the eighteenth century on, millions of men and women found themselves as free economic agents for the first time in history. Once again, Edward Shorter observes with profound insight

> In late eighteenth-century Europe, the sexual and emotional wish to be free came from the capitalist marketplace. . . . The logic of the marketplace positively demands individualism. . . . The free market engraves upon all who are caught up in it the attitude: "Look out for number one". . . . In the domain of man–woman relations, the wish to be free (the looking out for number one) emerges as romantic love. . . . Economic individualism leads to cultural egoism.[4]

The privatization of the family and the romanticization of the man–woman relationship changed the processes of mate selection profoundly. As Ellen Rothman has shown, from the latter half of the eighteenth century on, individuals increasingly expected to make their own selection of a mate, with a decreasing regard for parental wishes. Moreover, the basis of mate selection changed from considerations of property and propriety to considerations of emotional and sexual appeal.[5]

We know that the Jews were prevented from participating in the processes of economic modernization and civil rights until fairly late in the eighteenth century in the West, and were never fully allowed to participate in Eastern Europe. Therefore, Jewish family organization did not really begin to be affected by these modernizing trends until after the great political revolutions at the end of the eighteenth and the early nineteenth century. Intermarriage, like romantic love, entered into Jewish life arm in arm, so to speak, with economic and political liberty.

But as we saw in Chapter One, as soon as Jews were able to enter the economic and political mainstream of their host societies, the romantic ideology quickly began to influence their family arrangements as well. The legendary matchmaker was rapidly replaced by cupid, and love became the *sine qua non* of marriage for Jews as much as it had for Christians. With it, the private world of "the couple" displaced the collective world of the *mishpachah*, the family or clan, as the primary consideration for men and women who would marry.

One of the key effects of the privatization of the family, write Berger and Kellner, is that "in our contemporary society, each family constitutes its own segregated sub-world, with its own controls and its own closed conversation."[6] As they pointed out, in earlier society the family was coterminous with the larger community within which it was embedded. Both the family as a unit and the marital relationship itself were part of "a considerably larger area of conversation." The primary focus of what men and women spoke about, who they spoke about, and to whom and how they spoke about each other included a wide circle of kinfolk and neighbors and all their shared concerns.

"Unlike the earlier situation," Berger and Kellner continue,

> . . . in which the establishment of a new marriage simply added to the complexity and differentiation of an already existing social world [one, we might add, that would be all-important to the newlyweds], the marriage partners now are embarked on the often difficult task of constructing for themselves the little world in which they will live.[7]

Because romance very likely precedes marriage, and becomes an ideological desideratum afterward, there is a strong internal as well as a strong external pressure of each partner on the other to construct a warm and sheltering emotional haven out of a continual sharing of feelings and thoughts through conversation.

> Every social relationship requires objectivation, that is, requires a process by which subjectively experienced meanings become objective . . . become common property (to be shared with another). . . . A relationship that consists of only two individuals

called upon to sustain, by their own efforts, an ongoing social world, will have to make up in intensity for the numerical poverty of the arrangement. . . . The establishment and maintenance of such a social world makes extremely high demands on the principal participants.[8]

Berger and Kellner suggest that the traditional family had an identity that depended on the communal and kinship context in which it was formed, whereas the modern nuclear family, and the young couple in particular, must create their own collective identity precisely because they are free to do so. In other words, the freedom of marital choice requires that a joint effort at identity and reality construction be made.

The Zangwillian image of the Jewish David and the Christian Vera, walking hand in hand into the sunset of the melting pot to redefine themselves and their world, represents the extreme of nineteenth-century Romanticism. It was a rather unrealistic model of a man–woman relationship which suggested that two human beings can forge a new reality from love and sheer personality. But whereas modern marriage partners are impelled to create their own shared system of meaning, their own reality, they can never do so without reference to their individual as well as their collective past. The intimate conversations generated in the familial dyad cannot continue to depend on the shared affections of the couple only. They must inevitably draw on the same cultural wellspring in which their preromantic and premarital characters were formed.

We thus come to the final irony and the most subtle potential of intermarriage. Marriage in our modern society, write Berger and Kellner,

is a dramatic act in which two strangers come together and redefine themselves [more or less on their own terms without any interference from others]. The drama of the act is internally anticipated and socially legitimated long before it takes place . . . and amplified by means of a pervasive ideology, the dominant themes of which (romantic love, sexual fulfillment, self-discovery and self-realization . . . the nuclear family as the social site for these processes) can be found distributed in all strata of the society. . . . It should be added that, in using the term "strangers," we do not mean that the candidates for the marriage come from widely discrepant social backgrounds—indeed, the data indicate that the contrary is the case.[9]

In other words, marriage partners are only "strangers" to one another—relatively speaking—because of the level of intimacy they are expected to achieve in the process of becoming a married couple. In fact, they share a great deal of social familiarity, which, in no small measure, contributes to a more personal intimacy.

In traditional societies, marriage partners were no less "strangers" to one another. In fact, they probably shared a greater degree of social familiarity, that is, familiarity with each other's social backgrounds, although not with each other as persons. The point is that the roles marriage partners would be expected to play *vis-à-vis* one another for their entire adult lives were fairly specifically prescribed by their social groups. The husband or wife did not expect any great expressions of individuality from the other. Rather, what they expected was that each one conform to the normative ideals prescribed by their groups. Thus, the home was expected to be the arena in which the stylized role performances of husbands, wives, children—and often other kinfolk—were enacted and transmitted from one generation to the next. The home was not a place in which "strangers" became intimates on the level of personality or self-awareness. Indeed, at that level, traditional husbands and wives probably remained "strangers" to one another throughout a lifetime.

The modern home, on the other hand, is no place for strangers. It is a locale for intimacy, for self-disclosure, and for self-discovery. In fact, Berger and Kellner compare modern marriage with the socialization experience of childhood and adolescence, the main difference being that in the earlier phase "the individual was in the main socialized into an existing structure."

In marriage, he and she actively collaborate in their mutual socialization. "The re-construction of the world (and of one's self)
in marriage occurs principally in the course of conversation,"
and principally in the privacy of two people alone.[10] Therefore,
stylized images must give way to self-disclosure.

The question that Berger and Kellner do not address, and
which is of key importance for us here, is just what it is that the
marriage partners talk *about* when they are striving to achieve
intimacy, to reconstruct their world? What is the nature of the
self that husband and wife need to share, to disclose, to discover? In its nascent state, writes the lyrical Francesco Alberoni,

> falling in love is an experience of authenticity, of transparency, of
> truth. Lovers spend hours on end telling each other in detail
> about their lives because each wants to make the other participate
> in the totality of his (and her) being.[11]

All the nuances of the other's body, gestures, moods, and attributes are objects of fascination, as are one's own reactions to
them. There is, then, clearly no lack of things to share and talk
about when two people are falling in love. And all that they
share can be easily limited to the seemingly eternal present.

The rule that "the past does not count"—although incomprehensible in the routine course of everyday life—is, in
fact, one of the governing principles of the process of falling in
love. Beyond that nascent state, however, as the love relationship itself becomes progressively routinized, the past of
each person, along with the full range of their social relationships, needs to be integrated into the couple's newly established universe. As Alberoni writes,

> The couple thus constructs not only a present reality, but recon-
> structs past reality as well, fabricating a common memory that
> integrates the recollections of individual pasts. Similarly, there
> occurs a sharing of future horizons.[12]

Bringing these themes, now, back to the issue of intermarriage, we are in the position to see the profoundly revolutionary

potential of a marriage between people of different religious and ethnic backgrounds. We can also now appreciate the inevitability of the persistence of some attachment to one's heritage in the intermarriage.

That young men and women fall in love across traditionally great social barriers is attributable largely to the opportunities and human drives unleashed by the economic and political revolutions of the previous centuries. Under the influence of a romantic ideology, it was thought that once those relationships became institutionalized in marriage, a new form of marriage would emerge in which the partnership could be sustained solely by the sentiments and the personalities of the individual partners.

However, that ideology has tended to overlook the process by which love emerges and by which love is sustained between two individuals. In an attempt to disect this process, Ira Reiss interviewed a group of college student couples in 1960. He discovered that what people commonly call "being in love" is a feeling that develops in four steps. Moreover, staying "in love" seems to require the continuous re-enactment of these steps. Reiss called it the "wheel theory of love." The feeling states it describes seem to flow in an orderly and predictable cycle.

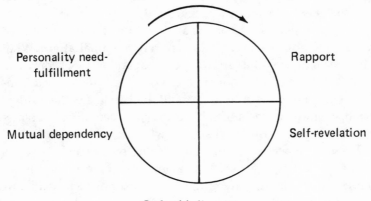

Cycle of feeling states

At first, there is simply the sense of rapport that one experiences between himself/herself and the other. This feeling stimulates a willingness and desire for self-revelation, which in turn yields to a feeling of trust. The sense of trusting and being trusted leads to mutual dependency, and it is in that mutually dependent state that two individuals will find, consciously or not, that certain basic personality needs of each is met by the other (e.g., the need for nurturance by one is met by the need to give nurturance by the other).

But "being in love" is not a terminal condition. As a matter of fact, it is a highly fragile and tenuous state. Mutual dependency is continually tested by the freshness of daily experience. Trust is always having to be renewed by the willingness of each to ask and to answer the question, "What are you thinking?"

The astute social-psychology of modern married life, suggested by the work of Berger and Kellner, and of the inner process of loving, suggested by the works of Reiss and of Alberoni, make the link between love and self-revelation inevitable. The very love that unites the individual man and woman into a couple compels them to explore each other's identities; indeed, to remake each other's identities. But, it is precisely that activity which forces the individual to confront his or her own past and the past of the other. Where man and woman share a common group background, a common cultural heritage, a general sense of social similarity, the confrontation with the past can easily remain a purely personal affair. What each reveals to the other are the personal and family secrets, so to speak. However, when man and woman do not share a common set of ground assumptions about their collective memories, the most minute aspects of self-expression become broad statements about one's cultural history—whether one likes it or not.

How unexpectedly and powerfully such confrontations with one's heritage can arise was brought home for me in an interview with Sam L., a young Jewish attorney, who had participated in our survey of intermarried couples.

Sam was born in the United States, in the Bronx, to be

precise, in 1948. His parents were Holocaust survivors who came to the country in 1946 with Sam's older sister and a grandfather. Sam attended a yeshiva in the Bronx until the eigth grade. Tragically, both his parents died, one of cancer and one of a heart attack before he turned thirteen. He was raised into adulthood by his older sister and grandfather, both Orthodox Jews.

At the time when we met, Sam was married to Lorraine, a social worker, a Methodist of German-English ancestry, born and raised on Long Island.

Sam recalled that when he and Lorraine had already been living together for sometime (in Buffalo, New York, where both were in graduate school), he took her, once, to a kosher delicatessen. When the waiter came to take their orders he was going to order a "kashe knish" for himself. But as the first syllable of his order passed his lips, he caught himself. It occurred to him that Lorraine had never heard of such a dish, that it sounds very foreign, and he felt that she might think him "too Jewish" for ordering such a distinctly Jewish sounding food. He asked the waiter to bring a corned beef-on-club with a side order of cole slaw.

That episode led Sam to break-up with Lorraine for almost two months, and to seek pre-marital counseling afterwards.

When they walked out of the delicatessen, Sam recalled, he felt as if had had betrayed his parents and the memory of all those Jews who perished in the Holocaust because he lacked the courage to order a "kashe knish" in Lorraine's presence. And if he did not dare to order the "kashe knish" with her on a date, how would he dare to raise his children as Jews once they were married? He felt guilty, angry—at her and at himself—and most of all, he felt confused. He was sullen with Lorraine for several days thereafter. He could not answer satisfactorily her question: "What are you thinking?" And, he wasn't sure he wanted to know what she is thinking. Arguments followed. Break-up followed.

At the time of our interview, some two years after the episode, he credited Lorraine with having had the insight to find a pre-marital counselor who was able to bring the two of them into a conversation where all the subtle feelings (loyalty to deceased parents, gratitude toward an Orthodox grandfather and an Orthodox sister, fear of anti-Semitism and hatred for the anti-Semites who had killed and persecuted his ancestors, attachment to Lorraine but fear of her parents and brother, who did not seem to like Jews much, but did seem to like Sam a lot) could be raised to the level of articulate conversation.

Feeling-talk, sex-talk, self-talk are the emotional imperatives of modern marriage. But that same imperative makes it inevitable, for intermarrieds and those who contemplate entering an intermarriage, that one's past and all the cultural ingredients of the self be scrutinized, reflected upon, and accepted (if not cherished) by the other. Failure to do so—witholding self-disclosure—is a sign of "bad faith," lack of trust, and ultimately a sign of an absence of "true" love. The home is not merely where the heart is. It is also where the self is; where the open heart, so to speak, is a gateway to the full measure of the person; where, through the medium of mutual affection, man and woman acquire the power to know as well as to remake each other's identities.

While the nascent moments of falling in love evoke a feeling of an intense and lasting present, in which the past and the future are irrelevant, the maintenance of love seems to have the opposite requirement. It seems to call for the probing of the past and the charting of the future. It also brings into its discourse the selfhood of the lovers, which inevitably implicates their cultural heritages. There is simply no self that is not linked in some fashion to an ancestry, a familial network, and a history. Certainly, there is no Jewish self that lacks such anchor points. But, in all likelihood, such anchor points are universal. Therefore, the intermarriage conversation is, inevitably, a converstion also about culture, history, and the personal feeling about tradition.

Thus, the revolutionary potential of the intermarriage reaches its full articulation not because the marriage partners will ignore or eradicate each others' cultural heritage. Were they to do that, only their own lives and the lives of their immediate families would be affected. That is hardly a revolution. Modern intermarriage has become revolutionary, particularly for Jews, precisely because the marriage partners are working at integrating different heritages, customs, memories, and histories that have been tragically at odds for thousands of years.

Through the process of conversions, as in the case of the Steinmans, as well as in mixed marriages in which no conversion has taken place but in which Jewishness has nonetheless *not* been fully relinquished, Jewish society and culture are being transformed through the inclusion of non-Jewish cultural ingredients into its primordial inner sanctum, the *mikdash m'at*, the family—upon which so much of the rest of its social order is founded.

From this perspective, it should be easy to understand that intermarriage poses much more than a demographic threat to such a survival-conscious group as the Jewish people. It poses the threat of cultural transformation, or—as Lewis Benjamin wrote in his book *The Passing of an English Jew* (1907)—"what centuries of persecution had been powerless to do has been affected in a score of years by friendly intercourse."[13] It is also quite easy to understand, in the light of those centuries of persecution and the passionate commitment to group survival that was bred by them, why Jews would be so concerned about the intermarriage of their children.

What is not well understood, because until the present time there had been no social scientific studies to probe the matter, is just exactly how does intermarriage affect the lives of the people who are most directly involved in them: the intermarriers, their parents, their children, and their larger communities. Also not well understood is the deeper philosophical–psychological question of why Jews and other ethnic and religious groups have been so resistant to marriage with "outsiders." It is these questions that will be discussed in the chapters that follow.

Chapter Three

PATHS TO
INTERMARRIAGE

Paths to Intermarriage

An ancient rabbinic parable relates the following concerning the subtle dynamics of love and marriage (as part of a commentary on how the Patriarch Jacob came to find his beloved wife Rachel):

> A Roman noblewoman asked Rabbi Yose bar Chalafta, "How long did it take your God to create the world?"
> "Six days," he replied.
> "And what has your God been doing ever since then?" she inquired.
> "He pairs people off, bringing husband together with his future wife," Rabbi Yose informed her.[1]

The story underscores the mystery of mate selection. Why does a particular man choose a particular woman as a marriage partner and vice versa? Even with the strict controls of the ancient world, the question of why particular individuals ended up together was a mystery. How much more so is it a mystery for us moderns who largely follow the directives of our private passions? The parable is the answer to the question: Why did these two marry? The answer is, so to speak: Only God knows.

Since the reason any two particular people end up as husband and wife remains mostly a mystery, it is hardly a subject on which a social scientist would have the last word. But why certain *types* of people get married at particular moments in history, that is another matter. A typological analysis of who marries who at particular points in history can, indeed, yield meaningful clues to the reasons for intermarriage—even though the mating choices of specific persons will continue to elude us.

Chapters One and Two painted a broad canvas of the long-term cultural and psychohistorical trends that have led to contemporary intermarriage. Processes of society, though, are only abstracted by the observer from the concrete actions and recorded thoughts of individuals—one at a time and in groups. Having delineated the overall trends, we will now begin to focus on individuals and social types.

The distinction of being the first American Jew to marry a Christian went to a well-known doctor in Maryland, one Jacob Lumbrozo, who took a Christian wife in 1660, according to the annals of the American Jewish Historical Society.[2] That is a mere six years after the first small group of some twenty-three Jews landed in New Amsterdam (New York) in 1654. Evidently marital blending began nearly from the start in the New World. Then, of course, the Jewish community was but a mere handful of families, most already related to one another. Therefore, the young were virtually forced to choose marriage partners from outside the Jewish fold. Indeed it is possible that Jacob Lumbrozo was the only Jew in Maryland in those days, or perhaps the son of the only Jewish family. His marriage to a Christian woman was a demographic inevitability.

Regrettably, the name and family history of his wife is lost to history. The more interesting question would be to find out why this Christian woman was willing to marry the Jewish doctor. Perhaps it is not coincidental that the marriage took place in Maryland, because that colony was established in 1632 as a refuge for non-Protestants, particularly for Catholics. It is likely that the spirit of tolerance for religious pluralism was more advanced there than in the other colonies—even though full political rights were not granted to Jews until as late as 1824 (nearly fifty years after religious discrimination against Jews was abolished in New York). I suppose it is also likely that a Jewish doctor was as valuable and as rare a matrimonial "catch" then as he or she is today.

There were few Jews in America, even well into the nineteenth century, especially in the more remote sections of the country away from the key Jewish settlements in New York, Philadelphia, Boston, and Baltimore. Studies published by the American Jewish Historical Society show, for example, that Jewish pioneers who had lived in Kentucky before 1836 had disappeared through intermarriage by the second or third generation—their descendants can be traced only by their Jewish surnames. In our own day, the well-known senator from Arizona, Barry Goldwater, is an example of the Christian descendant of Jewish ancestors, the product of intermarriages that took place among German Jews in the middle of the nineteenth century.[3]

Records of the Gold Rush days in California provide colorful instances of the adventurous Jews in the hinterlands and their intermarriages.

> John Jones, an English Jew, came to Los Angeles in 1851 and established a wholesale grocery business. He soon amassed a fortune. He married a Christian, Doria Deighton of San Francisco, while remaining prominent in the Jewish community. Jones' wife became a leading member of the Ladies Hebrew Benevolent Society. . . . Their daughter married the son of Isaac Lankershim (a Jew by birth and a leading citizen of Los Angeles). Ironically, Lankershim had been converted to Baptist Protestantism, and his descendants were lost to Judaism.[4]

Max Vorspan and Lloyd Gartner, who compiled some of these colorful accounts in their valuable book, *History of the Jews of Los Angeles* (1970), point out that there was an oversupply of Jewish young men as compared to Jewish young women in mid-nineteenth–century Los Angeles. This demographic constraint, coupled with the relatively open and easygoing relationship between Jews and Christians in the burgeoning city, made intermarriage a ready possibility.

> The marriage records of Los Angeles County from 1858–1876 show seventeen marriages involving Jews. Seven of these were performed by Joseph Newmark (a religiously observant leader of

early L. A. Jewry). Six were performed by Rabbi Abraham Edelman, and four (obviously intermarriages) by pastors or justices of the peace.[5]

These figures, small as they may be, reveal that of all marriages of Jews during the period, 24 percent were intermarriages. If we bear in mind that we are speaking of thirty individual Jews (i.e., thirteen Jewish couples and four Jews married to Christians) who married between 1858 and 1876 in Los Angeles, we see that 13 percent chose Christian partners.

Who were these early intermarriers? Although their biographies are shrouded in historical oblivion, we can surmise that they were sufficiently adventurous—mostly young men, hard-bitten by their quest for financial success and the power and fame that might come with it—to leave the more familiar surroundings of established Jewish communities in the East Coast cities and in Europe. They were not so much escaping the hard life of persecution or economic privation as they were seeking out the good life as promised by the image of the California El Dorado. They included men like the aforementioned John Jones (undoubtedly an anglicized name), merchants, speculators, tradesmen, and the like. One such merchant, Joseph Leventhal, who married a Mexican woman in 1868, made history not so much by his intermarriage but by the fact that his two children made the local headlines some years later—one for murder, the other for grand larceny.

Even more colorful is the story of Bernard Cohn, who came to Los Angeles in 1854. After prospecting for gold in Colorado for some thirteen years, he returned to Los Angeles in 1876. In the 1880s, he served for a period as President of the City Council and Mayor Pro Tem. It seems that between his arrival in the city in 1854 and his death in 1889, he managed to establish and raise two families simultaneously: one Jewish and one Catholic. With his Jewish wife, Esther, he raised three Jewish children. With his Catholic wife, Delfina Verelas, he raised six Catholic children. Oddly, this same Bernard Cohn had been President of Congregation B'nai B'rith, as well as the Hebrew Benevolent Society.

After Cohn's death, Delfina sued his estate for a share of the inheritance that she believed was rightfully hers. Cohn had apparently left her out of his will entirely, even though his Jewish wife had died earlier. In a curious twist of Jewish solidarity, Rabbi Abraham Edelman testified on behalf of the Jewish Cohn family, asserting that

> Bernard Cohn was an Orthodox Hebrew and rigorously observed the rules of his faith [therefore, he would never have married a Catholic]. He [Rabbi Edelman] had officiated at Cohn's home a number of times, dealt with him, and never heard of his being married to Delfina. He had heard, however, that Cohn had kept a mistress.[6]

The court ruled against Delfina, although her children who were fathered by Cohn were deemed entitled to a share of the Cohn inheritance.

Although Cohn's relationship with and treatment of Delfina Verelas hardly does him—or, indeed, his rabbi—much credit, it can be said on his behalf that he adhered to the letter of Judaic law and the law of his own congregation. In 1862, the constitution of his congregation denied membership to anyone who married out of the faith.

However, other intermarriages of the period reflected far more favorably on the community and also showed that intermarriage was not solely the province of the adventurous Jewish man.

> In 1880, soon after the arrival of Rabbi Abraham Blum, Los Angeles Jewry received its only known nineteenth-century convert. The daughter of L. B. Cohen, the pawnbroker, began to keep company with a Spanish fireman, Edward Kinney. Cohen refused paternal permission for the marriage unless Kinney would embrace Judaism. Kinney agreed, and under Rabbi Blum's tu-

telage he renounced his Catholic faith and was converted and married. Mrs. Kinney became a soloist in the [synagogue] choir and her husband one of the congregation's most regular worshippers.[7]

Although Edward Kinney was probably the first convert to Judaism in California, the first American conversion to Judaism probably occurred nearly a hundred years earlier, in Philadelphia. According to documents compiled by Jacob R. Marcus, the flagship synagogue of American Jewry—Shearith Israel of New York—had forbidden the acceptance of proselytes or marriage with a proselyte as early as 1763. Its rulings were sacred to all other synagogues of the time.

In 1793 a member of the Philadelphia community, Moses Nathans, brought his problem of intermarriage before the congregation. He and the gentile mother of his children [i.e., his civil law wife] had never been married according to Jewish law. However, she was willing to become a Jewess and sought the privilege of conversion and of a Jewish marriage. The husband's friends were sympathetic to the request. Nevertheless, they felt that they could do nothing on their account and referred the matter to the ecclesiastical court of the Spanish–Portugese synagogue in London. . . . The *hazzan*'s records show that he [Nathans] married the woman in 1794 in accordance with the Jewish ritual.[8]

Men like Moses Nathans and women like the daughter of the Los Angeles pawnbroker Cohen reveal the multivalent emotional attachments of Jewish young men and women in the eighteenth and nineteenth century. Although many were drawn into marriage with Christians, some clearly clung tenaciously to their Jewishness—even to the point of bringing their formerly Christian spouses into the Jewish fold; this was at a time when neither the Christian community nor the Jewish community were quite ready to accept the conversion of Christians to Judaism.

Other Jews who intermarried but did not bring their partners into the Jewish fold nevertheless seemed to persevere—at least in some notable instances—in their attachment to the Jewish community. In the 1750s, one Michael Judah, a small-town merchant who resettled from New York to Norwalk, Connecticut, married Martha Raymond, a Christian. It appears that he had his son circumcised by the qualified religious *mohel* he had brought to Norwalk for the occasion. It also appears that he had attempted to maintain a kosher household, and in his will he bequeathed the bulk of his modest estate to Congregation Shearith Israel in New York and to related Jewish charities. His son David, whose descendants include General Henry Moses Judah and Theodore Dehone Judah, the promoter of the Pacific Coast Railroad, lived his life as a Christian.[9]

Several themes emerge from the examples given thus far. One is that the type of Jew who intermarried was often an adventurer or an economically driven settler. The other is that most intermarriages were conditioned by a short supply of available Jewish women, particularly in the more remote areas of the country. Related to this point, of course, is the rather obvious observation that in most instances Jewish intermarriers were usually men. Finally, it appears that even in the earliest instances of intermarriage, some Jews felt sufficiently free in the American environment, and sufficiently committed to their Jewish heritage, that they sought and effected the conversions of their Christian mates to Judaism.

One other social type emerges from the historical record, reflected in the person of David Franks, one of the earliest Jewish settlers in Philadelphia. The son of an observant Jew, he married into one of the well-known Christian families in the city and moved in the highest social circles. His daughter Rebecca was raised as a Christian and married a Christian gentleman, Lt. Col. Henry Johnson.[10]

The Franks' family fortune was first established by Jacob Franks, who arrived in New York in the first decade of the 1700s, and by his two sons, Naphtali and Moses. According to Jacob R. Marcus, the Franks were the most successful and influential Jewish family in America in the eighteenth century. Their fortunes were made in military and government supply on a large scale. Evidently, by the third generation the attractions of the Christian aristocracy proved powerful enough to draw some of their descendants into intermarriage and apostasy, although other members of the family continued to uphold family tradition and married only within the Jewish fold.

The model of marital assimilation into the upper echelons of the American Christian elite, however, would be epitomized in its consummate form nearly one hundred years after the Franks had become fully integrated into that society. The man who set the tone of that model for the descendants of German Jewry in the nineteenth century was August Belmont (previously Schonberg), born in 1816. A son of a modest German-Jewish family, August was apprenticed to the House of Rothschild in Frankfurt in his teens. He came to New York upon the heels of a great financial upheaval, with the expressed purpose of turning a calamitous situation to personal advantage. He was an aggressive speculator. Upon landing in New York, he changed his name to Belmont and cultivated a life-style as remote from the local German-Jewish community as possible. In 1847, already among the wealthiest men in the city, he married Caroline Slidell Perry, daughter of the famous Commodore Matthew C. Perry, hero of the Mexican War and the man credited with opening relations with Japan. The wedding was at Grace Episcopal Church, with such families as the Astors, Vanderbilts, and Winthrops in attendance. August Belmont lived out his life among the elite as an Episcopalian and left no Jewish descendants. Indeed, he took great pains to camouflage his heritage.[11]

Belmont's intermarriage and apostasy were clearly the result of an almost transparent opportunism, but his model would be followed (in less extreme form) right up to the present day by highly upwardly mobile Jews—men and women alike—who saw marriage into the so-called "old American families," the

WASP elite, as a fitting crown to their achievement of wealth and power.

Or, perhaps, they saw (and many still see) marriage with a Jew as maintaining tribal loyalties that are inconsistent with their achievements in the public domain.

One contemporary example of this outlook might be a man like Henry Kissinger. Born in Furth, Germany in 1923, Kissinger was raised in an Orthodox Jewish family of solid middle-class standing.[12] His father was a highly admired teacher in an elite girls' high school. The family emigrated from Furth in the mid-1930s after the rise of Hitler, and settled in the Washington Heights section of Manhattan, which was already home to a large and growing enclave of Orthodox Jewish emigres from Germany. From all accounts of the family, Henry and his younger brother Walter continued to live an Orthodox Jewish life, actively taking part in the life of the local Jewish community. Some of the old-timers still recall that Henry participated in the Sabbath afternoon synagogue youth groups in the area.

In 1949, Henry Kissinger married his first wife, a Jewish young woman by the name of Ann Fleischer. They remained married for fifteen years and had two children. However, it appears that as his career leaped forward, his attachment to the Jewish tradition and to his Jewish wife diminished. He was divorced in 1964. In the 1960s and 1970s, as is well known, he began a meteoric rise to power and fame. In 1974, he married Nancy Maginnes, the attractive, intellectually gifted daughter of an "old American" WASP family. It would seem that Henry had finally acquired in the private sphere of domestic life the status commensurate with his achievements in the public domain.

Interestingly, Henry's brother Walter Kissinger—whose rise to the heights of financial accomplishment as an industrialist and financial wizard antedated Henry's own ascendancy to power—skipped the first stage of domestic drama. He married some nine years after Henry in 1958, although he is but a year younger. But his first (and thus far only) marriage was to a Protestant woman, Eugenie Van Drooge.

The number of well-known and accomplished American Jews who have married Christians is legion. Certainly this cannot be the place to catalog them. But it is important to reflect upon such men as the Kissinger brothers, August Belmont, and David Franks. Their mating choices tell us of the apparent price that the Jewish family system, and perhaps all minority family systems, feel they must pay when some of its members reach the pinnacle of wealth, status, and power in the wider society.

Glancing over the brief list of examples of Jews who have intermarried since the days of Dr. Jacob Lumbrozo in the seventeenth century, we are left with a paradox.

On one hand, the rising tide of intermarriage came in the wake of the economic and political revolutions of modern Western society. Intermarriage followed quite naturally from the emancipation of the individual in matters of mate selection, and signified the triumph of romantic ideology over tradition. Men and women could fall in love without regard to traditional group barriers and have the reasonable expectation that they might enjoy a lifetime of marital partnership with the object of their affection.

But one of the principles of the romantic ethos is that affection between men and women arises naturally, without any social constraint or rational calculation of advantage. In fact, it is a commonly held view that intermarriage, because it transgresses normative barriers, is based on more passionate feelings or a greater irrationality on the part of the lovers.

On the other hand, we have seen in the examples here that love is by no means blind. Cupid's arrows seem to be guided by compelling social influences, although tradition or religious heritage are not among them. Presuming that all the examples mentioned above were couples who "fell in love" before they married and that they chose to marry primarily because they were in love, their choices nevertheless have a certain rationality, even inevitability to them.

The shortage of suitable Jewish women made it inevitable that young Jewish men would more or less have to fall in love with and marry Christian women. The open, fluid social milieu of the newly settled communities of the American West in the nineteenth century broke down barriers between Jews and Christians, and the relatively free socializing between men and women paved the way for romance and intermarriage. Love did not break down those barriers. It simply filtered through the cracks that were being rapidly opened by other forces. And with the opportunity open to talent, it was virtually inevitable that some men—like David Franks, August Belmont, and Henry Kissinger—would rise to such high positions of power and status that they would consider marrying within the Jewish fold as marrying down.

The paradox that this line of analysis leads us to is that in an age of romanticism and emancipated mate selection, intermarriages—at least those we have looked at so far—reflect an undercurrent of realism; a tendency to choose marriage partners not so much as to oppose tradition, but rather to conform with the normative constraints of the present (i.e., one must marry at least one's social equal if not one's social better). Put more simply, the constraints of the past seem to have been replaced by the constraints of the present.

Is intermarriage, then, really a product of the romantic complex? Indeed, is any marriage, or is it based upon less ethereal emotions? The question sounds a bit sophomoric, but it is inevitable. In fact, it is probably a question that nearly all modern couples ask themselves and each other when they begin to seriously contemplate the possibility of marriage. In most cases, these questions are probably not resolved by the head, but by the heart. Lovers can allow themselves the luxury of being sophomoric in any century and at any age, but, in the context of our discussion, we cannot. Nor can we be presumptuous enough to make declarations about the mental or emotional states of men and women who claim to "be in love" without some further analysis of that delicate condition.

Fortunately, we have the benefit of some brilliant analyses of the processes of couple formation, and the role of love in it, by earlier students of American courtship. These studies, known in general as sequential theories of mate selection, all emphasize that becoming a couple is a developmental phenomenon and not a singular sudden event.[13]

Long before two people can "fall in love" they have to be within each other's field of eligibles, that is, a socially legitimate category from which each recognizes that it is appropriate for them to consider choosing a partner. Before one falls in love with a person, he or she has a mental image of the kinds of persons who might be considered suitable. That mental image, perhaps not even an image, but rather merely a set of abstract attributes (e.g., she has to be a college graduate, not over thirty, without children, etc.; he has to be successful, not wear white socks with brown shoes and a black suit, etc.), may not even be consciously articulated. People's particular "lists" may vary, and we may not stick to them too closely, but these attribute lists or mental images act as a kind of filter to screen out those one simply would not consider.

Those who intermarry generally come from backgrounds in which they have had sufficient social encounters with people outside their own ethnic and religious group so that their mental construct of their field of eligibles is more inclusive, to begin with, than those who do not intermarry. For example, Henry Kissinger married his first wife, who was Jewish, when he was twenty-six years old. As a young man from an Orthodox Jewish background, his field of eligibles clearly did not readily include Christians, regardless of his intellectual breadth. When he married for the second time, he was already the Secretary of State, and forty-nine years old. It is also instructive to note that Kissinger met his second wife while they were both in the employ of Governor Nelson Rockefeller. The situation of familiarity that led to intimacy was the workplace and the political arena, which, at least in the United States, permit men and women to socialize on emotionally neutral grounds.

In our survey of intermarried couples around the country, we found that nearly half of them met either at college or in their place of work. The rest met through friends or blind dates, or through an assortment of chance encounters.

The predominant mode of meeting is upon emotionally neutral ground, where erstwhile strangers can discover whether they might be suitable for one another. But for that discovery to be made, the strangers have to meet. In other words, there has to be an opportunity. The values of each person have to be such as to enable him or her to come to evaluate the other as ultimately acceptable. Cupid does not shoot his arrows until each man and each woman has judged the other a suitable target. Love does not make another person a suitable potential mate. The recognition of that potential precedes the emotional verdict "I am in love with. . . ." Ira Reiss's "wheel theory of love," which sees the feeling of love emerging in successive stages, from rapport to commitment, is the inner mechanism that drives this process. But, its outer social shell is held together by a series of role relationships as envisioned in the figure below. As this chart suggests, the opportunities (or dangers) of break up dog every step of the mating process.

Not surprisingly, we find that those who intermarry have a

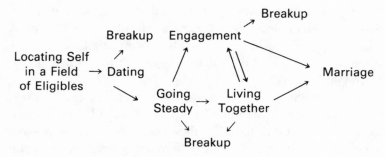

From meeting to mating: A flow chart

broader vision of their field of eligibles than those who do not intermarry. Given the sequential relationship between dating and marriage, the pattern of interdating is a good reflection of Jews' concept of their field of eligibles. The earlier mentioned National Jewish Population Study of 1970 inquired into the dating habits of Jewish adults with the following results. Those Jews who were intermarried were about four times more likely to have dated non-Jews during their late adolescent courtship period than were those who did not intermarry. To express it more specifically, among those couples who were not intermarried, 40 percent had never dated a non-Jew. In our survey of intermarried couples, we found that less than 10 percent had dated Jews exclusively prior to meeting their non-Jewish spouse.

Disproportionately, intermarriers are also people who marry at a somewhat later age than those who marry within their own ethnic and religious groups. As likely as not, intermarriers are also men and women who have already been once divorced. In our study of intermarried couples, we found that about 22 percent of the born-Jewish spouses and about 15 percent of the born-Christian spouses had been previously married. Erich Rosenthal, in his pioneering studies of intermarriage among Jews in Indiana and Iowa (1970), had also found that—to a significant degree—those who were intermarried were more likely to have been previously divorced from a first marriage than those who were not intermarried. Overall, second marriages were about 50 percent more likely to be intermarriages than were first marriages.[14] In fact, a prior divorce leads to such a high incidence of intermarriage the second time around, that some have suggested that divorce is the leading cause of intermarriage.

The combination of later age at marriage and prior divorce significantly serves to limit one's traditional field of eligibles, on the one hand, and to significantly expand one's field of potential eligibles, on the other. A failure to marry within the customary age period limits one's choices of potential mates within one's own ethnic and religious group. If the delay is also attended by frustrated desire after several marriageable years have passed without finding a suitable mate within the group, the taboo against intermarriage tends to diminish. "At least she (or he) is married and happy." "At least I can hope to live to see grand-children." These are some of the comments Jewish and Chris-tian parents make to reconcile themselves to the intermarriage of their daughters and sons when they have waited to marry within the group for too long without result.

Divorce channels men and women toward intermarriage partly as a result of the age factor and the diminishing pool of eligibles. It is also often accompanied by a mixture of shame (about marital failure) and resentment at the very value of endogamy, as well as the people (such as parents) who most represent that value. The divorced certainly resent their former spouses (and, by extension, their spouse's same-sex peers with-in the group). Taken together, these factors both impel and free the divorced man or woman to seek a new partner from outside his or her group.

In our study, the Christians who married Jews had also had an established circle of friends that included Jews as well as non-Jews, and only about half said that they had not dated any Jews until they met their present spouse. Considering the fact that Jews comprise less than 3 percent of the population, and non-Jews 97 percent, it is quite remarkable that nearly half the Chris-tians who married Jews had also dated Jews before they met their present spouse. Their field of eligibles was clearly much more heterogeneous or inclusive of Jews than one would expect from demographic norms. What shaped that field, besides the vagaries of demography and coincidence, is a set of values by which each was judged worthy of the other.

We also found that the circle of friends of intermarrieds, when they were still adolescents, was less mixed than their circle of dating partners. The table below conveys this point

Social Composition of Friends and Dates of Intermarrieds

	Born-Jewish respondents		Born-Christian respondents	
Composition	Friends	Dates	Friends	Dates
All/most Jewish	47	34	4	6
Mixed	29	36	11	18
All/most Christian	23	30	75	76
Total	100	100	100	100

with percentages. In our survey of intermarried couples, we asked each person to indicate whether their friends and their dating partners during adolescence were all or mostly Jewish, mixed (including Jews and Christians), or all or mostly Christian.

First, these numbers make the demographic point referred to earlier. Christians, being the overwhelming majority, are much less likely to have had Jewish friends or dating partners as adolescents. On the other hand, Jews, who are in a very small minority, are much more likely to have had either a mixed group or even mostly Christian friends and dates.

The second point made by these numbers, which is more pertinent to the present discussion, is that mixing between Jews and Christians seems to have been greater at the dating stage than at the friendship stage. Presumably, adolescents establish friendships before they begin to date. At the earlier stage, they are more under the influence of their parents, and therefore their friendships tend to be more limited to their own social group. As dating begins at a somewhat later age, their choices of dates seem to reflect a broadening of their concept of their pool of eligibles. To be sure, the differences are not great, but the trend is consistent with our analysis.

In a 1984 study of a nationwide sample of Jewish college students (sponsored by the American Jewish Committee), Rela Geffen Monson asked respondents questions similar to our own about the composition of friendship circles and about dating partners.[15] Monson divided her sample into three separate groupings according to their level of participation in Jewish student activities on campus (which is a good barometer of ingroup solidarity): high, medium, and low. The table below summarizes her findings.

In other words, a person's informal and voluntary ties to his or her ethnic community in a free environment, like the college campus, reflects the value he or she places on those ties. Given the fact that it is also through such ties that one's pool of potential mates is formed, the connection between values and ultimate mating choices seems quite clear. As we can see from the numbers, those Jewish college students who dated Jews exclusively tended to be largely (55 percent) students with a high

Composition of Friends and Dates, by Level of Participation in Jewish Student Life

| Composition | Level of participation (%) | | | |
	High	Medium	Low	Total
Proportions of close friends/Jewish				
All	52	31	17	100
Some	21	40	39	100
None	16	32	52	100
Proportions of serious dates/Jewish				
All	55	29	16	100
Some	22	41	37	100
None	16	32	52	100

degree of involvement in Jewish student life. Among the exclusive Jewish daters, only 16 percent had a low degree of involvement in Jewish student life. Similarly, those Jewish students who dated only non-Jews were also largely (52 percent) the students who had a low degree of involvement with other Jewish students in campus activities.

These figures also underscore the sequential model of mate selection referred to earlier. Who one dates and, ultimately, who one comes to fall in love with, is first of all a function of the social circles in which one moves, the ways in which one evaluates those circles, and the way one is evaluated by them. In other words, you may or may not love the persons you are with, but you cannot love the ones you are never with.

Our own survey data also showed that both Jewish and Christian intermarriers achieved significantly higher levels of education than those typical for their population as a whole. As the table below shows, over 90 percent of the Jewish men and over 80 percent of the Jewish women had at least a bachelor's degree. Indeed, nearly 50 percent of the men and about 40 percent of the women had advanced graduate degrees. Of their spouses who were not born Jewish, about 84 percent of the men

Percentage of Intermarrieds at Various Levels of Completed
Education by Ancestry and by Sex ($n = 450$)

Levels of education	Born-Jewish spouse		Born-Christian spouse	
	Male	Female	Male	Female
Less than college	8	18	17	23
College (BA/BS or similar)	42	42	27	45
Masters degree	14	31	22	23
PhD/MD/DDS/JD or similar	34	7	30	5
Other	2	2	4	4
Total	100	100	100	100

and 77 percent of the women had bachelor's degrees. More than 50 percent of the men had advanced degrees, as did about 28 percent of the women.

Further inquiry also showed that the great majority of our survey respondents had attended Ivy League schools, major private universities, or large state universities. Only about one-third had attended other small private colleges or state or community colleges. These broad descriptions all suggest that inter-marriers are generally high achievers, that they tend to move in cosmopolitan and liberal social circles, and that they are likely to have high aspirations for personal advancement.

What these facts also suggest is that the intermarriers of today, like their counterparts in the seventeenth and the eighteenth century, are likely to be on the frontiers of social mobility. Consequently, they are more likely to have a broadened sense of their "field of eligibles," they are more likely to meet people outside their own group who are tolerant of intergroup differences, and they are less likely to be subject to the traditional controls of family and community in their mating choices.

Chapter Four

THE HEART
HAS REASONS

The Heart
Has Reasons

The process of intermarriage, then, begins with a broad and inclusive vision of one's field of eligibles, which itself is shaped, to a large extent, by one's needs and values. But do intermarriers have needs and values that are substantially different from those who do not intermarry? This question has elicited several different opinions.

Social scientists who are most demographically inclined believe that individual behavior is largely determined by population composition and the constraints and opportunities it offers. They argue that intermarriers are no different from non-intermarriers; they are simply individuals who find themselves, in the prime time of mate selection (between the late teens and the early twenties), in a social environment where there is a high probability that they will meet and fall in love with members of the opposite sex who are not of their own ethnic or religious group. This argument certainly applies to such early intermarriers as Jacob Lumbrozo. It also applies to the many intermarriers found among small town Jews and Jews who lived in new suburbs in the 1950s, when Jews were more apt to meet non-Jews as peers and dates than they might have been in more densely Jewish neighborhoods.

A large body of psychological opinion, however, virtually disregards social realities and focuses, instead, on the inner needs or fears of intermarriers. This body of opinion was ably summarized by Louis Berman in 1968.[1] Among other factors, Berman mentions the following as some of the psychological marks of the Jewish intermarrier:

1. *Excessive attachment between mothers and sons, or between fathers and daughters.* Such attachment makes it difficult for the young Jewish adult to form a "normal" sexual attachment to a member of the opposite sex within his or her own group, due to overidentification with the parent of the opposite sex and the related fear of incest.

2. *Excessive mothering and/or fathering.* Overprotectiveness and control prevent the individual from achieving a sense of autonomy and self-mastery. They associate such stifling of their individuality with all members of the opposite sex within their own group.

3. *Repressive sexual training in puberty and adolescence.* The combination of Jewish inhibition of sexuality before marriage, and the prudery associated with upwardly striving middle-class life, leads Jewish young adults to see members of the opposite sex within their own group as "cold," "unsensuous," etc. By contrast, they see members of the opposite sex who are not Jewish as more sexually liberated, more fun, more loving and warm, etc.

4. *Existential insecurity.* Living with a history of persecution, forced migration, and other collective memories of minority status, Jews—particularly those who intermarry—see Christians as objects of emotional health and security for which they have a deep-seated need. This invidious view of the existential condition of the Jew and the Christian sometimes also produces a sense of "self-hate." Marriage with the more secure, emotionally healthier (and physically more robust) Christian enables the Jew to compensate for his or her own existentially conditioned flaws.

These psychological traits of Jewish intermarriers are synthesized from the clinical studies of scores of psychoanalysts and clinically trained rabbis from the 1920s on. The case material cited by Berman suggests that these psychological insights are particularly useful in accounting for what Karl Abraham called "neurotic exogamy."[2]

As is often the case with clinically based concepts, it is difficult to determine the extent to which such traits would be found throughout the total population of Jewish intermarriers. Indeed, if these traits are to be found among Jewish intermarriers in general, one would expect that they are even more to be found among those Jews who are not intermarried. After all, they, too, are subject to excessive attachment to parents, overprotective parenting, prudery in sexual training, and existential insecurity. Thus, either these traits are not to be found among most Jewish intermarriers, and therefore their explanatory value is highly limited, or they are to be found among all Jews, intermarried or not, in which case they beg the question of why they lead to intermarriage among some (a minority of) Jews and do not lead to intermarriage among the majority.

In addition to the psychological traits outlined above, Berman also mentions several familial traits that may have psychological impacts that foster intermarriage. These include difficult relations with parents in adolescence (which fosters rebellion), the breakup of the parental relationship during childhood or adolescence (especially by divorce), few or no ties with extended kin (cousins, aunts, uncles, grandparents), and being the youngest child or an only child. But these traits also emphasize abnormality in the backgrounds of intermarriers. Therefore, they fail to tell us much about the majority who, in fact, tend to be "normal" (i.e., not rebellious, not from "broken homes," not alienated from their relatives, and not the youngest or only children).

As a matter of fact, all the research cited by Berman—and it is voluminous—refers to studies done at a time when intermarriage was a rather uncommon, highly stigmatized phenomenon, both in the Jewish community and in the wider society. Therefore, it is quite likely that for most of the period that is covered by Berman's work (1920s to 1960s), those who intermarried did tend to be psychologically different from those who did not, in more than one respect.

However, with the great increase in the numbers of Jews marrying non-Jews since the mid-1960s, not only in outlying areas with small Jewish populations, but also in cities with centers of Jewish population, it is difficult to sustain the familiar demographic explanation and even more difficult to sustain the psychological one.

The greatest explosion of Jewish intermarriage in the modern world has occurred in America, precisely at a time of permissive parenting, sexual liberation, and great Jewish self-assuredness. It has also occurred primarily among second, third, and later generations of American-born Jews who have little reason for "existential anxiety," at least as Jews. Thus, the social trends of the past twenty years have rendered those explanations obsolete. Perhaps they were valid at an earlier time; they are not valid at present.

A possibly more durable explanation is offered by the work of Robert K. Merton, a sociologist, in a 1941 essay, "Intermarriage and the Social Structure."[3] Merton points out that, according to the then available data, intermarriers most often differ on two dimensions of social status: *ascribed* status (i.e., status into which one is born, such as being black or being a Brahmin) and *achieved* status (i.e., status that one achieves through personal effort and accomplishment). Focusing on black–white marriages, Merton observed, "the most striking uniformity in the statistics is the marriage between White females and Negro males." Merton goes on to suggest that this pattern of marriage between the racial castes in America is "understandable in terms of social structure." Specifically, he argues that in such marriages the female usually enjoys a higher ascribed status (because she is white) than the male, but most often the male enjoys a higher achieved status. Thus, Merton suggests, the marriage represents a kind of "exchange" in which the female acquires, as it were, a higher achieved status by association, just as the male acquires a higher ascribed status by assocation.

The model of exchange outlined by Merton is a simple one, and probably too simple. And although it may have worked reasonably well to account for black–white marriages in the first half of the twentieth century, it probably does not work nearly as well in the last quarter—neither for marriages between blacks and whites nor for marriages between Jews and Christians. Nevertheless, Merton surely put his finger on at least one dimension of the mate selection filter: the unconscious desire on the part of all men and women for status consistency at the level of their highest status. Given the assumption that, in a predominantly Christian country like the United States, being Jewish means that one has a lower ascribed status than Christians, it would not be at all surprising if a substantial number of intermarriages might be explained by highly achieving Jewish men marrying less accomplished non-Jewish women.

Of course, this explanation still leaves wide open the question of why Christian men marry Jewish women. As we have seen in Chapter Three, intermarrying Christian men also constitute a group of high achievers who presumably have available to them a wide field of Christian women. It must be added, parenthetically, that, during the late 1970s and early 1980s, the greatest growth in the rate of marriages between Jews and non-Jews had been between Jewish women and Christian men. One answer might be that relative to Christian women, Jewish women are, in fact, high achievers—a fact that is strongly suggested by the table on p. 94 as well as by other research. Therefore, Christian men might be selecting Jewish women because of their relatively higher achieved status. On the other hand, Jewish men might be selecting Christian women because of their relatively higher ascribed status. The resolution of these conjectures will have to wait for future research.

What the psychological and sociological theories make abundantly clear is that there are probably far more conscious factors operating in the decisions of men and women to marry one another than are tapped by the subtle conceptions of social science. Whatever intrapsychic or societal forces impel people into marriage, it is clear that those forces are themselves filtered through conscious value judgments.

We have seen earlier that Jewish intermarriers cannot be distinguished from non-intermarriers by either their demographic isolation from the centers of Jewish population or by their psychological traits. Perhaps they can be distinguished by the values they hold. Values are those symbols, ideas, objects, or states of being that persons hold to be good, beautiful, and worthy of pursuit and possession. From the perspective of social science, values are the meaningful goals that stimulate the individual to follow a certain course of action. Do intermarriers hold values that are significantly different from the values of non-intermarriers?

The answer that one is most inclined to give to that question is an emphatic "Yes." Yes, intermarriers do have values that differ from those of non-intermarriers! Having said that, however, one is hard put to demonstrate just exactly how they differ.

The simplest level on which one might be able to establish the differences between the two types of Jews and the two types of Christians is to say that those who do not intermarry place a higher value on marriage within their group than do those who intermarry. But the National Jewish Population Study found that when a large sample of non-intermarried adult Jews were asked to agree or disagree with the statement "It is alright for Jews to marry non-Jews," 38 percent agreed that it was. When intermarried adults were asked to agree or disagree with the statement, nearly 10 percent disagreed. Although they themselves were intermarried, they did not think that it was alright for Jews to marry Christians. One presumes that they were either divorced or that their Christian mates had converted to Judaism.

The point is that more than one-third of America's Jews

who are not intermarried nevertheless think that it is alright to intermarry, and a minority of intermarriers do not think that Jews and non-Jews should intermarry. In fact, the same National Jewish Population Study showed that in about one-third of the intermarriages, the Christian spouse converted to Judaism.

In the study by Rela Geffen Monson, *Jewish Campus Life* (1984), which deals with the attitudes of Jewish college students toward marriage and family life, it was found that only 15 percent of 1,300 modern American Jewish college students throughout the United States said that they never date and never would date a non-Jew. One of the women in Monson's study expressed some insights into her own feelings that probably reflect the feelings of others as well.

> Being raised as a caring and committed Jew, I cannot foresee marrying out of the religion. Especially since my grandfather was a rabbi and my grandmother was a past president of Hadassah and a devoted Zionist. Yet, the sparse number of Jews on campus, combined with their devotion to academics, makes dating Jewish males difficult. In addition, I tend to like the "jocky" fun-loving type of guys. Unfortunately, because of this I have yet to date a Jew. . . . I only hope that when I am ready for marriage I will meet a "nice Jewish boy" . . . but I can't say that I wouldn't marry someone because he was not Jewish.[4]

What makes this particular student's comments so telling is her family background. Her grandparents were both highly committed and active Jews. The fact that she refers to them suggests that they are very much on her mind in dealing with this issue. Yet her desire to be in the company of "jocky," fun-loving types of guys takes precedence in her mental calculus when choosing dating partners. Apparently being from a highly committed Jewish family background is no sure deterrent to interdating. In fact, Monson found that those who came from highly religious homes were five times less likely to interdate than those who came from non-religious homes. But even among those who did come from highly religious homes, only 30 percent said that they never date and never would date non-Jews, and 70 percent either do or would.

Some of those 70 percent who currently do interdate or would if the opportunity presented itself, and who all come from religiously observant Jewish homes, will end up marrying Christians. Can one, then, say of those who will end up inter-marrying that their values differed from those who did not inter-marry? It is very difficult to say!

It is the conventional wisdom among Jews that those who intermarry do so because they come from families in which there was no emphasis on Jewish values and the practices of Jewish living. On purely statistical grounds, that bit of conven-tional wisdom seems to be true. Intermarriage seems to occur with far greater frequency among those people in the Jewish community who have a low level of religious observance and a low degree of involvement with Jewish community life than those who have a high level of religious observance and commu-nal involvement.

Yet, as Monson's data suggest, when one probes the thoughts and feelings of young adults who come from those highly observant, committed Jewish homes, it is not at all clear that their values are substantially different from those who come from less observant, less committed homes.

Other values besides the value of in-marriage—or endog-amy, as social scientists call it—energize American Jewish life. It is probably impossible to identify all of them in detail, and even more impossible to determine how they are weighed in the hearts and minds of different groups of Jews. But through the works of such thoughtful students of American Jewish life as Marshall Sklare, Charles Liebman, and Steven M. Cohen, it is possible to piece together a more or less coherent view of its basic value system.[5] First, American Jews are committed to their own group survival. They are committed to the defense and support of Israel as a tangible symbol of their determination to survive. American Jews are committed to fighting against (as opposed to quietly tolerating) anti-Semitism and remembering that millions of their brethren were killed in the Nazi Holocaust perhaps because not enough men and women of goodwill fought back. American Jews are also committed to helping those Jews in need through volunteer work and charitable giving.

Naturally, the degree to which different segments of American Jewry adhere to these values varies considerably. What courses of action different segments will follow as a result of these values varies greatly as well. In a statistically elegant study, Steven M. Cohen has shown that such factors as age, education, income, occupation, number of generations in America, and stage in the family life cycle all play a significant role in shaping the behavior of individual Jews with respect to these values.

A more introspective essay on the American Jewish world view was Charles Liebman's *Ambivalent American Jew* (1973). He suggested that the value system of American Jews is fundamentally divided between their commitment as Jews to remain culturally different and socially separate and distinguishable from their Christian neighbors and their commitment as Americans to be full and equal participants in the wider society. According to Liebman, this ambivalence is endemic to the American Jewish outlook, regardless of which segment of Jewry one belongs to, and regardless of one's demographic traits. Indeed, the ambivalence, part and parcel of modern Jewish consciousness, places every Jew simultaneously into a rapidly changing and universally shared present and a timeless and highly particularistic historical past.

Given this pervasive ambivalence, it is indeed very difficult to say with conviction that intermarriers differ from non-intermarriers in terms of their awareness or acceptance of basic Jewish values. Perhaps it is only by some unfathomable coincidence or the grace of God that they end up on different sides of a shared chasm of ambivalent feelings.

In our study of intermarrieds, we devised a scale of Jewish values comprised of five affirmative statements that respondents were asked to agree or disagree with. The five statements were: (a) "Being Jewish is very important to me." (b) "American Jews and Jews in Israel are part of one people." (c) "It is important to me that there should always be a Jewish people." (d) "A Jew has a greater responsibility for other Jews than for non-Jews." (e) "I would be quite surprised and upset if my children did not regard themselves as Jews when they grew up." Although these statements obviously do not exhaust the range of values in the American Jewish *Weltanschauung*, they provide a useful measure of the core value of group survival and of the sense of interconnectedness of Jews the world over.

Agreement with each statement earned the respondent one point on the five-item scale. The highest score on the scale was five and the lowest score was zero. When we compiled the average score for our entire sample of 450 intermarrieds, we found an average score of 2.87. That means that the average respondent agreed with nearly three out of the five statements. In the absence of a non-intermarried group of typical American Jews with which they might be compared, we subdivided our intermarrieds according to the classifications shown in the table below, and calculated the average score of each on our Jewish value scale.

These seemingly cryptic numbers suggest that intermarriers do differ significantly among themselves in the affirmation of core Jewish values. Therefore, one expects that they would also differ significantly from non-intermarriers, but not by all that much.

Of the five items that comprised our scale, we found that 80 percent of all the intermarriers agreed with the statement "Being Jewish is very important to me" and 87 percent agreed with the statement "It is important to me that there should always be a Jewish people." However, only about one-half agreed with the statements "A Jew has a greater responsibility

Average Scores of Categories of Intermarriers on Jewish Value Scale

Category	Group average
Total sample	2.87
If parents of intermarrier had been synagogue members	3.12
If type of synagogue to which parents belonged was	
Reform	2.89
Conservative	3.11
Orthodox	3.20
If the non-Jewish spouse converted to Judaism under the auspices of	
Reform	3.98
Conservative	3.87
Orthodox	4.56
If the intermarriage was performed by a rabbi (even without conversion)	3.49

for other Jews than for non-Jews" and "American Jews and Jews in Israel are part of one people." Similarly, only one-half agreed with the statement "I would be quite surprised and upset if my children did not regard themselves as Jews when they grew up."

In short, the differences in degree reflect differences in the kind of values that are affirmed or not affirmed. The overwhelming majority of the intermarriers are committed to a broad and somewhat abstract sense of group continuity. This they would undoubtedly share with non-intermarried Jews as well. However, only about one-half share in the more specific and particular ramifications of that general value. This sets them apart from those other intermarriers who share in the broader range of the value of group continuity. It would probably also set them apart from non-intermarried Jews.

Having taken this somewhat circuitous excursion around the issue of American-Jewish values, we now come back to the questions that inspired it. Do intermarriers differ from those Jews who have not intermarried in terms of their basic Jewish values? Are those value differences useful in explaining why American Jews intermarry? Is the conventional wisdom, that one main cause of contemporary Jewish intermarriage is the insufficient grounding of young adult Jews in their traditions, valid; that if they had had a more thoroughly Jewish upbringing, they would not have intermarried?

Neither the scholarship of the last thirty years nor recent survey data permit an unqualified endorsement of the conventional wisdom. Many non-intermarried Jews believe that it is alright for Jews to marry Christians. Many Jews from religiously observant Jewish homes interdate, or would do so if the opportunity presented itself. And many intermarried Jews, in fact, share some of the deepest and most widely adhered to values of American Jews, in general.

Moreover, this analysis of Jewish values, and the varying commitments of different groups of Jews to them, has not yet taken into account the values of the Christians who have married Jews. A 1983 Gallup opinion poll found that the percentage of non-Jewish Americans who approve of marriage between Jews and non-Jews has increased from 59 percent in 1968 to 77 percent.[6] The fact that the majority of American Jews are two or three generations removed from their immigrant ancestors and have moved *en masse* into the mainstream of America's middle and upper middle class, has made Jews not only socially acceptable, but even desirable as marriage partners. Justified or not, the Jewish reputation for thrift, hard work, economic skill, and sobriety, and the reputation of the Jewish family for warmth and mutual caring, has made young Jews prime marriage targets in the eyes of a number of non-Jews. Given the rapid social mobility of Jews, their passion for education, and their achievement in such highly visible areas as literature, the arts, films, and journalism, it is not at all surprising that Jews should come to be seen in the eyes of a number of non-Jews as "culture heroes."

There is yet another ingredient to be added to the image of Jews in the eyes of Christians in the mid-twentieth century. Since the 1960s, America has witnessed and welcomed the return of ethnicity. Tastes, expressions, and group memories that were once thought to be appropriate only to immigrants were suddenly thought to be venerable and quaint objects of nostalgia by their American-born descendants. Because Jewish group identity is a complex mixture of religious as well as ethnic affinities (and since the founding of the state of Israel, it has also taken on the added patina of the rugged, resourceful pioneer–soldier), Jewishness reemerged in the 1960s as a culturally positive image.

All these factors, taken together, have made intermarriage a more frequent occurrence not only because of Jewish proclivities, but also (and equally so) because of Christian preferences.

John E. Mayer, who in his book, *Jewish-Gentile Courtship* (1961), studied four dozen young couples, recorded some of the images that the Christian spouses had of Jews, in general, and their own Jewish partners, in particular. A Catholic woman, who met her husband in a company cafeteria, assumed at first that he was a Christian. "I thought, now there's a man with brains. He didn't go on with the usual silly office chatter." A Protestant woman is quoted by Mayer:

> What I liked most about my husband were his interests. . . . My husband was interested in philosophy and lots of other things. . . . I thought that with Steven my life would be changing and growing all the time.[7]

Another Catholic girl is quoted:

> When I went into nurses' training . . . at the hospital there were only a few Jewish doctors, but they were the outstanding ones, and everyone admired them. . . . After I was through with nurses' training I wouldn't have refused to go out with anyone because he was Jewish.[8]

A Protestant man, raised in a small town in Arkansas, was taken to a Jewish party by a friend from school:

> They sang Russian and Jewish songs which had a vitality I'd never known before. And the strangeness and the newness had an exotic effect . . . it burst upon me that here are people that had a rounded cosmopolitan, as opposed to a provincial, outlook, against which I rebelled without finding an outlet. I admired them and what they stood for, and I wanted to rise to their stature. They interested me in things I had never dreamed of.[9]

And he met his Jewish wife in the same group.

Although these words come from anonymous interviews in social scientific studies, they might as well have been uttered by such famous personalities as Diana Ross, the electrifying black singer and movie star, who married Robert Silberstein, son of a well-to-do Jewish garment manufacturer, in 1971. Ross met Silberstein quite by accident in a Los Angeles men's shop where she was shopping for a present for a friend. According to *People Magazine*, she asked Silberstein for some help and "discovered a rare thing, a gentleman who was young, alive, and very handsome—all the fantasy things you think of in a husband."[10] The two had three children together before they divorced in the early 1980s.

At age 45, the star of film and television, Mary Tyler Moore, was recuperating from a broken second marriage (with Grant Tinker, head of NBC) and sorrow over the death of her younger sister (in 1978) and the self-inflicted death of her only son (in 1980) when she met and fell in love with Dr. Robert Levine. She married the New York cardiologist—fifteen years her junior—on Thanksgiving Eve, 1984. Perhaps the vivacious actress only saw youthful charm and sex appeal in the young Dr. Levine, but according to published accounts, the two spent Rosh Hashanah, a month preceding their marriage, quietly attending synagogue in Manhattan—even though Ms. Moore is a Roman Catholic.[11] What makes this marriage even more striking is that Levine is from a highly committed Jewish family. His father is a high level administrator in a major Jewish organization and his sister is a devout Orthodox Jew living a completely traditional Jewish life in a closely knit Jewish community.

If such a marriage had come about fifty years earlier, or even thirty years earlier, which is highly improbable, a man like Dr. Levine would have changed his name—perhaps to Linn or Livermoore—and tried to pass into his wife's obviously more exciting and elite social circle. He certainly would not have taken her with him to Rosh Hashanah services, nor would she have had the slightest interest in entering his ethnic and religious milieu.

Whatever may be the basis of Mary Tyler Moore's attraction to Robert Levine, and vice versa, the social vocabulary of the marriage, and her style of relating to his family heritage, clearly speak of the highly favorable image that the man *qua* Jew has in the eyes of his Catholic bride. It also speaks of a degree of pride and commitment that Levine has in his family heritage, which remains uncompromised despite his marriage to a highly attractive Catholic woman whose social status is clearly superior to and more secure than this own.

Whether any marriage is made in heaven, or by some intervention of divine powers, is a topic for romantics and theologians. But it is quite clear from our analysis, both of numbers and of people, that intermarriage involves a complex sequential process. For the most part, love itself enters the process fairly late in the game.

Ira Reiss, one of the foremost students of the sociology of modern "coupling," has suggested—on the basis of years of observation and careful survey work—that relationships that end up as love and marriage often begin merely as mutual interest or a generalized empathy.[12] Often they begin as simply the willingness of two people to go out on a "blind date" in which they are unaware of each other's background.

Once a relationship has begun, even on the most casual basis, the willingness of the partners to continue it, to see each

other again, is not a sure sign of any deep attachment, at least
not yet. Some of the interviews recorded in John Mayer's study
speak to this point quite openly. A Protestant husband:

> For the first six months I enjoyed going out with her, but had no
> serious intentions of getting involved. . . . I was really kind of a
> snob. When I was first dating her I felt I couldn't get interested in
> a Jew.[13]

A Jewish husband:

> I had been going with gentile girls before, and I was aware that it
> could happen [marriage]. But I felt that I would not let it happen
> to me.

A Catholic husband:

> About a month after we met, we went steady and we liked each
> other a lot . . . but I didn't think it would become serious. At the
> time I was just going out and enjoying myself.[14]

Another of John Mayer's Jewish interviewees remarked rather
soberly,

> We were not a big romance—we just drifted together as we got to
> know each other.

A Jewish husband put the same experience into a more dramatic
perspective:

> I never had any thoughts of marriage . . . never gave the matter
> any thought. As far as marriage was concerned, I felt that it was
> best just not to bother pondering about things like this. . . . One
> day I just found myself trapped.[15]

Although marital permanence may be far from people's
minds when they are just beginning to explore their interest in
one another, during that early state, Reiss observes, the couple
begins to indulge in varying amounts of mutual self-revelation.
Their values and tastes, from food to music, from people to
clothes, from films and literature to cars, are explored and com-

pared. Family histories are gradually unpacked and measured up, one against the other. The cast of characters in the lives of each is slowly introduced to the other, first only as idealized abstractions ("my brother majored in economics at Holyoke"), later as three-dimensional personalities with warts and all ("my sister had an abortion when she was sixteen, but we never told my parents").

The function of mutual self-revelation is not only to build familiarity (which can repel as much as attract), but also, and perhaps even more importantly, to build a sense of trust ("he has disclosed so much of his thoughts and experiences to me, that I feel I can trust him with my innermost secrets"). As we have seen from the comments of John Mayer's subjects, the stage of mutual self-revelation can last from weeks to months, and sometimes even to years. In my own survey of 450 inter-married couples, I found that the marriage partners knew each other and were dating, on the average, for two years before they actually got married; 45 percent of them were dating only for a year or less: and 29 percent for a period of between one to three years. The remaining 26 percent had dated for more than three years before getting married. Given current premarital mores, 35 percent had also lived together before marriage.

Interestingly, living together is no guarantee that a couple will end up marrying. In fact, in their landmark study, *American Couples* (1983), Philip Blumstein and Pepper Schwartz found that 29 percent of the cohabiting couples they interviewed in the course of the national survey had broken up within eighteen months after their survey was completed.[16] The remainder were either still cohabiting or had married. By contrast, only 14 percent of the married couples they interviewed had broken up. Although Blumstein and Schwartz did not focus on the inter-marriage issue *per se*, there is no reason to think that interfaith and interethnic POSSLQs (the U. S. Census's acronym for "persons of the opposite sex sharing living quarters") would have less than a 29 percent breakup rate. Given the pressure on such relationships, their rate of breakup is probably even higher.

Clearly, intermarriage is not something that most intermarriers rush into. They seem to tread cautiously toward it. Indeed, it is probable that the period of courtship preceding intermarriage is longer than that preceding marriage in general. Certainly there is a greater need for mutual self-revelation because not only self and family must be introduced into the couple's conversation, but also subcultures, and they must build a sense of trust and trustworthiness across foreign cultural terrain.

The courtship, or dating period, takes a dramatic turn toward permanence when the couple comes to realize that they are dependent upon each other in some profound and emotionally satisfying way. As Professor Henry Higgins sings of his Eliza Doolittle in the ever-popular *My Fair Lady*, "I've grown accustomed to her face." But he pines for her only when it seems he has lost her. The dramatic realization of mutual dependency only occurs in any courting relationship when the couple has had to face a challenge together.

"The nascent state," writes Franceso Alberoni,

> both with collective movements and with falling in love, always encounters a dilemma. . . . Tristram is divided between his affection for the king and his love for Iseult; Iseult between her affection for the king and her love for Tristram. Both Romeo and Juliet want to crush the inexorable laws of kinship and hatred, but they do not hate their parents.[17]

It is ironic that the dilemma that most intergroup couples face prior to marriage is the skepticism—if not the directly hostile opposition of their parents, siblings, and other relatives—concerning intermarriage. In our survey of intermarried couples, we asked both the born-Jewish and the born-Christian spouses to indicate whether their parents had opposed their interdating, in general, and their plans to intermarry. As we see

Percentage of Respondents Whose Parents Opposed Their
Interdating and Intermarriage

	Jewish parents		Non-Jewish parents	
	Father	Mother	Father	Mother
Opposed interdating	43	50	16	19
Opposed intermarriage	59	62	29	33

in the table above, Jewish parents were generally in opposition
to their children on both these grounds.

Christian parents are less opposed to their children dating
or marrying Jews than are Jewish parents, at least as reported by
the intermarrieds themselves. But in nearly two-thirds of the
cases, either one or both parents of the Jewish partner oppose
the intermarriage. Consequently, one of the major tasks the
dating couple must confront during their courtship is the dilemma of parental opposition, most often of the Jewish parents, but
in about one-third of the cases, of the Christian parents as well.

It is also important to point out here that—among these
very same respondents—less than 10 percent of the Jewish parents and less than 5 percent of the non-Jewish parents are reported to have shown any opposition to their children when, at
an earlier age, they had friends of either the same or opposite
sex from outside their own ethnic and religious group. Thus,
parental opposition to interdating and intermarrying presents
the couple with a surprising challenge.

One Jewish psychiatrist, Phil, married to a Catholic woman,
recalled—with a lingering sense of incredulity and much bitterness—his mother's violent reaction when he announced that he
was going "seriously" with his future wife.

> She started raving about how my father would have a heart at-
> tack; how I dishonored my grandparents; how I had no respect
> for the memory of six million Jews who were killed by the Nazis.

She just went "off the wall." Mind you, this woman hadn't been on the inside of a synagogue in maybe ten years, yeah, since my Bar Mitzvah. My father had this clothing store that he kept open seven days a week, year 'round. He never even closed for Yom Kippur. And here was my mother screaming at me about the shame I was bringing upon the Jewish heritage.

Phil's reaction to his mother was probably not too different from the reactions of thousands of others who have had similar experiences. He and Regina began to live together soon after that fateful battle. In a year they were married by a justice of the peace, without either of their parents present at the ceremony, and soon after marriage the young couple moved from New York to California.

Of course it would be silly to suggest that the two would not have married had it not been for Phil's mother's violent reaction to their courtship. In fact, probably many such courtships have been broken up by such parental outbursts and the sustained emotional pressure they exert on a budding relationship. But as likely as not, strong parental or other familial opposition to a fledgling romance between people who are already autonomous adults will tend to galvanize the couple. The opposition will constitute the challenge or dilemma, the overcoming of which will catapult the two into a sense of interdependence impelling them toward marriage.

The irony, here, is that the very people who are in opposition to intermarriage often help to bring it about by the style of their opposition. Ironic, too, is the fact that in many courtships preceding intermarriage, the overcoming of the opposition of families (and by extension, of the larger group tradition) is the primary basis for testing and proving the love that each has for the other. Overlooked is the fact that a much more profound test of the emotional ties of the couple will come only after marriage, when they actually have to integrate their respective cultural heritages into their life together.

The language, the visceral experiences, and the thousand

gestures of love that accompany the social fact of being a new couple lead to an ideology that pits the new "us" against the old "them." The sexual pleasure that most often attends the relationship is primary proof of the potency of the ideology. "We" can show "them" that the differences between our groups are not going to prevent us, as free and loving individuals, from forming a family that either ignores or bridges those differences. Love will triumph over tradition.

Intermarriage, like all marriage, then, is the outcome of an intricate developmental process in which emotions, values, and perceptions are reflected upon and negotiated within and between the partners, as well as between the partners and their respective families. However, unlike most other marriages, the process by which intermarriages come to life ends not only with a new couple becoming a family, it also ends with an implicit ideological affirmation that has grown out of the contest between love and tradition, between the individuals entering the marriage and their ancestors. It is an ideology of evolution, of rebirth, of boundless human potency for novelty and new beginnings. Although all marriages are personal testimonials to an abiding faith in life, intermarriages are also testimonials to a belief in the changeability of culture and society, to the changeability of the very core of the self.

Looked at in the light of its ideological component, intermarriage represents the very human and personal consequences of the predominant world view of all modern American Jews, indeed, of most modern ethnics and religious minorities. The belief that one can live, and the desire to live simultaneously as a minority committed to group survival and also as equal members of an open society, produces a level of ambivalence that will inevitably lead significant numbers to try to overcome that ambivalence. Ethnic isolationism and religious orthodoxy is one solution to that problem. Intermarriage is another. Both have progressed significantly in America since the mid-1960s, among Jews as well as others.

The path of ingroup isolationism tries to shut out the psy-chological challenge posed by the availability of alternate values and life-styles in a culturally pluralistic society. The path of in-termarriage, however, would nullify the reality of group diver-sity by blending cultural differences in the family melting pot.

But as we shall see, such a blending does not occur readily in the marriages between Jews and Christians. Personal dif-ferences in values, aspirations, behavioral style, and kinship loyalty, which are rooted in each person's family heritage as much as in their unique personalities, persist in the very woof and warp of the intermarried family. How these differences are worked into the texture of intermarried life is the subject of the remaining chapters.

Chapter Five

DIFFERENCES MATTER— SOMETIMES

Differences Matter— Sometimes

I was riding uptown from an appointment in Greenwich Village, reading a journal article that included in its title the word "intermarriage." Sitting next to me in the midday subway car was a young woman, thirtyish, casually dressed—jeans, loafers, a knapsack filled with books; probably a graduate student from New York University. She glanced over to what I was reading and gave a muffled but audible chuckle.

> Excuse me for laughing. I couldn't help noticing what you were reading. I thought it was about marriages between blacks and whites. Is that really an article about marriage between people from different religions?

Since she did not look like a typical subway "nut," I engaged her question. "Yes," I said, "Why do you find that amusing?" "I didn't think those things mattered anymore to anyone. You must be a professor." "I am, and they still do, at least to some people, sometimes," I replied. Neither of us cared to pursue the matter. We turned back to our reading and soon arrived at 59th Street, where I got off.

That chuckle, her incredulity, however, articulated a feeling that I was to encounter among many of my colleagues as well as friends and even intermarried research subjects. For many people, "intermarriage" is an arbitrary label attached to a marriage that, in fact, carries little or no meaning to the couple themselves.

Which differences matter? For whom? When and why? Are the differences in religious beliefs important, or are there more

123

subtle differences in attitudes, habits, or world view that really differentiate partners in an intermarriage? Are differences more important at some points along the family life cycle than others?

For example, Marshall L., a forty-four-year-old chemical engineer in Philadelphia, has been a member of a Unitarian church for the past eighteen years. He is a fourth-generation American of German-Jewish ancestry. His parents were nominal members of a large Reform temple when he was growing up, but were not particularly observant Jews nor in any way involved with Jewish community life. He hardly recalls anything particularly Jewish about his upbringing. Marshall's wife, Mildred, was born into a Midwestern Baptist family, with very little serious religious involvement. The two joined a local Unitarian church soon after their first child's birth. They felt the need for some kind of spiritually meaningful ethical community, but neither had much feeling for their ancestral religion or community. One of Marshall's coworkers invited them to visit the church one Sunday. They liked the people they met there and the quality of the minister's sermon, titled "Love and Reciprocity in Human Relations," as Marshall recalled. He and Mildred were sufficiently impressed to want to return a few Sundays later. Slowly they became regulars and, eventually, they took the formal step of becoming members.

Marshall and Mildred found it odd that I would even consider including them in a study of intermarriage. For them, the question of family tradition had never been a source of either personal or familial divisiveness. To be sure, Mildred often complains that Marshall spends too much time reading his professional journals as well as other literature. She much prefers an evening out with friends; she loves to watch basketball and even an occasional game of hockey, either on TV or live. He enjoys classical music more than she does, and he finds it harder to laugh at Woody Allen movies. As a descendant of a socially respectable German-Jewish family, he finds it hard to identify with the Eastern European immigrant *angst* projected by Woody

Allen characters. The fact that they are portrayed by a Jew only makes him uncomfortable. But neither of them has ever connected these differences in their preferences and temperaments to the fact that one is of German-Jewish and the other of Midwestern Baptist ancestry. They are a handsome American couple in the prime of life, comfortably middle class, with two typical teenage children. Mildred has returned to school after a hiatus of some twenty years and expects to get a degree in journalism.

The differences that matter to Marshall and Mildred are far less related, at least as they see it, to their ancestral differences than they are to their personality, sex, and intellectual orientation. Marshall is more of a scientist, while Mildred is more of a humanist. I politely suggested that, from my vantage point, some of the differences that they chalked up to personality were probably rooted in the cultural traditions of their ancestors (Marshall's bookishness and rationalism has a distinctly German-Jewish flavor), but it seemed to matter little to either of them.

It would seem that the specific values or traditions of an ancestral heritage were so little a part of either's upbringing that neither could think about it in anything but the most intellectual and depersonalized manner. For Marshall, the fact of his Jewishness was an abstraction, on a par with what anyone would feel about his or her genetic traits. They may be interesting to speculate about, but one cannot and need not do much about it, and certainly one cannot keep it in normal everyday consciousness. It is a neutral fact of biography.

For others, however, the differences born of ancestral heritage may be either a source of emotional stress or of ultimate family enrichment and, at times, both.

"What do you think you most wished was different about him when the marriage was still good?" I asked Linda. We had been talking together for nearly an hour about her marriage to John C., a second-generation Chinese-American, a civil engineer of Baptist parentage. The marriage had ended in divorce some years earlier, and I was trying to understand what difference it had made to her that she and John came from such different backgrounds.

Linda was Jewish, born and raised in Brooklyn (although not of particularly religious parents). She had had a rather lonely and tumultuous childhood, with incessant moving from one neighborhood to another and virtually no friends until the age of thirteen, when her father died. John was born and raised in New York's Chinatown, one of six children of a hard-working, success-oriented immigrant family that was strong in its Baptist faith and proud of its Chinese heritage. The two met at the New York securities firm where both worked. After marriage, they settled in Brooklyn close to Linda's widowed mother. The mother was quite fond of John and was not much troubled by the fact of his background. Linda went back to college and developed a close circle of friends, all of whom were Jewish women with Jewish husbands.

Linda thought for a long while before she answered my question. "You know," she began,

> I think deep down I always wished he were Jewish. Not just because he was Oriental. I just think I would have felt more "right" with him. He was so uncommunicative. I always felt I had to guess what he was thinking or feeling. He just couldn't express himself. I think that had something to do with our different cultures. The man I am dating now is Jewish and when we have any fights or disagreements, I have no doubt about what he is thinking or feeling. With John, I would know that something was bothering him, but it would take days, sometimes weeks, before I could pull it out of him what it was. Maybe he didn't know himself.

As I recorded her reply, I could not help but wonder how often John C. had wished that Linda were Chinese, or at least a Baptist. Linda said that it took her a long time after the marriage broke up to realize that she really wanted a Jewish husband. The marriage broke up, after eleven years and two children, for reasons that apparently had nothing to do with cultural or religious differences, but Linda's retrospective wish left us both wondering to what extent those differences were implicated in their breakup after all. Living in a Jewish community with an almost exclusively Jewish circle of friends, and raising their children as Jews, must have placed strains on both of them. Inevitably, John wanted out, despite a basic love for his wife and children. And Linda wished she had a Jewish husband (although the issue of conversion for John never came up).

Probably for all marriage partners, there are times and ways in which they wish that their personal differences would just disappear. Professor Henry Higgins, in the musical *My Fair Lady*, sings "Oh why can't a woman be more like a man . . . oh why can't a woman be more like me." Such sexual narcissism has its counterpart in the relationships between different ethnic and religious groups as well. Andrew Greeley has shown, in a book by the title *Why Can't They Be Like Us?*, that one of the characteristic ways in which different groups respond to one another is with the tacit wish "Why can't they be like us?"[1] In the context of intermarriage, the occasional individual narcissism blends with group narcissism, compelling husband and wife to face their feelings about both heritages.

For many, the differences simply will not go away; they cannot be wished away. And unlike the sexual difference, they also do not become a source of natural pleasure. Under the best of circumstances, husband and wife learn to build bridges across the differences. For some, however, the cultural gaps require more or less constant bridging, and bridge building can become wearisome even for the hardiest souls.

There are probably as many ways to build those bridges as there are couples building them. One of the difficulties in trying to capture that range of diversity is that all the fine nuances of individual temperament and inventiveness are lost in broad categories. Yet, those broad categories can serve as mirrors in which individual reflections may be compared, refined, or more meaningfully understood. In describing what differences emerge and how they are reconciled or not, I expect, we will move closer to understanding what love does to tradition and what tradition does to love in the modern intermarriage.

In her book, *Crosscurrents* (1980), Evelyn Kaye presents a type of bridge building that is probably a paragon of one of several alternatives to handling the differences in a marriage between a Jewish man and a Christian woman.[2]

Edward is thirty-eight and a professor of English literature. . . . He grew up in a suburban Jewish community where he was Bar Mitzvahed in the local Reform temple to which his parents belonged. "I went to Hebrew school and to the public high school," Kaye quotes Edward.

> There was some anti-Semitism in high school, but since about
> 40% of the students were Jewish . . . it never affected me very
> much. . . . I knew that most of the gentiles in school were not
> particularly observant of their religions, and were not committed
> to their Christianity.[3]

After high school, Edward went to college, where he majored in English and ran the college newspaper. He returned after graduation to teach in a local college. He met Donna through a friend who invited him to double date.

Donna said of their first date,

> I remember that very well, that first time, because although we
> liked each other immediately, we talked even at that early stage
> about religion, and we decided very quickly that we should not
> see each other again. We felt we just should not go on with this
> because of the religious differences.[4]

At their first meeting, Edward and Donna recognized their mutual attraction and, perhaps for reasons they could not define then, immediately came to the mutual decision that they had no future together. It was not based on any argument, any comment, any disagreement (much less on any parental objections).

They had enjoyed each other's company, but—observes Evelyn Kaye—in an unthinking response to taboos of which they were only partly conscious, both thought it prudent to adopt a "don't touch" reaction, although their emotions cried out to the contrary.

Edward's don't touch reaction was based largely on an inchoate sense of tribal loyalty, a feeling instilled since early childhood that, in their most intimate connections, Jews belong with other Jews. Donna's concerns were based on a deeply held commitment to Christianity.

> Before I met Edward, I was involved with two men, both of whom later became ministers. I even considered going to divinity school myself, but there were no scholarships for women. For me, being a Christian was an important part of my identity. Many of my closest friends were Christians.[5]

Donna was an active member of the Lutheran church, although of one of the more liberal of the Lutheran churches, which was not part of the Missouri Synod (the more conservative branch of American Lutheranism).

Edward and Donna's was not a case of a disillusioned Lutheran meeting a disaffiliated Jew. It involved, rather, a self-aware Jew, comfortable with his identity, encountering an equally (or more) committed Christian. Apparently the attraction they had for one another was not to be resisted for long. They continued to date, trying to discover the points of their commonality. The emotional attraction soon became embedded in a serious intellectual relationship as well. "Over a period of three years, we kept going together and then breaking up," said Donna, smiling. "We were so aware from the beginning that we should not get married, that we talked about it incessantly."

"The question of children really bothered us," said Edward.

> We discussed that a great deal. How could we bring up a child in one religion when neither of us wanted to reject the other? We met people from different religions and asked for their solutions. But most of them said that one partner gave up his or her faith

and took up the other one, or else it was a matter of indifference to them, and they didn't bother with any religion for their children.[6]

Edward and Donna felt that neither of these solutions was right for them. Edward began to go to church with Donna, and she went to a Reform temple with him. She also went to a series of Hebrew classes at a local temple, where she attended a Yom Kippur service with Edward. Both of them became much more aware that Jesus himself was Jewish and had been educated by rabbis. Although Donna could see more clearly that the roots of Christianity were in Judaism, Edward began to see the connections between Christian thinking and its Jewish sources. "It was the substance of what our faith did for us that was important, and we saw that we had far more in common than in separateness," Edward explained.

After agonizing for three years over their relationship, and facing no small opposition from Edward's parents, the two decided to marry and to bring up their children in both their traditions. The wedding ceremony took place in a Lutheran church with a specially designed ceremony to take into account Edward's Jewish background. Both sets of parents came to the wedding. ("They had seen both of us going through so much pain and suffering, that it was a relief when we said we would get married.") It was a joyous occasion that both recall happily.

A couple of years after their marriage, Donna and Edward had a son whom they named Joseph. "The old neat distinctions were not relevant anymore," said Donna. "We knew we wanted to bring him up in both our faiths, to share both our backgrounds." They followed the biblical tradition of circumcision a week after his birth, with a rabbi and a *mohel* (religious circumciser) present to perform the ceremony. The ceremony itself was held in the home of a Lutheran pastor friend, and other friends from both faiths were there to read from the Book of Genesis and to recite poetry and other carefully selected texts. When the baby was a few months old, a special welcoming ceremony was also held at the church, led by the pastor. Babies are usually baptized in the church, "But we were sure we did not want a baptism, because we didn't feel it was authentic," explained Edward. "It's clear to me that a child is *born* Jewish," Donna said (although according to traditional Jewish law, her children would have to convert in order to be regarded as Jews), "whereas there's no way you can be born a Christian." In Donna's view, that was something that little Joseph would have to choose later. "That made me realize," she continued, "that no matter what he decides later, it is important that Joseph have a Jewish education so that he knows who his people are." As an afterthought, she added,

> But I do think of him as being raised more Jewish than Christian. Though he goes to church with me now and I want him to understand some of his mother's faith, the family emphasis will probably be more Jewish.[7]

Since the early months of Joseph's life, Evelyn Kaye reports, the dual family commitment has continued. At Christmas time, the family visits Donna's parents in the Midwest. The family also celebrates Hanukkah, lighting candles all eight nights in the traditional menorah (an eight-branched candelabrum). Passover, too, is a significant part of their ceremonial lives, and Edward has even introduced its observance into Donna's church group. Edward said,

> One of the Sunday school teachers invited me to talk to her class about Passover, so I brought in some matzoh [the unleavened bread] and grape juice [in lieu of wine] and explained what the seder was like and what happened.
> She suggested that we might have a seder at the church the next year, and I agreed. But I insisted that it be authentic, with kosher food, and following the traditional pattern of observance.[8]

That year, at Passover, about eighty parents, children, and church members attended a seder at the church, led by Edward, which was based on a temple seder written by a rabbi in Philadelphia.

So ahead of young Joseph lie seders at the church, and Christmas celebrations with his grandparents enlivened by the eight days of Hanukkah, which usually coincide with Christmas. He will go to Hebrew school and perhaps to Lutheran Sunday school as well, although one wonders when he will have the time for that, given the claims of a child's usual activities. His parents are united in their approach and wholly commited to their dual solution. Indeed, the time, energy, and enthusiasm they spend on the religious aspect of their lives amazes their friends and family. "No one we know does as much as we do," said Donna, "and some people think we're crazy. But we've found it very satisfying so far, and it doesn't seem too much for us."

Evelyn Kaye is also quick to point out that the sympathy and support that Donna and Edward found in the intellectual academic community in which they live is the exception, not the rule. Moreover, it is quite clear that this couple represents an extreme of commitment to constructing a family life that fully reflects their dual heritage. Donna and Edward spent a long painful time—three years—examining their own beliefs and deepest feelings about their values and attitudes (and about each other) before they decided to marry and form a family. "It wasn't easy," Donna said, "and other people may not want to do it, but it was right for us."

From everything we learned from our studies of intermarrieds, it is clear that Donna and Edward chose a most difficult way to bridge their differences. Their blending of traditions is not only very difficult (requiring a great deal of study about each other's heritage, a great deal of sustained conversation about deep philosophical issues, and a great deal of external social support), it is also very unusual.

I talked to Donna some five years after Evelyn Kaye had interviewed the two of them, and found that she and Edward were still very much on the path they had chosen earlier. They have remained active members of a Lutheran church and a Reform temple. Joseph, participating in the life of both, was attending a Quaker school where, Donna said, there were a number of families that were raising their children as "Jewish Christians." But she did acknowledge that although Joseph was enjoying the pleasures of a dual religious heritage, he was not too keen on going to Sunday school in either faith (not an uncommon reaction for eight-year-old boys in any faith). Although Joseph did ask his mother, "Do you feel jealous that I have two religions and you only have one?" Donna also reiterated that as much pleasure as she and Edward derived from the path they had chosen, their solution to intermarriage is a very difficult, time-consuming, and often painful one. "I do not recommend it for others", she says without regret. One wonders what Joseph makes of it all.

Marshall and Mildred, Linda and John, and Edward and Donna each represents a type of response to the differences of family background and its impact on a relationship, yet each couple is atypical. In our survey of intermarried couples, we found that most Christians who marry Jews are but minimally committed to their heritage. We asked those who did not convert to Judaism what the religion of their birth was, and with which religious group they identified currently. As we see in the table below, the majority have relinquished their identification with their religious heritage.

Religion of Birth and Current Self-Identification

Religion of non-Jewish spouse	At birth (%)	Currently (%)
Protestant	45	26
Catholic	30	10
Other	6	7
None	19	57
Total	100	100

John C., of Chinese-Baptist parentage, is perhaps the most typical in his orientation to his heritage. Except for a feeling for Chinese cooking, he had lost interest in his heritage even before he married Linda. After their divorce, he moved in with a Catholic Puerto Rican woman. Mildred L. drifted from her Baptist background to Unitarianism, which she now shares with her husband. Donna is the only one of the three Christians who remains loyal to her own religious heritage.

The Jewish partners in the three examples are more typical, except for Marshall. In our survey, we found that most Jews in intermarriages continued to identify with their religion of birth. In fact, when we asked the same question of the born-Jewish partners as we did of the born–non-Jews, we found the following pattern.

A large proportion (19 percent) of the non-Jews married to Jews who do not convert to Judaism perceive themselves as not having been born with a religious identity to begin with, yet only 6 percent of the Jews in intermarriages see themselves as not having had a religious identity at birth. Similarly, the majority (57 percent) of the non-Jews married to Jews who do not convert see themselves as having no particular religious identity as adults. By contrast, only 17 percent of the born-Jewish re-

Current Self-Identification of Born-Jewish Respondents

Religion	At birth (%)	Currently (%)
Jewish	94	73
Protestant	—	7
Catholic	—	—
Other	—	3
None	6	17
Total	100	100

spondents regarded themselves as having no religious identity. Marshall's apparent complete disregard of Jewishness is therefore fairly atypical.

Linda and John's divorce is probably more typical of the irresolution of many intermarriages than are the resolutions of either Marshall and Mildred or Edward and Donna. To be sure, not all or even most intermarriages are doomed to fail. They probably remain more or less happily intact, as do most marriages. But the disproportion in the number that do end up in divorce is great enough to suggest that the difficulties posed by intermarriage are every bit as difficult to resolve as Donna and Edward told us.

Although reliable current statistics on divorce rates among intermarrieds are not available, a study done in Indiana in the mid-1960s is quite convincing. Sociologists Christensen and Kenneth Barber followed up a sample of couples, who married in 1960, five years later. The overall divorce rate in Indiana at that point was 8.4 percent. By establishing that rate as a standard and assigning it an index value of "1," they were able to determine that the rate of divorce for marriages between two born Jews who had married five years earlier was at an index value of .31 (about one-third the average rate). By contrast, the index value of divorce between Jews and Christians who had married five years earlier was 1.83—nearly six times the rate for endogamous Jewish marriages and nearly twice the average for the population as a whole.[9]

My own study of the client population of a large Jewish family service agency, the Jewish Counseling and Service Agency in Millburn, New Jersey, found that of all the married or formerly married clients who came to the agency in 1983, a total of 18 percent were either separated or divorced. Of 666 non-intermarried clients (both partners Jewish), 10 percent were either separated or divorced. Of the 131 intermarried clients, on the other hand, 60 percent were either separated or divorced. Clearly, both studies leave a lot to be desired as a basis for generalizing on the connection between intermarriage and marital failure. One study is based on data that have been made obsolete by dramatic changes in the American divorce rate since the 1960s. The other study is based on data from a clinical population, which can never be used to make reliable generalizations to a normal non-clinical population. However, in the absence of better research, it is still quite striking that two such different studies, so widely separated by time and geography, should both indicate that the divorce rate among intermarrieds is about six times that of the rate among endogamous Jewish couples.

Divorce, on the one hand, and the creative blending of traditions, on the other, stand at the opposite poles—so to speak—of a continuum of strategies for resolving the tension between love and tradition, between Jews and Christians in a marriage; between the need for unity in the home, and the need of individuals to keep in touch with their roots. But the majority of intermarrieds do not follow either of these paths; they follow the somewhat more conventional path of either religious apathy and disaffiliation, or conversion.

The National Jewish Population Study found in 1970 that in nearly one-third (31 percent) of the intermarriages in their survey, the Christian spouse converted to Judaism. By contrast, that study also found that only about 3 percent of the Jewish spouses who had married non-Jews converted to another religion. My own study of intermarried couples (1977–1979) found a somewhat lower rate (25 percent) of conversion to Judaism on the part of non-Jews married to Jews, but it also found a significantly lower rate (7–10 percent) of conversion out of Judaism on the part of born-Jewish marriage partners. The predominant pattern found in both studies, with respect to conversion in intermarriages, is that the great majority of intermarrieds do not embrace their spouse's faith, but neither do they make very rigorous efforts to perpetuate their own respective heritages for themselves or for their children.

Therefore, Marshall L.'s turn to Unitarianism stands out in

sharp contrast to Edward's continuing Jewishness. But, in fact, they are both quite atypical in their treatment of their Jewish heritage. They stand out in sharp contrast to the far more typical example of Kenneth G., a thirty-nine-year-old Jewish psychiatrist in San Diego, married to Jenny, a thirty-five-year-old social worker of a religiously uninvolved ("vaguely Methodist") background. The two met while Ken was in residence at a local VA hospital where Jenny was training to be a social worker.

Ken had grown up in a small town in Pennsylvania outside of Hazelton, being one of three Jewish students in his high school class. "I was the only Jewish kid I knew who wanted to be on the football team—and who had the build for it." His father, himself a third-generation descendant of German-Jewish merchants who settled in the area in the 1860s, was a lawyer in town. Ken's mother had a similar background. The family belonged to the Reform temple in Hazelton for three generations, although Ken recalls attending services only three or four times a year and for special occasions like weddings and Bar Mitzvahs. Ken was Bar Mitzvahed and confirmed in the temple.

When he began to date in his sophomore year, his parents made an effort to get him to Jewish youth activities in Hazelton or Wilkes-Barre, either at the temple or at the Jewish community center. He had gone to Sunday school at the temple for three or four years preceding his Bar Mitzvah and knew a number of kids there. But Ken was becoming a popular "jock" in his local high school—a good quarterback, by his own estimation. He was mostly hanging around with his football friends and their girlfriends. Inevitably, he dated mostly Christian girls. "I think they saw in me a combination of Woody Allen and Joe Namath— though I doubt they knew who Woody Allen was."

When he got to Johns Hopkins in 1965, he met many more Jewish students, particularly as a pre-med.

I tended to feel somewhat uncomfortable around most of them. They were mainly from places like Boston or Long Island and Westchester. They had grown up primarily among other Jews and therefore seemed more comfortable amongst themselves. To me, they all seemed much more "Jewish" than I ever felt. They were intense about everything; about their courses, about their politics, about their love affairs. They just didn't seem to know how to loosen up, to have a beer and some laughs in a bar on the weekend. And still, none of them played football. The Jewish girls I met were just like the guys, in many ways. They were either out husband hunting or were bleeding hearts with horn-rimmed glasses, out to remake the world; they were always so enthusiastic about some cause or another. They just didn't seem to know how to have fun.

Once again, Ken gravitated mostly toward a Christian social circle. He had some pre-med friends, mostly as lab or study partners, but his closest "fun friends" were the guys on the football team. They were only dimly aware of his academic self-discipline, although he was a strong student who had every intention of becoming a doctor. They had no interest in his course work, and Ken didn't miss the "shop talk" of his pre-med classmates, of which he had more than his fill during the course of the semester. Throughout college and medical school, he casually dated mostly Christian girls. In fact, it mattered to him very little what the ethnic or religious background of his dates were. "I just didn't have any strong feelings about that kind of stuff. Besides, I wasn't planning to marry any one of them." His main interests were medical science and sports, as well as having a good time with friends.

During the first two years of medical school, he had little time for either friends or fun, but as the rigors of medical training eased up, or he became more adept in handling them, he was able to find like-minded peers among his medical school classmates who also knew how to enjoy sports and leisure.

He dutifully went home to Pennsylvania to be with his parents for the High Holidays, Rosh Hashanah and Yom Kippur, although a few times he was forced to cut short his visit because of his schedule of medical school classes. He continued to go to the Reform temple with his parents three times a year. Indeed, he enjoyed seeing old friends of the family there over the years. Although he was not particularly religious in terms of feelings, and had some difficulty in reading the prayers in Hebrew, he felt a certain sense of satisfaction in fulfilling the annual ritual. Passovers were also generally spent at home, at least for the seder night. Over the years, Ken even learned to appreciate his father's rather mechanical recitation of the Haggadah (the legend of the Egyptian exile and the Passover redemption). There would always be other members of the family and friends around the seder table, and somebody would soon turn the conversation to contemporary issues of civil rights or the relations between the Arabs and Israel, so the liturgical history of the Haggadah would quickly be transformed into a discussion Ken could feel at home with. But these annual family occasions were Ken's only involvement with any formal religious aspects of Jewish living.

Ken never doubted his own Jewishness, nor was he in any way uncomfortable about being Jewish. In fact, he claimed to be quite proud of it. During the Six Day War in Israel in 1976, he even participated in a campus fund-raising effort on behalf of wounded Israeli soldiers. He felt a great deal of pride in the macho image of the Israeli military, but, on the whole, Jewishness occupied a relatively small space in his self-concept.

After finishing medical school, he joined the Navy, was stationed in San Diego, and found the life there sufficiently appealing to want to settle there. His parents were planning to retire to a Florida condominium in another few years, and his older sister was married and living in Los Angeles.

It was at the end of his second year in the service that Ken met Jenny—a trim, quite good-looking, athletic woman with strong feelings about poor people and children and a strong commitment to helping them. Jenny was an animated conversationalist, not unlike Ken's own mother and sister.

Like Edward and Donna, Kenneth and Jenny immediately liked each other but, unlike Edward and Donna, these two had

no reservation about falling in love. They soon moved in together and, after a year and a half, got married.

Jenny was born and raised in Cleveland. After her parents
divorced, when she was thirteen years old, Jenny moved with
her mother to Los Angeles. Not having any close family around
and not being part of any ethnic or religious community (her
mother had long ago lost any interest in religion), Jenny found
her closest ties through school friends and extracurricular activities. She was on the swimming team and the school newspaper. Her school-centered activism continued through her college years at UCLA.

Living in Los Angeles, she inevitably had many Jewish
friends, both in high school and in college. In addition, her
mother worked as an administrative assistant to one of the partners, who was also Jewish, of a local film production company.
In fact, all the principals of the firm were Jewish. As a result,
Jenny's mother was always off from work on the Jewish High
Holy Days.

Jenny recalled that, as a little girl in Cleveland, she would
go to a local Methodist church with her grandparents from time
to time, and one year she was even sent to Sunday school.

> We learned some Bible stories and some hymns, and did all kinds
> of arts and crafts. That's all I can remember. And of course we
> had a big Christmas party. I guess we must have done stuff
> around Halloween and Easter as well.

Christmas was really the only holiday that she and her
mother celebrated regularly, but not as a religious holiday. They
never went to church, but would have friends over to the house
and visit with others to exchange gifts and enjoy the general
spirit of the day.

Jenny's mother was delighted with Ken. She had always
had a high regard for the Jewish men she met in the course of
her work. In fact, she had dated a few herself, and would have
married one had she been asked. Ken's parents expressed only

mild reservation about his decision to marry Jenny. "How are you going to raise your children?" Ken's mother asked. "As Jews, of course," Ken answered. Then, as an afterthought, he added, "There are a couple of temples in San Diego. I don't think we should have any problems." The truth of the matter is that, at that point, he and Jenny had never even discussed that issue. It had not seemed important enough to either of them, and Ken simply assumed that his children would be Jewish, just as he was. Ken was twenty-nine years old, a doctor, a veteran of the Navy, and his parents did not think they should get too deeply entangled in how Ken and Jenny would run their lives or raise their children. They were quite taken with Jenny as a person, and were pleased to see that their son was happy and getting ready to settle down to a stable married life like his older sister.

As a reserve officer, Ken was married to Jenny in a Navy chapel in a Jewish ceremony conducted by a Reform Jewish chaplain. Ken did recall,

> The year we got married was the first time my parents sent me, sent us, a Jewish New Year's card. We didn't get to go back to Pennsylvania for the holidays so, I guess, they just wanted to remind me. I suspect they were more concerned about the intermarriage thing than they showed. But they really needn't have worried.

Although Ken did not "find religion" by any stretch of the imagination after he got married, he and Jenny did join a local Reform temple after the birth of their first child. Ken wanted to have the little girl named Naomi, after his father's mother, and felt the need to have the baby "officially" named in the temple. Jenny found the idea quite touching and was pleased to go along with it; she was perfectly happy to have the child raised as a Jew.

> I guess not having had any deep roots myself, I found the whole idea of naming Naomi after one of her grandmothers in a temple ceremony surprisingly satisfying. I felt like we were all being

woven more closely together into something that was greater than just ourselves. I felt it was also drawing Ken and me closer together. I think the rabbi must have sensed it, too, because he really went out of his way to make me and my mother feel a part of the ceremony. We all went up to the ark in front of the congregation. I thought it was pretty dramatic, and I was glad we did it.

The only time the issue of their religious differences might have led to conflict, was the Christmas right after their daughter was born. "I was surprised," Ken said,

> though in retrospect, I probably shouldn't have been, when Jenny announced sometime in mid-December that she was really looking forward to having our own Christmas tree for the first time. It never crossed my mind that she would want that. The idea of having a Christmas tree in my own home just bothered me. We never had one in my parents' home. None of our relatives did either, though I knew some Jews who did. It just didn't sit well with my own self-concept, and I wasn't very gracious about it at first. Jenny was confused by my reaction, and I wasn't quite sure how to explain myself to her.

Until their daughter was born, they had always gone to visit with friends or with Jenny's mother on Christmas, so the issue of a Christmas tree of their own just never came up. Jenny's mother, of course, always had a tree, as did their friends. The celebration of the holiday had nothing religious about it; it was simply a time of joy, togetherness, food, laughter, and gifts. It was the kind of fun that both Ken and Jenny enjoyed, but the idea of having a tree of his own just struck Ken as a step toward "un-Jewishness" he didn't want to take. The symbolism of it felt wrong.

"I thought we'd celebrate Hanukkah," Ken responded to Jenny's wish for a Christmas tree. The fact was that Ken had not celebrated Hanukkah since he had been out of his parents' home. He did not even own a menorah. But Jenny's request triggered an almost instinctive reaction. Jenny knew of the Jewish holiday well enough; many of her friends had celebrated

Hanukkah. She also had a number of friends who had celebrated both. "Why can't we have both?" she asked. Ken had more or less anticipated that that would be her reaction, to do both, and he really did not have a good reason to give her as to why he was opposed to such a combination. Something in him sensed that celebrating Hanukkah, together with a Christmas tree, would do little to salve his antipathy to the Christmas tree. On the other hand, if having a Christmas tree would please Jenny, particularly since it had no religious significance to her, it seemed a small price to pay for the fact that, in all other ways, Jenny was perfectly willing to go along with Ken's way of being Jewish and with raising Naomi as a Jewish child.

In the next couple of days, Ken went and acquired a handsome Christmas tree, tinsel and a string of lights, and an electric menorah in which they would light one amber bulb on each of Hanukkah's eight nights. Thus, Ken and Jenny's home acquired a new family tradition. The following year, Ken took the initiative himself, surprising Jenny with a nice-sized Christmas tree before she even had a chance to ask him about it. The forbidden quality of the tree's symbolism had simply become irrelevant for him. Nothing in their lives had changed the previous year as a result of having celebrated Christmas. Besides, he really liked the atmosphere and aroma of the tree in their den. The tree in the middle of the room and the menorah on the windowsill had become natural complements in the seasonal esthetics of the home.

In each of the cases discussed thus far, there appears to be a partial encounter with tradition; both with the Jewish tradition and with whatever Christian tradition is joined to it in the particular marriage. In the case of Marshall and Mildred, as we have seen, there was a relinquishing of the traditions of their respective families and the embracing or creating of a new family tradition through Unitarianism.

Linda and John C. were apparently quietly grappling with

the psychological constraints and images of their respective traditions. Perhaps the failure to articulate the meaning that their respective traditions really had for them, at a conscious level, ultimately led to their estrangement and divorce.

Edward and Donna are apparently gripped by the religious symbols, values, and rituals, as well as the liturgy and congretional ceremonies, of their respective traditions. Their conscious, intense involvement with these aspects of their heritage have made sharing and mutual religious instruction a major force in their life together as a family.

None has entirely rejected involvement with a religious and/or ethnic tradition in their self-concept or in their routine family life. Indeed, for both partners, each in his or her way, some aspect of tradition has played a key role in shaping their lives together. It is also obvious that none of the families we have examined has taken either partner's tradition in its doctrinal entirety. Each has taken some fragment—some more, some less, some entirely new fragments—that will lend color, substance, and personal meaning to their lives.

Some, like Edward and Donna, struggled for three years of courtship, agonizing about how their love for one another might affect the tradition each held dear. Others, like Linda and John C., probably should have examined more closely, before their marriage, the meanings their traditions held for them. Still others, like Ken and Jenny, recaptured and made important for themselves, fragments of their traditions only after their first child was born.

These examples suggest that perhaps the very nature of family living impels men and women to recollect, to reevaluate, and to reconnect, with some portions of a tradition they had once experienced, or maybe wished they had. In Chapter Four, we have seen that the social psychology of falling in love and becoming a couple impels people toward self-disclosure and therefore toward greater self-examination of their own and the other's heritage. Here we see that the family life cycle—from the marriage ceremony to child rearing, to the celebration of the more or less normative cycles of the calendar, to later life cycle events, such as the rites of passage of children into adulthood, and ultimately to death and burial—all impel people to reclaim bits and pieces of their traditions. Indeed, what is incredible is that anyone should have ever thought that it is possible for tradition to be completely overcome by the force of love. But, writes Alberoni, "The rule that 'the past does not count,' although incomprehensible in everyday life, is valid in the nascent state [of falling in love]."[10] Hence, a certain element of surprise among intermarriers arises when they discover in each other a thirst for aspects of their respective heritages as they proceed through the life cycle.

In a profound book, called *Tradition* (1981), Edward Shills notes that

> the human beings alive at any given time are rarely more than three generations away from any other members of their own lineage alive at the same time. Their range of direct contact, physical and symbolic, with things, with works, words, modes of conduct, created in the past, is far more extensive and reaches much further back in time.[11]

Through the sheer act of recollection, through continual contact with both objects and people of the past (e.g., parents and grandparents), through society's own veneration of objects and ideas of the past (e.g., in museums and libraries and through public ceremonies), we are all inevitably "in the grip of the past." However, that grip is not, by any means, intractable.

> Every orthodoxy in tradition is in incessant danger of breaking into heterodoxy. It may break at the point where the tradition passes from one generation to the other or it may break while in the possession of a single generation. . . . There is no tradition, no transmitted and received symbolic pattern in any field of human creation which is wholly free from ambiguity, obscurity, and uncertainty when viewed from within its own postulates, as well as from outside them.[12]

Consequently, traditions always undergo a process of change through reinterpretation, through adaptation to new conditions, and through simple confusion and forgetfulness. In turn, any individual's relationship to his or her tradition is necessarily fragmentary. Some may go to great efforts to reconstruct out of the fragments, a coherent and "authentic" whole, either as an object of study or veneration or as the basis for a life cycle. Others may try to ignore some disturbing fragment of tradition that intrudes into what otherwise seems to be a modern, untraditional life-style. Most will simply respond to the evocations of images, feelings, and associations of the past, as they occur in routine living, and try to integrate the past and the present with the least amount of friction. But the fragments of each person's biographical, as well as cultural past, are ubiquitous and ever ready to present themselves in the normal course of life as objects of meaning and renewed attachment.

It is probably fair to say that all modern men and women have a fragmentary relationship to their traditions. Perhaps, with the exception of Hassidic Jews in Brooklyn, Amish brethren in Pennsylvania, or Krishna devotees in an ashram, all modern people are far more involved with the exigencies of the present—the pursuit of happiness—than they are with the imperatives of the past. However, because the cultural and/or religious heritage of each is rather opaque to the other in an intermarriage, Jewish and Christian husbands and wives are more likely to be surprised (or confused or troubled) by each other's fragmentary attachments to their respective traditions than would be the case for couples who share a common religious and ethnic background. At least in the latter case, each knows intuitively where the other is "coming from."

Hence, there is a much greater need in an intermarriage for an ongoing serious conversation about fundamental issues of meaning and cosmology—topics that are ignored by most modern families. This explains the marital breakdown between Linda and John C., the intensity of the religious conversations between Edward and Donna, and the drift toward religious homogeneity between Marshall and Mildred and Ken and Jenny.

The fragmentary memory of tradition resides quietly in the recesses of normal consciousness. How richly laden that storehouse is, and to what extent one is inclined to draw upon its resources, is largely a matter of historical coincidence and personal upbringing. A person who is born into a group with a richly textured, well-articulated tradition is apt to have a richer repository of cultural fragments in his or her consciousness than a person who is heir to a less clearly articulated tradition. Similarly, a person who is raised in a family in which the tradition of the family and its group has been cultivated is also likely to have a keener sense of the fragments of his or her heritage than a person who is raised in a family in which there is but slight attention paid to such matters. In other words, the history of a group and the socialization of its individual members in particular families converge in shaping the consciousness of each and every man and woman. The extent to which fragments of a religious or ethnic tradition will rise to salience from the recesses of a person's consciousness will depend, therefore, both on the exigencies of the ongoing life cycle and on history and biography.

Even endogamously married partners are likely to vary in their awareness of and attachment to the norms, values, artifacts, and customs of their heritage. For example, in the premodern Jewish community of Eastern Europe, boys and men were typically much more involved than women in formal religious learning (the Bible, the Talmud, etc.) and the regular recitation of prayers. Consequently, men had much more awareness of the tradition than their mothers, sisters, and wives. On the other hand, because of their relative isolation from the roots of tradition (religious text, liturgy, and communal prayer), women often played the more innovative role in that society. It was often the women who learned a useful trade like sewing; who learned to read and write in the common language of the gentiles (Polish, Russian, etc.); who brought new ideas into the community via novels or newspapers, and even fashions. Women were to be found in large numbers in the marketplace as small merchants. They were also to be found as distillers, innkeepers, meat processors, and bakers—often working to sustain a large family and a husband who spent a good part of the average day in a *beis hamedresh* (house of study and prayer).

Of course most men worked, too, but their greater familiarity with religious texts, and their day-to-day involvement with synagogue and community life, tended to act as a buffer against acculturation. Women's link to the tradition was more pragmatic, through the obligations of family care and obedience to their fathers and husbands.

As a matter of fact, one of the functions of the *shadchan* (the matchmaker), who was traditionally relied upon to arrange marriages, was to make sure that the prospective husband and wife were well suited to one another in terms of their degree of religiousness and feeling about Jewish traditions. But in that distant world, men tended to be more religious and more tradition bound than their womenfolk.

For many reasons, the mass immigration of Jews into the United States changed the relative attachment of men and women to the Jewish tradition; women became somewhat more attached than men. As a result, the first decades of this century witnessed considerable conflict within families, between Jewish husbands and wives, over religious observances and traditionalism. The conflict also contributed to a virtually unprecedented phenomenon in Jewish family life: the desertion of wives by their husbands.

The point of this brief historical excursion is that, since the entry of Jews into modernity, Jewish men and women have had to face their own private dilemmas, as well as occasional battles, with one another over the issue of how to incorporate the tradition into the life of the family. To keep a kosher house or not? To keep the sabbath or not? To send the children to a Hebrew school or not? To belong to a synagogue or not? To make friends with Christian neighbors and colleagues or not? To allow one's children to date Christians or not? These, and many other related issues, are not at all unique to intermarriages. They are the familiar problems of countless American-Jewish couples who have a common ancestral heritage. The differences in exposure of individual men and women to their own tradition has made it just about inevitable that there will be considerable gaps in their memories and associations with, and attachments to, the fragments of tradition.

Jews are surely not alone in having a fragmentary recollection and an uneven attachment to their tradition. Probably all groups, religious or ethnic, that lay claim to any tradition, suffer such a fate. Thus when two Italian Catholics, or two Mormons, or two Chinese Baptists marry, they must face occasional disparities in their attachments to their own tradition, just as Jews do.

The differences in cultural affinity between intermarried couples (e.g., Christmas versus Hanukkah, Passover versus Easter, Baptism versus circumcision, Bar Mitzvah versus Confirmation), however, are more intractable than those that arise between husbands and wives of a common heritage. A common group identity gives each the same right to deviate from—or to appropriate fragments of—the tradition, without making the other feel that he or she is being "invaded," as it were, by an alien culture. A shared universe of discourse about heritage also makes each privy to the ambivalences and confusions, as well as commitments, of the other. So if a husband is less traditional than his wife or vice versa, if they are both Jewish or Italian or Chinese, they each are likely to feel at least some of the pangs of nostalgia or conscience or ambivalence of the other. By the same token, a lack of awareness or rejection of some aspect of their common heritage by one marriage partner is less likely to make the other feel that he or she is being symbolically rejected as a person, when husband and wife have a common heritage.

For example, David, an Orthodox Jewish lawyer and a graduate of a yeshiva high school with a thorough grounding in Jewish scholarship, married Nancy, a lawyer at his firm who came from a Reform Jewish background. Nancy had two years of Hebrew school before her Bat Mitzvah, attended synagogue with her parents maybe three or four times a year, and had very little feeling for, or familiarity with, much of Jewish tradition. Although she and David were deeply in love and had much in common, including their professions, they consistently split over issues of religious observance and the extent to which they wished to have their life-styles colored by their Jewishness. However, both were proud of their Jewishness and had a common fascination for Jewish history and antiquities; both were equally strong in their feelings for Israel; Nancy did *pro bono* work for a major Jewish women's organization. Although they often argued over particular observances, they never interpreted the differences between them as either's rejection of the other's identity. After all, they were both Jews. They could focus their attention on those aspects of their common heritage to which they were equally committed.

Had theirs been an intermarriage, there would have been greater pressure for one to yield (probably Nancy) a sense of one's tradition in favor of the other, or for both to ignore their backgrounds. When intermarried couples focus on their commonality, as they must for the sake of their marriage and out of the affection they have for each other, they inevitably do so at the cost of their respective traditions, unless one spouse converts to the faith of the other or they both make the extraordinary efforts that Edward and Donna made. The drive to create a shared universe of discourse between married partners leads to a yearning for and a straining for a reconciliation of traditions, but contrary to the Zangwillian image of some familial melting pot, the blending process does not usually favor or disfavor the two traditions equally.

Chapter Six

THE TENACITY OF
JEWISHNESS

The Tenacity of
Jewishness

When Phil and Regina were finally married after a tumultuous two-year courtship, there had been so much conflict between them and their respective parents that they were just relieved to be moving to southern California, 3,000 miles from either set of parents. Both looked forward to pursuing their chosen careers; he a child psychiatrist, she a journalist. Over the previous two years, both had developed a profound distaste for each other's heritage, as well as for their own. "All I saw of Jewishness, particularly in Phil's mother," Regina recalled, "was paranoia, hysterics, and abusiveness." Phil did not contradict her, but added,

> I always felt that Regina's father had to consciously restrain himself from calling me a "dirty little Jew boy." He was a Pole who took his Catholicism—and his anti-Semitism—seriously.

"That's just one of the many reasons that I always hated him and his religion," Regina interjected.

Long before she ever met Phil, Regina had decided that she would have nothing to do with Catholicism once she left her parents' home. As for her Polish heritage, it had never meant much beyond certain foods that the family would eat at Christmas and Easter time. Her father was American born and her mother was a fifth-generation Irish-American. It was more Catholicism than any sense of ethnicity that defined the group identity of her family, and she wanted out of that.

Phil's parents were American-born Jews and nominal members of a Reform temple in their home community on Long

Island, but hardly observant. Although Phil grew up with mostly Jewish friends and always went to schools with large Jewish student populations, he never had much exposure to, or interest in, religion as such.

> I guess I was Jewish by osmosis. I knew when and what the holidays were. I knew a little about Jewish history—very little. I even knew how to make out a few Hebrew words in the prayer book. I was Bar Mitzvahed in the temple. I knew about the Holocaust because some of my mother's cousins were killed. Since 1967, I've also had a strong identification with Israel. As a psychiatrist, I was also fascinated by the fact that some of the giants in my field, beginning with Freud, were Jews.

If anyone would have told Phil and Regina that within the next five years, after they had settled on the West Coast, they would be members of a local Reform temple and would hold their first seder in their own home, they would probably have dismissed it as sheer fantasy, but—in fact—that is what happened.

Soon after they moved, Phil became friends with one of his colleagues at the hospital. He, too, was from the East Coast and he, too, was married to a Christian woman. Soon the two couples became quite close, spending a lot of their free time visiting together, going on outings, and so forth. With the approach of the High Holy Days, Phil's friend said that he and his wife were going to "try out" a small local Reform temple. Would he and Regina like to join them? "I hear that the rabbi has a Ph.D. in psychology, so how bad can he be?" After some cautious conversation around the issue, Phil and Regina decided that they would give it a try. After all, they would be with friends whose company they always enjoyed. Regina had never been to a synagogue service, so she was curious. Phil had not been to a synagogue in such a long time that he was also curious about how it would feel now that he was an adult.

To their joint and pleasant surprise, they enjoyed the experience much more than they had expected. They met several other young couples, some intermarrieds like themselves, who had also recently settled in the community. The rabbi, an athletic-looking man in his mid-thirties, with a California tan, gave a thoughtful sermon on the meaning of guilt and forgiveness in the Jewish tradition that was filled with appropriate psychoanalytic references, as well as Jewish textual allusions. Regina was very much taken with the warmth of the communal singing during the service and with the sense of intimacy that seemed to pervade the congregation. The rabbi made a point of coming over to them after the service, of asking them a little about themselves, and of inviting them to come again. It all made a favorable impression. Some weeks later they were at their friends' house on a Sunday afternoon for a barbecue, and met the rabbi again, this time with his girlfriend. There also were a few other couples they had seen at the temple on Yom Kippur. They were all young professionals, an active and attractive group, with whom it was quite natural for Phil and Regina to feel a sense of ease and intimacy.

In the beginning, they were drawn to the congregation for unabashedly social reasons.

> Being transplanted Easterners with no previous friends in the community, we were literally starved for some companionship of like-minded individuals. The temple was almost like a club for us,

said Regina. I could not resist asking her, "Don't you think that a church just as easily could have filled the same function?" "Perhaps," Regina replied, "but neither Phil nor I would ever have gone to services at a church." However, after awhile Regina became interested in learning more about the substance of the customs and the meaning of the services. She even took an introductory class in Hebrew. Phil found himself looking forward to the holiday celebrations that he, in fact, never had as a child. He also found it enjoyable to engage in rather heady conversations with his temple friends about religion, Israel, Jewish political concerns, and the like.

Three years after they had settled in the community, Phil and Regina were also expecting their first child. When the little boy was born, they both agreed that he should be named in the temple and also have a circumcision ceremony amidst the sheltering friendship of the congregation.

"We literally drifted into the Jewish community, almost in spite of ourselves. I am sure there are many people in the temple who don't even know that I am not Jewish," Regina said. "Nowadays, I sometimes forget that myself. I have even had my own anti-Semitic incident", Regina said, with some measure of pride.

One day soon after we moved in, I bought some furniture at a local store. When the man asked my name and address for the delivery and I'd given it to him, he repeated it in a slow and deliberate voice. "That's a Jewish name, isn't it?" he said. "Yes," I replied, and he didn't pursue the matter. But it was obvious to me that his inquiry was neither casual nor benevolent. It made me aware, for the first time in my life, what it must be like to be Jewish, and why Phil was often terribly sensitive when non-Jews made certain remarks. I haven't been back to that store since.

Phil, like Ken and Edward in Chapter Five, had a tenuous connection to his Jewish heritage before he married Regina. The life cycle of the marriage seems to have impelled him toward a renewal of group identity and an activation of interest in various aspects of his Jewish tradition. Typically, except for Donna, neither Jenny nor Regina showed much interest in renewing their connections with either Methodism or Catholicism.

These examples illustrate what appears to be a major trend in modern intermarriages between Jews and Christians. Jewishness, in whatever fragmentary form, plays a stronger role in defining the group identity of the intermarried family than the cultural heritage of the Christian spouse. Our survey of some 450 intermarried couples between 1977 and 1979 underscored this point.

Whereas about 78 percent of the Jews who intermarry retain

their self-identification as Jews after the intermarriage, only about 58 percent of the Protestants, and about 33 percent of the Catholics, retain their original religious self-identity when they marry a Jewish partner. We also noted that although somewhere between 25 to 33 percent of the non-Jews in an intermarriage convert to Judaism, only between 3 to 10 percent of the Jews in intermarriages actually convert from Judaism to another religion.

But one partner's conversion to the religion of the other tends to be the solution for only a minority. Yet, in the majority of cases, we have found that, even in the absence of conversion on the part of the non-Jewish spouse, Jewishness diffuses into the culture of the intermarried family in a variety of ways.

At the outset of our inquiry with intermarried couples, we had asked both spouses how important their religion was to them before marriage. As seen in the table below, the born-Jewish respondents rated their religion as "important" to them by a majority of nearly 20 percent over their Christian spouse's rating of their religion.

These numbers suggest that the majority of Jews and Christians who intermarry come to the marriage with somewhat different attitudes toward their religious heritage. Whereas about 67 percent of the Jewish spouses are at least favorably disposed to their own heritage, only 45 percent of their Christian partners

"How Important Was Your Religious Background to You before Marriage?"

	Jewish respondents	Christian respondents
Very/somewhat	64	45
Unimportant	30	42
Negative/was against it	6	13
Total	100	100

"Are You More or Less Involved with Your
Religious or Ethnic Heritage since Marriage?"

	Jewish respondents	Non-Jewish respondents
More involved	28	7
No change	46	51
Less involved	26	42
Total	100	100

are similarly disposed toward theirs. This premarital difference
in attitudes seems to continue into the marriage.

Both Jewish and non-Jewish partners in intermarriages
were asked whether their involvement with, or feelings toward,
their heritage had changed since their marriage; had they become more or less involved, or experienced no change? A summary of their responses is shown in the table above.

As the table illustrates, intermarriage serves as a catalyst to
increase their interest and involvement in their own heritage for
substantial numbers of Jews, be it in lighting Hanukkah candles
for the first time, taking a more serious interest in Jewish history, or simply intensifying their awareness of Jewish and Israeli
affairs.

For a similar minority of Jews, intermarriage has the opposite effect, lessening their interest and participation in activities related to their heritage. However, the impact of intermarriage on the interest and involvement of Christians in their
own heritage appears to be considerably more negative: 42 percent indicate a lessening of interest and involvement in their
heritage.

About 40 percent of the intermarried couples we surveyed
had some objects of Jewish art in the home and also some Jewish
books and a Jewish Bible or prayer book. About 60 percent had a

menorah as well. Displays of non-Jewish ethnic or religious artifacts are found in fewer intermarried homes.

Except for Christmas, which enjoys a very wide appeal in intermarried homes, Jewish holidays appear to mark the holiday calendar of intermarried families at least as much as if not more than Christian holidays. The table below lists the holidays that respondents were asked to indicate whether they had celebrated during the previous year. The percentages in the table reflect the answers in the affirmative. Because differences between conversionary and mixed marriages are quite significant in this area, their patterns are reported separately (below).

As expected, Jewish holiday celebrations are far more prevalent among conversionary families in which the non-Jewish partner has converted to Judaism than in mixed marriage families. But even among the former, some kind of celebration of the Christmas holiday is widespread. Among the mixed marriages, on the other hand, Hanukkah and Passover are favored by a substantial minority.

It is important to point out that the meaning of "holiday

Percentage Celebrating Jewish and Christian
Holidays

Holidays	Conversionary families	Mixed marriage families
Christmas	65	95
Easter	19	80
Hanukkah	92	33
Passover	100	37
Rosh Hashana	88	21
Yom Kippur	88	20
Weekly Sabbath	50	6

celebration" varies considerably between some of the Jewish and Christian holidays. For the overwhelming majority of inter-marrieds, be they in conversionary or mixed marriages, celebrating Christmas or Easter entails largely a home-centered activity with family and friends. The same holds true for Hanukkah and Passover among the Jewish holidays. Rosh Hashana and Yom Kippur, the High Holy Days of the Jewish calendar, on the other hand, require participation in synagogue services.

In fact, we have found that only a minority of non-Jews (22 percent), and an even smaller percentage of their Jewish partners, actually participate in Christian religious services as such. On the other hand, it appears that the overwhelming majority (80 percent) of conversionary families, and about 20 percent of the mixed marriage couples, go to synagogue services at least a few times a year.

Differences in the pattern of synagogue and church attendance are also reflected in the attitudes of Jewish and non-Jewish marriage partners toward worship. Both were asked how they felt about religious worship in the faith of the other and whether they would like to learn more about the religious services of the other. As the two tables suggest (below), non-Jewish

"How Do You Feel about Worship Services in Your Spouse's Religion?"

	Jewish respondents	Christian respondents
Like it "very much" or "somewhat"	18	43
Don't care about it	38	17
Dislike it "somewhat" or "very much"	20	10
Don't really know enough to judge	14	30
Total	100	100

"Do You Feel That You Would Like to
Learn More about Services in Your
Spouse's Religion?"

	Jewish respondents	Christian respondents
Yes	15	30
No	85	70
Total	100	100

partners are more favorably disposed to Jewish worship and are more apt to be interested in learning more about such services than Jews are interested in Christian religious services.

As these figures further demonstrate, Jews and Christians who are married to one another frequently have an asymmetrical appreciation of, or an interest in, the others' ethnic and religious heritage, with non-Jews showing a greater interest in Jewishness or Judaism than their Jewish spouses in Christianity or other heritages.

The tenacity of Jewishness expresses itself in yet other ways, which reveals something about the Jewish value system. When asked about their wedding ceremonies, most intermarrieds told us that they were married either in a civil ceremony (28 percent) or in some other "creative" private ceremony, often with a Jewish judge or a justice of the peace presiding. Only 8 percent were married in a church or other non-Jewish religious ceremony, and 5 percent were married by both Jewish and non-Jewish clergy officiating at the wedding. By contrast, 23 percent were married in a Jewish ceremony with a rabbi officiating. These figures, once again, hint at the underlying resistance of Jews to any explicitly alternate ethnic or religious symbolism in their lives and the apparently greater receptivity of non-Jews to Jewish symbolism in their lives.

One of the important ways in which a heritage is maintained is through kinship ties, particularly with parents. Not surprisingly, we found that about one-half of the intermarried couples spent a holiday like Passover with the Jewish parents and Christmas with the Christian parents. The more interesting finding came as a result of a question concerning Thanksgiving, which is clearly a non-sectarian American holiday. We found that nearly half (47 percent) of the intermarried couples "always" spent this holiday with the Jewish parents, but only 34 percent "always" spent it with the Christian parents. The Jewish partner in an intermarriage was also more likely to live in closer geographic proximity to his or her parents than the non-Jewish spouse. Moreover, the Jewish partners in the intermarriages we studied were more likely to visit and to speak by telephone with their parents with greater frequency than their non-Jewish mates (see Tables below).

These figures on visiting and telephone communication with parents are noteworthy for several reasons. First, they add yet another bit of evidence to our point that the Jewish family tradition is more strongly represented in the intermarried family than the non-Jewish tradition. They also suggest that, although Jewish parents are more often opposed to their children's intermarriage than are Christian parents, such opposition does not seem to diminish the ties between the intermarrieds and the Jewish parents, in the long run. Finally, these figures are noteworthy because in our sample of intermarrieds, 66 percent of the

Frequency of Visiting with Parents

	Jewish respondents	Christian respondents
Once a week or more	40	20
Once a month or more	24	22
Less than once a month	36	58
Total	100	100

Frequency of Telephone Contact with Parents

	Jewish respondents	Christian respondents
More than once a week	50	13
Once a week	33	40
Less than once a week	17	47
Total	100	100

Jews were men and only 34 percent were women. Given the generally well-established fact that women maintain closer and more frequent ties with their parents than do men, it is quite striking to see that, in intermarriages, Jewish husbands outpace their non-Jewish wives in maintaining contact with parents. Of course, Jewish wives outpaced their non-Jewish husbands by even greater percentages in maintaining contact with their parents.

The more frequent contact with parents on the part of Jewish husbands and wives in intermarriages illustrates the persistence of Jewish family closeness, which is very much a part of Jewish tradition. But it hints at something else as well. One has the feeling, in looking at those seemingly cold statistics, that Jews maintain closer ties with their parents than do their non-Jewish partners precisely because through those ties they are able to sustain their connection to the Jewish tradition. Their need to nourish their connection to tradition appears to be somewhat stronger than it is for their non-Jewish spouses.

How the children are raised is probably the ultimate test of which tradition or heritage predominates in the intermarried family. Like the issue of conversion, it is a question that will be explored in greater detail later. For the purposes of this discussion, it is sufficient to observe that more children are raised in the Jewish tradition than are raised in another ethnic or religious tradition.

When our sample of 450 intermarried couples was asked whether they regarded their children as having been "born Jewish" or not, we found that 41 percent considered their children as being Jewish by virtue of their birth, but 26 percent considered their children as being Christian or having some other group identity by virtue of birth. A small handful (2.5 percent) considered their children as having a dual group identity—Jewish-Christian, Jewish-Unitarian, etc.—and 30.5 percent did not regard their children as having any religious group identity.

In a follow-up study of the children of these couples, also conducted on behalf of the American Jewish Committee in 1983, we found that 46 percent of the children (16 years of age or older) considered themselves Jewish, 32 percent considered themselves Christian or members of some other ethnic and/or religious group, and 22 percent thought of themselves as not having any particular religious group identity.

In sum, we have looked at eight indicators that point to the relative salience of the Jewish over the non-Jewish heritage in intermarriage. With the exception of the preference for celebration of Christmas (and to a lesser extent, Easter), they all suggest that Jewishness persists in the intermarried family in a variety of forms. Moreover, they suggest that, at least as far as giving the family a distinctive group identity, the Jewish role is stronger than any other ethnic or religious identification.

The saliency of Jewishness, as I have described it, is really quite a startling phenomenon. It flies in the face of Jewish conventional wisdom, as well as in the face of widely accepted sociological principles. For hundreds—perhaps even thousands—of years, Jewish parents and religious leaders have believed that "intermarriage is the last nail in the coffin of Jewish survival." As we have seen earlier, that belief seemed to be supported by both historical experience and by social science.

As recently as 1964, in a seminal work on the subject of minority group assimilation, sociologist Milton M. Gordon wrote,

> If marital assimilation takes place fully, the minority group loses
> its ethnic identity in the larger host or core society . . . eventually
> the descendants of the original primary group become indis-
> tinguishable . . . the price of assimilation is the disappearance of
> the ethnic group as a separate entity and the evaporation of its
> distinctive values.[1]

Clearly, intermarriage, which is what Gordon called "marital
assimilation," between Jews and non-Jews is not followed in
any lockstep by the inevitable consequences that Gordon pre-
dicted on the basis of sound scholarship.

The salience of Jewishness in intermarriages raises two essential questions. What are its causes? And what are its consequences? Why is it that Jews seem to adhere somewhat more
tenaciously to their group identity than do their Christian marriage partners? And what are the consequences of that tenacity
for individuals, their families, and the wider community?

However, before we turn to these questions, it is important
to clarify what I mean, and what I do not mean, by "the saliency
of Jewishness." Some will surely ask, Do you mean to say that
Jews who marry non-Jews are generally as committed to being
Jewish as those Jews who marry within their faith? Are intermarrying Jews as religiously observant as Jews who marry other
Jews? Are they as committed to perpetuating the Jewish people
as their endogamous brethren? Certainly, except for the conversionary marriages that constitute but a minority of all intermarriages, the answer to these questions has to be "No."

In the majority of mixed marriages, Jewishness finds expression only episodically (e.g., on certain holidays) and in a
highly fragmented form. Jewishness does not comprise a major,
much less a central motif in the overall style of such families. A
picture on a wall, a particular Jewish dish eaten on special occasions, certain gestures or jokes or colloquial expressions (such as
the Yiddish "gezuntheit" when someone sneezes—the equivalent of "God bless you"), the regular pilgrimage to visit one's
parents for the Passover seder, an intense interest in Israel, and

a lightening-quick sensitivity to any form of anti-Semitism may comprise the sum total of what is understood by Jewishness in such families. Now, to be sure, there are a great many non-intermarried Jews whose personal sense of Jewishness is equally fragmentary. But, on the basis of available survey data, it remains a fact that Jews in intermarriages do have a much more limited and fragmentary attachment to their heritage than do Jews who are not intermarried.

In what sense, then, can one assert that Jewishness is a salient source of group identification for them? Only in comparison to the attachment of their Christian spouses to their Christian heritage. Put simply, Jews in mixed marriages may be less "Jewish" than other Jews who are not intermarried. But they are more "Jewish" than Christian or Buddhist or anything else, and they are more inclined toward Jewishness than are their spouses toward their own traditions. The point being made here, then, is that Jewishness in the intermarried family is salient only in relation to the potential salience of the heritage of the non-Jewish partner. It is clearly not as salient in the lives of most intermarried Jews as it is in the lives of typical, endogamously married Jews. Commitment and identification are ultimately relative terms, matters of degree. One must always ask, As compared to whom?

So why is it, then, that Jewishness seems to matter more in most intermarriages? At the risk of repetition, let me reiterate an earlier proposition on which the answer depends. All recollections of one's heritage are fragmentary. How frequently, how accurately, and with what degree of commitment one recalls his or her traditions, depends on a mixture of ingredients: the culture of the group, the history of the group, and the biography of the individual.

Jewish history in the past hundred years, particularly in the United States, has converged remarkably with Jewish and American culture, as well as with a particular kind of upbringing (the latter especially in the past thirty years). This has made it increasingly possible for Jews to remain attached to their group heritage even when their spouses are not Jewish.

Jews entered America on a large scale, as we have seen earlier, at a point when the society as a whole was becoming increasingly pluralistic. The mass influx of different nationalities, coupled with the decline of WASP cultural hegemony, has made it relatively easy for Jews to establish a subculture within the larger society. Thus, since the end of the nineteenth century, American Jews have organized an elaborate network of religious, educational, social welfare, recreational, and political institutions that are unmatched by any other ethnic or religious minority group, except perhaps Catholics. The impetus for this extraordinary level of voluntary organizing among America's Jews stems from Jewish culture itself.

Given their marginal or pariah status for most of their sojourn in the Christian West, Jews have had to survive not only as a religion, but also as a people. In the absence of a nation-state, they evolved a communal structure and a sense of transnational peoplehood that comprises the secular husk of the religious community. Thus, Jewish culture has always been a complex amalgam of values and norms partly pertaining to community and people and social welfare of the folk and partly pertaining to the religion based on the Torah. With the rise of nationalism and concepts of social welfare in the nineteenth century, and, most significantly, with the birth of Israel in 1948, it has become increasingly possible for modern Jews to choose among the ways in which they would construe their own sense of Jewishness. They can choose to be Orthodox Jews, Jewish socialists, Zionists, religious Zionists, anti-Zionist Hassidim, etc. The current plethora of political parties in Israel is but the constitutional reflection of this unique development of Jewish culture. In the absence of a central religious authority, such as is found in the Catholic Church, Jewish culture has been fundamentally pluralistic.

Although this pluralism has never been without tension, it

has also been the source of a tremendous amount of creativity in the form of intellectual debates, movements and countermovements, and schisms and rebirths. It has probably been one of the forces that has catapulted Jews into the center of general cultural creativity in the wider society—in literature, the arts, mass media, science, and the like. From Freud to Woody Allen, from Einstein to Barbara Streisand, American culture, in general, has been enriched by tensions and passions born of the Jewish experience. One important consequence of this positive role that Jews have played in the wider society is that, specifically, Jewish role models have always been readily available to the wider population of Jews seeking to articulate their own personal sense of Jewish identification. Another is that—despite the fact that Jews are a small minority, less than 3 percent of the total American population—Judaism and Jewry have come to be regarded as the third faith community, alongside Protestants and Catholics, in the American pluralistic mosaic.[2]

The availability of positive Jewish role models has made it possible for Jews to select a pattern of identification suited to their individual tastes from a rather wide spectrum. The generally favorable view of Judaism on the American cultural landscape, on the other hand, has made Jews more and more acceptable to non-Jews—not simply as abstract fellow citizens in an egalitarian society, but specifically as Jews.

The rendezvous of Jewish culture with American history has not only made intermarriage an increasingly more frequent option for Jews and Christians, it has also made it possible for Jews in intermarriages to construct a form of Jewish self-identification that is suited to their unique marital circumstances.

Whatever the background of non-Jews who are married to Jews, it generally lacks the wide spectrum of identificational choices found in modern American Judaism. Unless they are religious, Christians probably find it more difficult to remain attached to their heritage than do Jews. Most other ethnic groups do not have such potent symbols as Israel or the Holocaust to energize the dormant loyalties of their members. Indeed, as we have seen in some cases, the very sense of some non-Jews that they lack a distinct heritage is precisely one of the factors that may lead them to marry a Jew. As a matter of fact, in those intermarriages in which the Christian partner is also heir to an amalgam of a religious and ethnic tradition (as is the case with Irish or Italian Catholics, Greeks, Chinese, or Poles), there is likely to be more tension between husband and wife over the issue of group identity.

There is yet one more ingredient in the matrix of forces that accounts for the persistence of Jewishness, as well as its peculiar forms in intermarriage. That is the trend in child socialization, upbringing, in the past thirty years—the time during which the rate of intermarriages has risen so significantly. Terms like *permissive, child centered, expressive* and *egalitarian,* and *other directed* have been used by many to describe this trend. The essence of this trend, the roots of which are traceable to the rise of the urban middle class as far back as the dawn of the Industrial Revolution, is that children have been raised less and less as carriers of a group tradition. Rather, they are raised to discover and fulfill their own unique potentials as individuals. In the United States, for a variety of reasons, Jews have been among the most enthusiastic practitioners of this mode of child rearing. Whereas traditional Jewish parents wanted *nachas* (joy and fulfillment) from their children, modern Jewish parents want their children to be joyous and fulfilled. Rather than expecting their children to fulfill the parents dreams, modern Jewish parents seem to want to do all they can to enable their children to fulfill their own dreams.

One result of this child-centered mode of upbringing has been the increasingly free rein given to young adults in their choice of life-style, which—in fact—has led to the increase in intermarriage for Jews. But the other result has been to make Jews increasingly introspective, self-aware, and self-assertive. Ironically, the very Jews whose child-centered upbringing probably increased their likelihood of intermarrying since the mid-1950s have also been the people whose upbringing has heightened their introspective sensibilities and their self-conscious desire for a meaningful identity. At the same time, the internal pluralism of Jewish culture and the external pluralism of the wider American society have made it possible for Jews, be they intermarried or not, to identify themselves as Jews and to retain a foothold in the tradition in a broad variety of ways: through varying modes and degrees of religious observance, through purely secular involvement with social welfare and civil rights, through a concern with and commitment to Israel, through the appreciation of Jewish literature (Bellow, Malamud, Mailer, Roth, Singer, and others), through Jewish humor (Woody Allen, David Brenner, Joan Rivers, and a multitude of others from the "borscht" belt to the Sun Belt), to Jewish cuisine (sour pickles, rye bread, bagels and lox, matzoh, and sweet wine).

I believe that the confluence of the patterns of Jewish culture, the history of Jews in America, and the social psychology of the modern Jewish family has produced the twin results of intermarriage. Although it has increased the incidence of intermarriage, it has also increased the likelihood that intermarried couples, Jews and non-Jews, will have their group identity defined more by the Jewish heritage than by any other ethnic or religious heritage.

But those very same forces have also increased the fragmentary nature of what constitutes Jewish tradition and Jewish identification. Thus, although Jewish culture survives and even flourishes in modern America, it does so less as an integrated whole and more as a kind of grab bag of fragments from which individual Jews choose more or less at will. Because the so-called tradition, now, is rich with many fragments, all Jews are able to fashion for themselves an identity that is well suited to their life-style. For Jews who are married to Christians, this has meant choosing very carefully the elements of the tradition that can be readily shared (e.g., food, humor, literature) or identified with in more universal terms (e.g., support of Israel, support of social welfare and civil rights, resistance to any expression of anti-Semitism). The elements of the Jewish tradition by which a sense of Jewishness is expressed in most intermarried families, mixed marriages in particular, also are only sporadically recollected or enacted. After all, each holiday comes but once a year. Books by or about Jews are read only from time to time, and even Jewish foods are not likely to be a daily diet. So being Jewish is mostly a sometime thing. Of course feeling that one is a Jew or not a Jew is a constant existential condition, but enacting or recollecting any of the cultural imperatives of that feeling are only episodic and subject to the choice of each individual. Therefore, we often find the anomalous situation of people who say, "Of course I am Jewish!" and who will even think of their children and spouses as Jews (when traditional Jewish law would not legitimize such a claim), while manifesting very little concrete expression of Jewishness in their daily lives.

The part-time and fragmentary nature of identification is certainly not unique to only those Jews who are married to Christians. It characterizes, to a greater or lesser extent, all Jews. Indeed, it is virtually the universal character of all forms of ethnic and religious identification in modern society, and it is precisely this part-time and fragmentary nature of Jewishness that produces much of the invidious distinctiveness among various factions in the Jewish community. Levels of commitment and degrees of identification are invariably measured by the amount of time and resources one spends articulating various aspects of the tradition (be it through behavior, the expression of attitudes, or affiliation with movements and organizations) and by the amount of knowledge one has of the tradition itself. Those who do more, spend more, and know more are generally considered by themselves and others as the more committed and the more identified. The problem with this seemingly sensible yardstick is that it does not reflect any of the subjective or emotional significance that those activities have for the individual. In other words, a person who attends a synagogue only once a year, or celebrates only Hanukkah or Passover, may derive as much subjective meaning from the experience—and therefore consider himself a "good Jew"—as a person who attends the synagogue much more frequently, celebrates all the holidays, and actively participates in the life of the Jewish community. The problem is analogous to comparing the large amount given to charity by a rich person and the small amount given by a poor one. It is difficult to say which of the two is the greater giver.

Among Jews in general, the distinctions in levels of commitment or degrees of identification result largely in the sorting out of cliques, the "right" and "left" branches of denominations, and diverse patterns of synagogue affiliation. Friendship patterns also come to reflect the various ways Jews define their links to their heritage, so that Jews who may not belong to any synagogue or Jewish organization, who practice no part of the religion, and who have but a little interest in Jewish history or politics, may nonetheless have an almost exclusively Jewish network of friends.

The feeling of ease among one's friends, and the interests and backgrounds one shares with them, often constitutes the basis of a tie to the Jewish community even among highly acculturated Jews.

However, the ways and extents to which intermarried Jews express their sense of Jewishness is frequently understood by other Jews, as well as by themselves, to result from the fact that they are married to non-Jews. The large variety of ways in which Jews in general identify and show commitment seems to take on special significance in the case of intermarriers, as if to say that the reason why intermarried Jews express their sense of Jewishness the way they do is because they are married to non-Jews. Therefore, our finding that Jewishness is more salient in cases of intermarriage than any other ethnic or religious identity, is unexpected, and forces Jews, as well as non-Jews, to rethink the relationship between love and tradition, between intermarriage and group identity. It also involves a stretching of the normative boundaries of what constitutes a legitimate form of Jewish identification, and this brings us to one of the more interesting consequences, the potentially revolutionary consequence, of Jewishness in modern intermarriages.

Regardless of the breadth of alternatives in the ways that Jews can accommodate the ethnic and religious aspects of their tradition in their personal lives, marriage to a Christian was always considered beyond the pale. The man or woman who took such a step was thought to have relinquished all interest in or claim to *any* of the alternatives in Jewish identification. Despite the pain often involved, the family and the community frequently broke off all contact with the transgressor, in effect expelling the intermarrier from the Jewish community. Some of the older intermarrieds who were part of our study, particularly the Jews who became Unitarians or Christians, told heart-rending stories of family rejection; Jewish parents who sat *shiva* (the traditional seven days of mourning) for them because they married a non-Jew; violent verbal battles that led to a lifetime of estrangement—later to be deeply regretted by both sides. One Jewish man of fifty told how his parents would not answer their door to let him into their house when he brought his first child—their first grandson—to show them, because in their eyes the child was not Jewish. It was then that he decided to join his wife's church.

The prevalence of the "rejectionist" relationship between Jewish intermarriers and their families and community, customary until the 1950s, more or less ensured the eventual assimilation of the Jew who married a Christian. Conversion of the Christian to Judaism was not only discouraged, but, in fact, was virtually unacceptable to either Orthodox or Conservative Jews (who made up the majority of the American-Jewish population). Although Reform Jews were accepting of intermarriage and conversion, they hardly went out of their way to make easy the entry of the intermarried couple into the Jewish community. In short, the Jewish community was not only opposed to intermarriage, it was steadfastly opposed to having any intermarrieds in its midst.

Perhaps that rejectionist approach helped to prevent some intermarriages from taking place, but it also guaranteed that when a Jew married a non-Jew, he would most likely opt out of the Jewish community, and the community, in turn, would wish to see him out. The strict prohibition against marriage between a Catholic and a non-Catholic prior to Vatican II in the mid-1960s had a similar effect upon Catholic intermarriers. This is probably why the Church liberalized its doctrines.

The great increase in the rate of intermarriers since the 1950s has made the rejectionist approach highly hazardous for the future of the Jewish community. But even more importantly, the tendency of Jewishness to prevail in intermarriages over alternate ethnic or religious identifications has emboldened more intermarried Jews to maintain their ties with the Jewish community. This tendency has pushed rabbis in all three branches of American Judaism to take a more tolerant and open-minded approach to non-Jews seeking conversion. It has convinced a large and growing number of Reform rabbis, in particular, to officiate at mixed marriages in which the non-Jewish partner has not converted, although all rabbinic associations remain opposed to such officiation as a matter of policy. It has also convinced at least the Reform movement to take two highly dramatic steps toward incorporating non-Jews into the Jewish community.

In 1978, at the annual meeting of the Union of American Hebrew Congregations in Houston, Rabbi Alexander Schindler, the president of that body, proposed that the Reform movement reach out to "unchurched" Americans, in general, and to the non-Jews who are married to Jews, in particular, "to make the congregation, the rabbi, and Judaism itself available to them and their families." That proposal reversed a nearly 1,600-year-old tradition on the part of Judaism of not only not seeking converts, but, in fact, discouraging non-Jews from entering the Jewish fold. The proposal was enthusiastically endorsed by the Reform movement and became the basis of a major organizational effort at "outreach." Moreover, it catalyzed the Conservative and Orthodox communities to begin reevaluating their long-standing resistance to conversion.

In 1983, Rabbi Schindler further opened the portals to Judaism, at least of the Reform movement, by reiterating and publicizing the position of the Reform rabbinate on the Jewish identity of children. That body, through the Central Conference of American Rabbis, proclaimed in 1947 that although traditional Jewish law has regarded children of a non-Jewish mother and a Jewish father as not Jewish, the Reform movement would consider a child as Jewish regardless of which parent was Jewish, as long as the child was, in fact, raised as a Jew. It made socialization, upbringing, the final test of Jewishness as opposed to matrilineal descent. The social trends of the previous thirty-six years made the position taken in 1947 worthy of repetition and publicity in 1983. Earlier, it served largely as a statement of an abstract principle, but by 1983, it served as the basis for a *modus vivendi* for tens of thousands of families.

The shifting attitude of the American rabbinate, as well as Jewish families, from a rejecting to a more accommodating approach to intermarriers illustrates, perhaps, the most subtle way in which Jewishness has persisted in the face of intermarriage. The fact that large numbers of intermarrying Jews have chosen not to assimilate has impelled Jewish institutions and their leadership to alter age-old policies and ideologies; to accommodate intermarried families within at least the more liberal wings of the organized Jewish community. Of course, such liberalization may make intermarriages even more possible, but it also makes it more likely that when an intermarriage takes place, the non-Jewish partner will be more apt to consider conversion to Judaism. It also makes it more likely that even in the absence of the conversion of the non-Jewish spouse, the intermarried family will feel comfortable in the midst of the Jewish community and will be more inclined to raise their children as Jews.

In concluding this chapter, two final points need to be emphasized. The persistence of Jewishness, perhaps even its salience in the intermarried home, does not mean that the heritage of the Christian partner is excluded. First, the general American culture, which is obviously not Jewish, pervades the intermarried home, as it pervades all American homes. But more importantly, spouses not from a Jewish background carry within themselves all the cultural fragments and memories their own upbringing has given them. Even in conversionary families, the partner who is a convert to Judaism will very likely have ties to a Christian family network with which relationships are maintained to a greater or lesser extent. Therefore, elements of Christian religious and ethnic traditions will inevitably filter into the life-style of the intermarried family. Indeed, it is these very elements that may provide the family with its distinct cultural richness, as well as its internal tensions.

Finally, it must be emphasized that whatever ingredients of each spouse's heritage are expressed in the life-style of intermarried families, in fact, neither's heritage is inevitable. No religious or ethnic tradition is permanently sealed in or out of the world view or climate of any family. Its salience and perpetuation, or erosion and ultimate loss, is the product of ongoing communication and negotiation between husband and wife. What individual men and women who are intermarried do with their cultural and religious differences is not the outcome of an impersonal social force. Rather, it is most often the outcome of decision-making. Therefore, in Chapter Seven we turn our attention to the ways of marital decision-making in the intermarried family.

Chapter Seven

TO LOVE AND
TO NEGOTIATE

To Love and
To Negotiate

To marry or not to marry? That is the burning question all couples in love agonize over, some to a greater and some to a lesser degree. For potential intermarriers, the throes of that decision are generally deeper and last longer than for men and women who share a religious and ethnic heritage.

If Francesco Alberoni, the lyrical Italian sociologist, likens falling in love to a revolution, we may liken marriage to the aftermath of a successful revolution in which a new state, a new regime, a new order is established. The prospect of such institutionalization is formidable indeed. Hence, the dilemma. And, writes Alberoni,

> The more complex, articulate and rich the order is, the more terrible the disruption, the more difficult, dangerous and risky the process is. . . . The person who has more ties, more obligations, more things to integrate and change is the one for whom falling in love is the more disruptive.[1]

Although Alberoni writes only of people with more or fewer social ties, one can easily extend this line of analysis to couples who have the greater differences between them—ethnic and religious differences—and are inevitably implicated in a more "revolutionary" romance than are people who come from similar backgrounds. Therefore, the decision to marry is itself likely to be more difficult for couples from different ethnic and religious backgrounds than for couples who have common backgrounds. Also, as we have seen in some earlier examples, the process of agonizing over the marriage decision (e.g., length

179

and turbulence of courtship) will vary considerably even among intermarriers, depending on the degree of the differences between prospective husband and wife.

But once that all-important question—to marry or not to marry—is settled in the affirmative, a multitude of other questions quickly follow, much like the challenges of statecraft follow quickly upon the heels of a successful revolution. Each question in its own way tests anew the commitments of the couple to each other and to their respective heritage.

How should we be married? By a rabbi? By a priest or minister? By both? By neither, but rather by a justice of the peace? What kind of ceremony should we have? Jewish? Christian? Other? Mixed? Neither, but rather a civil ceremony? Where should the wedding be held? In a synagogue? In a church? In a judge's chambers? In a private home or a catering hall?

In the planning of any marriage, such questions would be a necessary part of the logistics of setting up the new institution. In an intermarriage, they are pivotal to the identity that the new institution, the new family, is to establish. These questions, and many others that will follow, impel the couple—again and again—to reconcile the claims of love (the premise of their "revolution") with the multivalent tugs of their respective heritages.

Where love counsels self-sacrifice and a blind eye to one's traditions ("What do I care who marries us, or where and by what incantation or formulae?"), amorphous ancestral affinities may sometimes urge otherwise ("I really can't bring myself to be married by a rabbi; I just need to have a priest present"). These twin tendencies inevitably lead couples to negotiate just how their "new regime" will integrate their dual heritage.

From earlier examples and from most of my own research, it is clear that the events or situations that necessitate negotiating matters of family identity are primarily those having to do with the holiday cycles of the calendar and certain transition points of the life cycle. As one pundit summed it up years ago, we suddenly find religion or heritage important when we "hatch," "match," or "dispatch," as in birth, marriage, and death. Less glibly, the matters that necessitate negotiations over the issues of family identity among intermarriers are the wedding itself, how to raise children, what holidays to celebrate and how to celebrate them, and—to a considerably lesser extent— how closely to pattern the general life-style of the family on either of the couple's twin heritages.

It should be noted at the outset that on most issues pertaining to the family's collective identity, as in many other aspects of family life, marriage involves continuous negotiation throughout the life cycle. Although some matters can be settled once and for all, others may remain unsettled for a lifetime.

In an influential textbook on modern marriage and family life, the sociologists Letha and John Scanzoni devote two chapters to the role of power and negotiation in marital decision-making.[2] Many of their observations are pertinent to the understanding of the dynamics of intermarriages as well. The Scanzonis point out that people who believe that marriage can stand on love alone are likely to find themselves in a highly precarious relationship, or an imbalanced one at best. "Marriage," they write, "requires two legs—love and justice." Although the first may come from hidden wellsprings within each soul, the second is achieved through the sobering process of give and take.

As in all negotiations, be it in the realm of politics or commerce, write the sociologists,

> Marriage involves an on-going series of exchanges. Even a relationship that over the years seems to have settled into very routinized ways of doing things often is caught unawares by new circumstances and faces the issue of renegotiation.[3]

To be sure, the basic ground rule of marital negotiation differs significantly from the basic ground rule of most other types of negotiations. The tacit understanding of the partners in a marriage is that the outcome they seek is one that will provide a "maximum joint profit" for each partner. Most other negotiations are based on the assumption of a "zero-sum" outcome; that is, an outcome in which one party's gain must inevitably entail the other's loss. In such a zero-sum negotiation, each party tries to gain advantages for himself or herself at the other's expense. Given the unique ingredient of love in most modern marriages, at least at the outset, the negotiations that take place between wives and husbands most often include a sincere desire on the part of each to assure that his or her gain (profit) does *not* result in a loss for the other. The guiding motto of most marital negotiation seems to be "Let's follow that course of action that produces the greatest possible satisfaction for both partners or, if not satisfaction, the least possible dissatisfaction."

However, apart from its unique maximum joint profit ground rule, the marital negotiation—like all other negotiations—depends on the power, authority, and resources each partner brings to the relationship. The outcome of any particular sequence of exchanges also depends on what each party *believes* about the power, authority, and resources of the other party. For example, in most quarters of our society, there is a generally held belief that mothers have a keener sense of the needs and aptitudes of their children, particularly when they are young, than have fathers. This belief, be it correct or not, is likely to tip many negotiations between husbands and wives in the favor of the wife in matters of early child rearing, even when the husband may have more power and resources at his command.

But what constitutes power and resources in marital negotiations? Although there is considerable controversy among social scientists on these matters, there is general agreement that power is "linked with one's degree of involvement in the economic opportunity system." The capacity to give or withhold valued resources provides men and women with varying degrees of power in their relationships. Of course, to the extent that each can seek and obtain valued resources outside of their one-to-one relationship, the power that either has over the other by virtue of his or her resources will be limited.

Thus, a man who is the sole breadwinner of a family might have considerable power in his relationship with his wife. On the other hand, if his wife is a skilled professional who is only out of the job market voluntarily and for a limited period of time, his power is not likely to be as great as that of a man whose wife has never been employed and does not have the training for or aspirations to gainful employment.

The power and resource dimensions of marital negotiations are also tempered by the "relative competence and relative involvement of the spouses in specific decision-making areas" of family life. For example, despite a great deal of role equalization among modern men and women during the past two decades, men are still much more likely to be involved in the mechanical aspects of home repair than are women. Women, however, are still much more likely than their husbands to be involved with the aesthetic aspects of home decorating. (Note the difference between the so-called women's magazines—even *Working Woman*—and magazines targeted to men, such as *Mechanics Illustrated* or *Business Week*.)

How a couple finally comes to decide anything—be it in the area of sexuality, child rearing, or where to take a summer vacation—evokes the full gamut of decisional forces. As family research has shown, these forces include resource and power differentials between wife and husband, their culturally bred beliefs about the appropriate roles of men and women, as well as other cultural stereotypes; their personal interests in and competences concerning the issues about which decisions are to be made; beliefs about the legitimacy of trying to influence one another; and idiosyncratic personality differences in exerting influence (e.g., who speaks louder or longer).

The decision to marry probably does not come easily to a great many couples; hence, there is an extensive period of dating and courtship. Based upon our survey of intermarried couples, we found that the average couple "courted" for *a little over two years.* In fact, nearly one-third of the 450 couples I surveyed dated for *three years or more* before they married. The old cliché about love and marriage, "fools rush in where angels fear to tread," apparently does not apply to intermarried couples. Two to three years of courtship hardly seems like rushing.

This period of courtship is also the time when a great many of the couples confront some of the early consequences of their different heritages, including the reaction of their parents, decisions on how and where their marriage will be solemnized, questions about the "identity" of the family, and how children will be raised. Considering the weightiness of these questions and the uncharted terrain in which the new couple must find answers, it is not at all surprising that it does take the couple two to three years to finally arrive at the altar or under the *chupah* (the Jewish marriage canopy) or before a judge.

How they resolve these early questions during the courtship, how they will resolve all the other questions that occur in later life, will be determined not only by their love for one another, but also by the subtle workings of their decisional forces. The negotiation over the matter of heritage will, however, favor the person who has the greater interest in and commitment to his or her past.

The marriage of Paul and Maxine L. is a telling example of this last point. Paul is an interior designer, in his mid-fifties, and of Hungarian ancestry. Although he was born a Jew and survived the Holocaust by hiding out with Christian friends in Budapest, he comes from a family of intellectuals (his father was a journalist, his mother a concert cellist), and he has never regarded his Jewishness as more than a pure accident of geneology. Paul married right after the war. His first wife was Jewish, although he pointed out that her religious origins did not particularly interest him at the time.

That marriage dissolved soon after they immigrated to the United States in 1956, and Paul moved from New York to Los Angeles. He met Maxine, an artist, at a gallery opening of a mutual friend in the early 1960s. She was some twelve years his junior, which troubled Maxine as well as her mother at first. The fact that he spoke with a heavy foreign accent and was not an Episcopalian also disturbed Maxine's family, who were faithful church members. When Maxine finally agreed to marry him, she did so on the condition that he join her family's church. Paul did not hesitate for a moment.

The fact that Paul had no family in Los Angeles, nor any prior commitment or involvement with the Jewish community, apparently made his shift to Episcopalianism a relatively easy matter. Indeed, by doing so, he not only acquired a new wife and a new religion, but also an immediate acceptance within a family that might otherwise have had a great deal of difficulty thinking of him as one of their own.

Paul and Maxine's resolution of their difference in religious heritage is a good illustration of how personal status and the weight of interest in family tradition on the part of one spouse, as compared to the relative disinterest on the part of the other, results in the couple "choosing" to identify with one heritage.

The fact that Paul was a good deal older than Maxine, and an immigrant with no family connections, put him at a status disadvantage relative to Maxine, even though he was a successful and much sought after interior designer. Maxine's father was a successful land developer around Los Angeles, as were her uncles. She prided herself on being a third-generation Angelino, and Maxine's family was generally well represented in the city's various civic and cultural institutions. Although Paul was not seeking her hand in marriage for any ulterior motive (she was a strikingly attractive and exciting young woman who attracted Paul for her own qualities), he was not oblivious to the superior social standing of her family. As the family had been members of the same church for many years, attending services at least once or twice a month, it would have been unthinkable for Maxine to marry outside the church.

In sharp contrast to Maxine's family's attachment to the

church, Paul had had very little feeling for his Jewishness since childhood. He had not been Bar Mitzvahed and had never been to any synagogue service apart from having been invited by friends or distant relatives for ceremonial occasions. Therefore, when Maxine suggested that he join her at church a few times before their marriage, he did not hesitate. "I don't have a particularly exclusivistic idea about God. If He does in fact exist, I doubt that He cares whether I pray in a church or a synagogue," Paul commented.

> At least in the church I can understand what's going on. Hebrew never made any sense to me and, the few times I was inside a synagogue, I don't recall that the services made much more sense to anyone else around me. It was like all the Jews around me who were praying were mechanized to sway, sit, stand, murmur, or chant on cue, without any of them having the slightest idea of what their words or actions were supposed to mean.

Paul found the services in Maxine's church both dignified and orderly. He could appreciate the prayers in English, even though he never thought of himself as a particularly religious man. He found the high-minded sentiments of compassion, awe, charity, forgiveness, and social responsibility that he heard expressed in the prayers and the sermons appealing. To his pleasant surprise, once he began to attend services with Maxine, Paul also found a distinct warming of attitude on the part of her parents and relatives. He even made a few new acquaintances on his own among the Sunday regulars, so when Maxine suggested that he "join" the church ("it would really make my life a lot easier with my parents") and that they be married in it, Paul could think of no compelling reasons to resist her urgings. He loved Maxine deeply and he could hardly wait to marry her. Becoming an Episcopalian seemed like a relatively small "requirement" for the pleasure of having her as his wife.

Although it is unlikely that either Paul or Maxine ever thought of themselves as "negotiating" the terms of their marriage and Paul's religious identity, an objective view of their relationship suggests that they had indeed negotiated it. To be sure, they were also in love. But, clearly, Maxine—and somewhat indirectly, her parents—wanted the marriage to reflect certain other values than just the love of two people for one another. Moreover, they seemed to have somewhat greater leverage in bringing about the desired outcome than did Paul. Maxine's youth, her family status, her membership in an American majority group, and her obvious interest in maintaining her family's religious heritage all favored her in this particular aspect of family decision-making.

Let us consider one other example in which the issue between the couple specifically focuses on how the marriage should be solemnized.

Sam L. and his Methodist financée, Lorraine, have already been introduced to us. He was a Jewish lawyer raised as an orphan in the Bronx. She was a social worker raised in a modest middle-class family in Oceanside, Long Island. They met while both were in graduate school, and lived together for almost two years before they decided to marry.

"I think the very next sentence out of Lorraine's mouth after she said 'Yes' to my proposal," Sam recalled, "was the question, 'How are we going to get married?'" Perhaps because he was trained as a lawyer, Sam was anxious to establish in advance the "terms" of their marriage. "I am sure I can find a nice rabbi who will marry us in a catering hall somewhere out on Long Island near your parents", Sam replied. In the same breath, he made it clear to Lorraine that he would not get married in a church and that he expected their children to be raised as Jews. Lorraine was crestfallen. The happy moment of their affirmation of love was almost instantly tarnished by an obvious difference in their expectations about the very ceremony in which their marriage would be solemnized.

You may recall that Sam was the son of Holocaust survivors, both of whom died tragically when Sam was in his early teens. He was raised by his older sister and brother-in-law and by a grandfather he revered, all of whom were Orthodox Jews. Sam himself was sent to a yeshiva day school in the Bronx through eight years of elementary school.

Although Lorraine was lukewarm toward her Methodist faith, never having been much of a churchgoer, her mother and grandmother attended church fairly regularly. Over the years, the minister of their church had become very much a family friend. He was a frequent family guest, although they hardly ever talked of religion as such. With all that, however, Lorraine's mother had a great deal of respect for Sam. Perhaps because her own son had barely graduated from community college (he was working as a salesman in an auto parts store) and her husband worked as an advertising layout designer at a local newspaper, she was immensely impressed with Sam's career prospects as a budding young lawyer. "I think she saw Sam as probably the most successful man she had ever had in her immediate family," Lorraine admitted. The idea of having a son-in-law who was a lawyer obviously pleased her, even though Lorraine's grandmother grumbled from time to time about her granddaughter's "Jewish beau."

Nevertheless, whenever the subject of their marriage would come up, Lorraine's mother invariably turned the conversation to what sort of arrangements she should make at the church with her friend the minister. "Reverend N. has known Lorri all her life. He will perform a wonderful service for us," she would say. As invariably as Lorraine's mother brought up the subject of a church wedding, just as invariably would Sam and Lorraine duck out of it. "We have too many other things to think about, like finishing school first." Privately, Sam kept pressing Lorraine to tell her mother that there would be no church wedding, but neither could bring themselves to confront her.

"I just knew that my mother would make a big scene if I told her that he didn't want to get married in the church," recalled Lorraine, and I couldn't face her yelling. Since childhood, I always hated her yelling at me and, considering the few times a year that we would come home from school, I didn't want to spend an entire visit being subjected to her yelling—especially not with Sam in the house.

"I guess I could have confronted her myself about the church thing," Sam reflected, "but I just didn't think it was my place, as a Jew, to tell this Christian lady that her daughter couldn't get married in her church because of me."

Sam and Lorraine struggled for the better part of a year over the church issue. Finally, they devised a scheme whereby they would take Lorraine's parents to dinner at a restaurant and tell her mother of their decision not to marry in the church. They reasoned that her mother would be unlikely to make a scene in a restaurant and, indeed, she did not. Of course, by then the mother probably also sensed the reason for their hesitancy in talking about a church wedding. For whatever reason, Lorraine's mother managed to accept their decision against the church wedding a lot more easily than either Sam or Lorraine had expected.

However, neither had the heart to push their case so far as to deny Lorraine's mother and grandmother the pleasure of their minister's participation in the wedding ceremony. Lorraine herself had known the minister all her life, and she made it clear to Sam that she would also find it rather discomfiting not to have his blessing on their marriage. Having won the battle, so to speak, on the issue of the church, Sam did not feel up to pushing further either against Lorraine or against her family although, as he recalled, "I had no idea how I was going to tell my sister and grandfather that there would be a Protestant minister co-officiating with a rabbi at our wedding."

Sam's other main concern was that the wedding should be held in a catering hall where kosher food could be served, so that his Orthodox Jewish relatives could eat along with the other guests. This wish on his part had no particular significance to either Lorraine or her parents, especially since Sam reassured them that he would pay any difference there might be between kosher catering and a non-kosher alternative. They readily accepted Sam's proposal and thought it only a matter of etiquette that all guests partake of the food equally.

What is so striking about these accounts of bargaining, both on the part of Paul and Maxine and Sam and Lorraine, is precisely that they took place even before the marriage itself. At a time when love and romantic involvement are at their peak, one would expect the lovers to be "blind" to their differences of heritage or to overlook those differences in their haste to marry. Obviously, these couples were neither "blind" nor all that hasty.

The two accounts also illustrate the delicate strategy of what we have described as bargaining with maximum joint benefit as its goal. Whereas Paul found it quite easy to accede to Maxine in the matter of religious affiliation, the situation between Sam and Lorraine was made more complicated by the fact that both had certain sentimental attachments to their heritage. "I know that Judaism means much more to Sam than Methodism does to me," Lorraine acknowledged.

> It's so much more complicated for him, with his parents having been survivors of the Holocaust and then dying when he was so young. I didn't want to do anything that would make him feel that I was threatening his sense of belonging to his people. At the same time, I have a family too, and I just couldn't bring myself to hurt my mother and grandmother by denying them my minister at the wedding.

Sam had a slightly different explanation for the compromise.

> Lorraine really has a great deal of difficulty opposing her mother. I think when her mother raises her voice, Lorraine becomes a child all over again. I don't know what she is afraid of, but then my mother died when I was a kid. I have not had to deal with my

parents as an adult, so I really can't fault Lorraine. I don't know how I would have performed. I do know that I was very anxious about telling my grandfather that there would be a minister at the wedding. Given my own anxiety about that, I guess I knew pretty much what Lorri was feeling toward her mother and grandmother, so I didn't want to put any more pressure on her than I felt I had to.

Although Sam could exert some influence on Lorraine, at least up to a point, he imagined and feared that in her mother's eyes he was just a lower-class Jewish kid of immigrant parents. In his own mind's eye, as he imagined Lorraine's mother saw him, Sam was still in the West Bronx. Lorraine and her folks were real Americans, Protestants, and from Long Island, which to him had a certain cachet.

Odd as it may seem, a certain sense of status inferiority seemed to prevade Sam's approach to Lorraine's mother and grandmother, even though he was in the process of becoming a lawyer whose social and economic status would probably be greater than theirs. At the same time, Sam could also look beyond his feeling of status inferiority, as could Lorraine's mother, who was—after all—convinced that her daughter was making an excellent match.

Sam recalled that even as he was going along with the plans for the wedding ceremony, including the minister, he said to himself,

After we get married, we're moving to Washington. I'll be working at the Justice Department and we'll be independent. Lorraine won't see her mother much, and I'll be free to make the kind of Jewish life with her that is suitable to our situation.

In fact, Lorraine had agreed that they would raise their children as Jews. That was something of supreme importance to Sam.

The issue of the wedding and the marriage ceremony itself is frequently the first and most significant test of how a young couple will deal with the twin tugs of their love for each other and their dual heritage. Often that issue will affect all subsequent marital negotiations: questions concerning each spouse's familiarity with his and her respective traditions, emotional attachments thereto, attachments to parents, and varying degrees of embeddedness on the part of each in his or her community of origin.

The marriages of Paul and Maxine and of Sam and Lorraine illustrate the complex decision-making dynamics that lead up to a wedding. But, in fact, the choices of a church wedding for Paul and Maxine, and a ceremony co-officiated by a rabbi and a minister for Sam and Lorraine, turn out to be highly atypical for most intermarriers.

In his authoritative textbook on the American family, the sociologist William Kephart observed that, according to the National Vital Statistics Division, "most Americans prefer a religious ceremony . . . four out of five marriages are presided over by a clergyman."[4] Yet of the couples who were part of my survey of 450 intermarriages, the most typical marriage was a civil ceremony in which neither tradition was represented, followed by such creative alternatives as marriage by a Jewish or Christian justice of the peace. The table below lists the percentages finding different solutions to the dilemma of the wedding ceremony.

The "other" category in the table also includes the many cases in which the wedding was held at the home of either the bride or the groom, with either a rabbi or a Christian clergyman officiating. Such clergymen were generally not affiliated with any church or synagogue. They often held employment outside the pulpit and, therefore, were available to perform such wedding ceremonies outside an established religious institution.

Of the 450 couples surveyed, 150 had weddings that were solemnized by a rabbi either exclusively or, in a handful of cases, together with a Christian clergyman. In all but thirty-eight of the cases in which a rabbi participated in solemnizing the marriage, the Christian partners had converted to Judaism prior to the marriage. Most rabbis will not perform a marriage

Wedding Ceremonies of Intermarriers

Type of ceremony	Percentage
Synagogue ceremony	20
Ceremony in rabbi's study	7
Church ceremony	9
Ceremony officiated by rabbi and minister or other non-Jewish clergy	6
Civil ceremony	32
Other	26
Total	100

ceremony between a Jew and a Christian because to do so would be to violate not only *halachah* (the corpus of traditional Jewish law), but also the firm resolutions of all major rabbinic associations. Jewish law simply does not recognize marriages between Jews and Christians as religiously valid, no matter who performs them. Of course, these marriages have civil validity if they are performed by a duly recognized authority.

Seventy couples had weddings in which their marriages were solemnized by a Christian clergyman exclusively or together with a rabbi. The other 230 couples were married in ceremonies in which judges, justices of the peace, university or military chaplains, and a variety of other functionaries who are authorized to solemnize marriages officiated.

One of the advantages of a statistical analysis is that it is not affected by emotions. Therefore, the percentages outlined in the previous table do not reveal the tensions and arguments, the pleadings and guilt pangs, that undoubtedly went into the making of a great many of the marriages, or at least into the planning of the wedding ceremonies. The familiar strain over the issue of making up a guest list, which attends virtually all wedding preparations, is greatly multiplied when one can as easily offend one's relatives by failing to invite them as by inviting them to a wedding ceremony that they will perceive as strange or foreign at best, and downright threatening or offensive at worst.

As the statistical wedding portrait of intermarriages suggests, the majority opt for ceremonies that avoid the most direct expressions of each one's religious or ethnic heritage for a variety of reasons. Both families generally wish to avoid emphasizing the differences between them. The relative infrequency of wedding ceremonies under specifically religious auspices (e.g., synagogue or church) underscores yet another fact. Most couples who intermarry do not have such strong feelings or ties to their own ancestral communities as to face the potential conflicts that might arise were they to insist on a more "traditional" wedding ceremony, or they introspect that the other person feels the same ties; thus, they cancel out. Of course synagogues also prohibit marriages between Jews and Christians. That diminishes the number of intermarriages that might take place under Jewish congregational auspices.

The high proportion of non-denominational weddings among intermarriers also signifies that intermarriage is still regarded as "deviant" in the Jewish and Christian communities, professions of ecumenicalism and universalism notwithstanding. Families who face the prospect of an intermarriage most often prefer not to bring it to the attention of their communities or religious leaders. Therefore, they frequently opt for a civil ceremony or some creative variant thereof. Many will select a judge or justice of the peace who represents not only civil authority, but who also embodies one or another partner's religious or ethnic heritage. For example, Judge Marvin R. Halbert, a Common Pleas Judge in Philadelphia, boasts that he performs more marriages in a year than most clergymen he knows. Because so many intermarrying couples would not be married by a rabbi or a minister, they find it aesthetically and emotionally satisfying to be married by a Jewish judge. Apparently the knowledge that the secular figure of authority has some personal connections to the Jewish tradition, by virtue of himself being Jewish, satisfies some subtle need on the part of the intermarrying Jew to be connected to that tradition even minimally. Judge Halbert most likely has his counterparts in every major city in America.

The issue of the wedding ceremony is not only a matter of *who* shall solemnize the marriage. It is also a matter of *how* and *where* the ceremony shall be held, as we have seen in the case of Sam and Lorraine. Except for those who make a commitment to one or another tradition (e.g., as when one partner converts to the religion of the other prior to marriage), synagogues and churches are out of the question. They are much too potent as symbols of the difference between the bride and groom. Even when the partners themselves are willing to have their marriage "blessed" in the house of worship of the other, their respective families are generally not. Restaurants, country clubs, non-denominational chapels on college campuses, and family homes, when they are large enough, are the most frequent alternatives.

Particularly when the ceremony is co-officiated by representatives of both denominations, couples and their families frequently request of the clergyman (and many even insist) that no specific references to Jewish or Christian liturgical material be made. Etiquette and the fear of potential conflict demand that the distinctive marriage liturgies of the two different religious traditions be muted into harmonious generalities with which all can feel comfortable. References to the "laws of Moses and Israel," or to "the name of the Father, the Son," etc., are hardly the kinds of phrases that would bring peace and comfort to a newly formed intermarriage, unless one of the partners converted to the faith of the other first.

However wedding plans are finally resolved, most couples acknowledge that a great deal of their energies had been expended in trying to please their own families and in trying to avoid offending their respective in-laws. David R., a Catholic-born computer programmer, recalled that difficult interim stage, prior to getting married, with an obvious residue of bitterness.

> There was an aura of general unpleasantness around our wedding plans. No one was patting us on the back or congratulating us; at least not among our family. Only some of our close friends were really supportive, or at least curious about what Helen and I were going through. Our families were simply resigned to it. Naturally, we didn't want to do anything that would cause the raw feelings that were clearly there, just below the surface, to flare up into open hostility.
>
> For my family, the whole thing had nothing to do with religion. My parents hadn't been to church in years, although they're both Irish Catholics. They simply never had anything to do with Jews, didn't have particularly positive attitudes toward them, and felt very much outclassed by Helen's family. In their eyes, the son of an airplane mechanic and a stenographer had no business marrying the daughter of a Mr. and Mrs. Jewish lawyer.
>
> Helen's parents, on the other hand, kept talking about how they were the pillars of their congregation, and what would all their friends and family say when their daughter was not married by a rabbi under a *chupah*. We finally found a rabbi who married us in Helen's parents' home in Westchester, with *chupah* and all. My family really didn't know what was going on, and I think many of Helen's folks thought the wedding was kind of phony, since I wasn't Jewish.

Our survey of intermarried couples found that, in fact, about 43 percent of the Jewish parents and about 30 percent of the Christian parents openly disapproved of their child's choice of marriage partner because he or she was from outside their own group. About 20 percent in each category was openly approving, and the remainder were either ambivalent or non-committal ("It's your choice that matters. You're the one who is going to have to live with him/her"), as shown in the table.

The percentages of parents who disapprove of their children's mating choices or who do not totally approve, stand as a statistical reminder of the direct challenges that intermarriers

Reaction of Parents to Prospective
Intermarriage (percentage)

Typical reactions	Jewish parents	Christian parents
Approval	20	22
Disapproval	43	30
Ambivalence/ non-commital/ not applicable	37	48
Total	100	100

must face as they plan marriage. The discouragement of parental disapproval, or non-approval, in such a significant life choice as of one's mate, often serves as a powerful psychological stimulus for negotiations. As we saw in the case of the Episcopalian Maxine *vis-à-vis* her Jewish fiance Paul, as in the case of Sam and Lorraine, the explicit or implicit disapproval by the Christian parents pushed their daughters to negotiate with their Jewish fiances for concessions in favor of the Christian heritage. In fact, the anticipation of similar kinds of pressures led Sam to choose a job in Washington, D. C., hundreds of miles from his Methodist in-laws. He wanted to be sure that when it came time for raising children, he and Lorraine would not be thwarted in their plan to raise them as Jews.

Various forms of disapproval and pressure have been reported by the majority of intermarriers, particularly from the Jewish parents. Depending on the context, the style of these emotional sanctions and the quality of the relationship between the young couple and the parents have a broad range of consequences.

Selma G., a middle-aged Jewish schoolteacher, had married a black physician from Trinidad in 1949 when she was in her mid-twenties. Her parents and relatives, all second-generation

Conservative Jews in the Bronx, were outraged. Only her younger sister attended the wedding at City Hall. Selma did not see or speak with her parents for five years after her marriage, although she had two children in that time. Significantly, however, she ultimately raised her children as fairly traditional Conservative Jews, even though her husband did not convert to Judaism. Her children went to Hebrew school throughout their elementary school years. Her daughter was an active participant in Jewish youth groups through high school and college. Selma readily acknowledged that, perhaps in spite of her parents' disapproval, she wanted to demonstrate to herself as well as them that she could raise Jewish children and yet be married to the man she loved.

Phil R., a Jewish psychiatrist from Long Island, whom we met in Chapter Six, married Regina, a Catholic, against the violent opposition of his mother. Regina's father, of Polish-Catholic ancestry, was also quite unhappy with his daughter's choice of mate, but he was more subtle in his disapproval than Phil's mother. Right after the wedding, the couple moved to California. The cost of long distance calls, Phil observed, kept family arguments to a bearable minimum. Visits were not made more than once a year. Yet as we have seen, Phil and Regina drifted quite comfortably into a liberal Reform Jewish community and were planning to raise their children as Jews. Interestingly, however, when I asked Regina whether she thought about converting to Judaism, she replied without hesitation, "I would never give my mother-in-law that satisfaction."

Mildred F., a middle-aged housewife and mother of two children, and Jewish by birth, had tears in her eyes even after eighteen years of marriage to Tony, her Italian-Catholic husband, as she recalled for us her parents' reaction to her marriage.

> When my first daughter was born, we were poor. Tony had just gotten out of the army. He was looking for a job and we really had no money. When I went to my parents in Brooklyn, they

hardly were going to let me in the door. I asked if we could stay
with them for awhile until Tony found a job and we were able to
rent our own apartment. They said "No," so we went to live with
Tony's parents. His mother really warmed up to me after awhile.
I learned to cook and talk like an Italian. We ended up living with
them for almost two years. They were more of a family to me than
my own parents. Naturally, we all went to church together.
Tony's mother was big on going to church. After awhile, it just
made sense for me to convert to Catholicism. The way my parents treated me, I didn't see what good it did for me or my
children to be Jewish.

Interestingly, Margaret J., a formerly Catholic nurse and
mother of a six-year-old, tells an almost identical story, but from
the Catholic side. When she left her husband of ten years, also
an Italian-Catholic, her mother was furious with her. In her
mother's world, women simply did not leave their husbands
and Catholics did not get divorced. Her mother made it plain to
Margaret that she could expect no help from her in trying to
cope with being a divorcee and a single mother. For several
months after the divorce, Margaret lived with another nurse
friend of hers, and her son Nicky was taken care of by a variety
of babysitters and in daycare arrangements.

When Margaret met Sheldon, a Jewish stockbroker, at a
local Parents-without-Partners rap session, their friendship
blossomed quickly into romance. Sheldon brought Margaret for
a visit to his parents early in their relationship, and they responded warmly to her. Although they were fairly observant
Conservative Jews, they were also very anxious about the fact
that their son was trying to succeed in his profession and at the
same time raise his seven-year-old son from a previous marriage. His wife had left him, as well as his son, some two years
earlier.

For Margaret's mother, the prospect of a Jewish son-in-law
was like salt on the wound. She exploded at Margaret both for
her divorce and for her "irresponsibility" in falling in love with a
Jew. After Margaret brought Sheldon to meet her, they were

both convinced that the woman was anti-Semitic. Sheldon made it clear that he would have as little to do with her as possible.

In contrast to Margaret's mother, Sheldon's parents were so pleased at the prospect of their grandson having both a step-brother and a "mother" in the home, that they lavished a great deal of genuine warmth as well as gifts on Margaret. The issue of religion came up very delicately in the fall of 1973, right before the High Holy Days. Sheldon's mother asked Margaret if she would like to spend the holidays with them. With some trepidation, Margaret agreed. As fate would have it, that year Israel was attacked by its Arab neighbors on Yom Kippur. War broke upon the Jews on the holiest day of their religious calendar. By the afternoon of the holiday, the synagogue was filled with murmuring about the war in Israel. Margaret could see before her eyes a community that was suddenly praying not only for some abstract sense of personal salvation, but for collective survival. Perhaps the nurse in her could sense a group galvanized to face a mortal threat. Throughout much of the holiday, she had sat in the synagogue with Sheldon and his parents, who took great pains to explain to her—as well as to Nicky, whenever he would pop in—the order and meaning of the day. The prayer book was fully translated and, along with the rabbi's periodic directions, she had no difficulty following the service.

In the weeks that followed, Sheldon and his parents were much preoccupied with what came to be known as the Yom Kippur War, and Margaret inevitably found herself being caught up in their concern. She found herself included in the sense of the Jewish "we" that Sheldon's family assumed whenever they would talk about the war, and that was most of the time they were together. One day Sheldon remarked in a joking tone, "If you hang around with us long enough, you may become Jewish." Margaret wasn't sure if he was joking or not, but the comment struck home. A few days later, she brought up the subject seriously with Sheldon's mother. By this time, her future mother-in-law had virtually become a friend. Margaret recalled

that after about a three-hour conversation that involved considerable soul baring for both of them, Sheldon's mother called
their rabbi to inquire about what they should do. The following
week, Margaret and Sheldon met with Rabbi S. and worked out
a six-month program of study that would lead to Margaret's
conversion. They planned their wedding for the week following
her conversion.

The varied reactions of parents, illustrated by these cases,
all have their reverberations in the ultimate strategies followed
by their children in coming to grips with the differences in
heritage in the intermarriage. The necessity of negotiating their
religious and ethic differences was conditioned for each of the
couples by some of the pressures brought to bear upon them by
one or the other set of parents. But as we have seen, that pressure could result in outcomes that are in line with parental expectation, as was the case with Maxine and Paul, or could
"backfire," as in Margaret's reaction to her mother. It is safe to
surmise that reactions to parental pressures will be shaped by
the long-term quality of the relationships that prevail between
the parents and their children.

As a matter of fact, in 1960, when intermarriage was far less
common than it is now, the sociologist Jerold S. Heiss found
that intermarriers generally have poorer relationships with their
parents throughout life than do people who marry within their
own religious and ethnic group.[5] This point was confirmed in
yet another study of the subject in 1977 by the sociologists David
Caplovitz and Fred Sherrow.[6] Perhaps one important determi-
nant of what matters of heritage will be made the subject of
family negotiation between bride and groom, or between husband and wife, is the relative quality of each one's relationship
to his or her parents. Some of the logically possible emotional
tugs in either direction are outlined in the table below.

Because the table describes only abstract types, it must be
remembered that the terms "positive" and "negative" do not
describe any specific set of experiences. Rather, they describe

Types of relationships between intermarriers and their parents

Quality of Relationship
of Jewish spouse to parents

	Positive	Negative
Positive	I	II
Negative	III	IV

Quality of
relationship of
Christian spouse
to parents

the kind of evaluative judgments that people generally make
when they compare their own relationships with those of their
spouses. In the examples in this chapter, we might say, for
instance, that both Paul, of Hungarian-Jewish ancestry, and
Maxine, his wife of American-Episcopalian ancestry, appear to
have had equally positive relations with their parents. Of course
Paul's parents were not alive, so they were not pressing issue in
the marital negotiations. Both Mildred F., who converted to
Catholicism from Judaism, and Margaret J., who converted to
Judaism from Catholicism, seem to have had significantly
poorer relations with their mothers than their husbands had

with their parents. Phil R. and his wife, Regina, both appear to have had equally difficult relationships with their parents.

Lorraine, the Methodist wife of the Jewish attorney Sam, seems to have had a somewhat negative relationship with her mother, but Sam's parents were no longer alive and thus could not be used as a basis of comparison.

These examples offer ample evidence that the comparative emotional valences between intermarriers and their parents are a potential source of influence on both the content and the outcome of the negotiations concerning each partner's heritage. It is in these valences and the other factors outlined earlier, such as power, resources, and ideology, that we may expect to find the explanation for the varied ways in which intermarried couples come to grips with their differences.

Does it seem somewhat odd that the quality of relations with parents should play such a significant role in the married lives of adults, particularly in such important matters as dealing with one's heritage or religious tradition? It must be remembered that for the vast majority of adults, their parents were the ones who first introduced them to religion and ethnicity. Indeed, unless they took courses as adolescents or adults, which most had not done, their parents and grandparents were probably the most significant source of instruction regarding their heritage. Therefore, when the time comes to deal with heritage, a matter of utmost importance in an intermarriage or indeed any marriage, it is inevitable that those parental relations will bear heavily upon the negotiating process.

The positive or negative relations adults have, or recall having had, with their parents, may also be the result of experiences pertaining to the family heritage and religion itself. A slap or a reprimand at a Bar Mitzvah; a wrongful accusation of a "sin"; embarrassments, frustrations, or punishments recalled from childhood; excessive demands made by parents around some issue of religious practice, belief, or ceremony, continue to hurt in the recalling. Adults will often exact a full measure of satisfaction for those hurts; if not in their treatment of their parents, then in their treatment of the family's traditions.

A number of Jewish intermarrieds report that their relations with their parents were perfectly harmonious until they began bringing home non-Jewish dates. Some of the Christian respondents had similar experiences with their parents after bringing home Jewish dates. Although parent–child relations may have been fairly positive in all other areas of daily life, parents may have turned negative or punishing when it came to the transmission of family tradition. Such experiences may, themselves, have channeled some people into seeking marriages outside their own religion. But even if those experiences did not have a causal influence on the mating choices of intermarriers, they were apt to make them unsympathetic to religion in general and to their own family heritage in particular.

In sum, it may be said that each person in an intermarriage will bring as much of his heritage into it as is dictated by his personal familiarity with that heritage, as he feels impelled to by personal commitment and filial piety, and as he believes he has the power to influence his mate to accept. In this matrix of forces, the parent plays a significant role, as we have seen. But they do so mainly by what they have done with their children in the past, in childhood and adolescent socialization. Their direct and active role diminishes significantly in the everyday lives of their now-adult children. In fact, if they insist on continuing to play an active interventionist role, they will most often be perceived as meddling, and therefore resented and rejected.

Each man and woman is at the center of a web of social ties, some of which they may share. Many, in fact, will draw them to one another, which is probably one of the main reasons they choose to marry. But many of those social forces—such as their different friendship networks and ties to certain institutions that may characterize their ethnic group or differentiate between social classes—will push them apart because both desire to integrate the other in his or her own world. The figure on p. 205 is an attempt to represent this web of forces graphically.

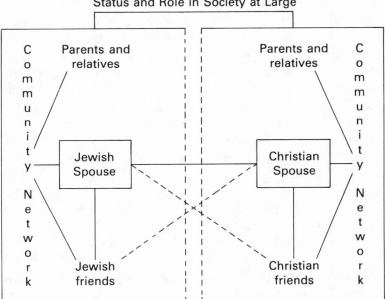

The social ties that surround the intermarrieds

In this diagram, each person is linked to others by bonds of kinship, friendship, and other more or less obligatory affiliations (e.g., job, club, neighborhood) in the wider society and community. The broken lines indicate that, for some intermarriers, their social worlds may not be as discontinuous as it is for others.

The figure helps us visualize not only the different social worlds to which intermarrieds are introduced through their parents, but also a host of other significant social ties that may hamper each one's ability to feel at home in the world of the other. Love frequently has to bridge great social distances. It is the building of such bridges and the need to shore up the foundations at each end of the span that allows intermarried couples to love and negotiate at the same time.

What the figure does not indicate is how the important issues to be negotiated, and the terms of the negotiation itself, change over the family life cycle. Experience and survey research suggest that the salient issues have to do with the transition points of the life cycle itself. Getting married, having and raising children, deciding on how to educate children and on what rites of passage to have them follow (e.g., circumcision, baptism, Bar or Bat Mitzvah, Confirmation) and, eventually, the question of how and where each one is to be buried at the end of the life cycle, each can rekindle the tension between love and tradition. Each necessitates negotiating again the way in which the ingredients of each spouse's tradition will enter into the family's handling of the particular life cycle event. The observance of holidays, subtle differences in food preferences, the fluctuating feelings of attachment and detachment to one's ethnic and religious group, and aesthetic values all crop up in the course of married life as matters to be negotiated across the cultural divide of husband and wife. But these latter issues generally do not engage feelings with the intensity that is evoked by the major points of transition in the life cycle.

The wedding itself, how and where it is to be solemnized, is an issue that engages intermarrying couples in intense familial negotiations. The handling of that issue often indicates how the couple will cope with subsequent significant events.

Cutting across all the issues of religion and tradition that intermarried couples are likely to confront, discuss, and negotiate is the question of conversion. All available evidence indicates that when one spouse converts to the religion of the other, or when both partners convert together to a religion that is new to them, the family's life-style will mirror the practices and values that are typical of members of their chosen community. Therefore, in Chapter Eight we turn our attention to some of the dynamics of conversion and its consequences for the life-style of the intermarried family.

Chapter Eight

YOUR PEOPLE ARE
MY PEOPLE

Your People Are
My People

And Ruth said: Entreat me not to leave from following after thee;
for whither thou goest, I will go; and where thou lodgest, I will
lodge; thy people shall be my people, and thy God my God;
where thou diest, will I die, and there will I be buried.[1]

These moving words of love and devotion were uttered not by a
bride to her groom, but rather by the ancient Moabite Ruth, of
biblical fame, to her mother-in-law, Naomi. The story is well
known, as the basis of numerous works of art and literature.
The image and words of Ruth have also been a model of what is
to be expected of an earnest convert to Judaism: selflessness,
total acceptance of faith and fate, and a transference of loyalty
from one's family of ancestry to one's family by marriage.

As is the case with a great many biblical characters, the
historical Ruth is cloaked in obscurity. No one is certain that
such a person ever really existed and uttered precisely those
words, but the legend of Ruth and the words attributed to her in
the Bible have shaped many of the expectations that Jews, at
least, have of a non-Jew who chooses to become a Jew. Although the image has been constant, rabbinic policy and practice toward the encouragement of conversion and the acceptance of converts has fluctuated throughout Jewish history, as
has the status of the proselyte in Judaism. A series of essays,
entitled *Conversion to Judaism*, edited by Rabbi David Eichhorn,
demonstrate that until the advent of Christianity, the Jewish
community was generally accepting of converts (even as rabbis
argued among themselves as to the proper criteria for their acceptance into the fold).[2]

After Christianity became the dominant state religion of the Roman Empire, a series of bans and edicts were promulgated by the Church that prohibited Jews from seeking or accepting converts. For example, in the year 339, the Emperor Constantine ordered the confiscation of the property and the expulsion of anyone who aided or abetted the conversion of Christians to Judaism. Constantine also made marriage between a Jew and a Christian, and circumcision of a pagan, capital offenses. Consequently, after the rise of Christianity, all rabbinic authorities forbade the seeking or the accepting of converts for fear of jeopardizing their own lives as well as the lives of their communities.

It is probably a fair generalization to say that the Jewish community has been nearly closed to converts for the past 15 or 16 hundred years. However, despite the community's closed door policy, and despite the great personal dangers associated with conversion, there has always been a handful of non-Jews who chose to become Jewish. The *Universal Jewish Encyclopedia* (1943) records the names of some of the most renowned ones, such as Bishop Bodo of France, who was confessor to the king. He converted to Judaism in the year 838, adopted the name of Eliezer, and later married a Jewish woman.[3] In the seventeenth century, a Polish nobleman by the name of Valentin Potocki died a martyr's death for choosing Judaism, as did the Franciscan Father Diego de Assuncao, who converted to Judaism in Portugal in 1603. The *Chronicle of Solomon Bar Simson* (an account of Crusades that date from the eleventh century) records the slaughtering of Jews as well as "sincere proselytes" in the vicinity of Worms and Mainz.[4]

Perhaps because of the great dangers associated with conversion to Judaism or because of the almost unattainable ideal set by Ruth, people seeking to become Jewish were strongly discouraged by rabbinic authorities. In fact, conversion came to be strictly forbidden by Jewish law if the prospective convert had any non-religious motive—such as marriage to a Jew—for seeking it. Consequently, the flow of conversions into Judaism since the rise of Christianity in Europe has been but a trickle.

In sharp contrast to Judaism, Christianity has always been profoundly committed, both theologically and programmatically, to the conversion of heathens and Jews through proselytizing by missionaries. From time to time, this commitment actually expressed itself in the forced conversion of Jews; most notably during the Crusades and the Inquisition. As late as 1858, a seven-year-old Jewish youngster, one Edgar Mortara, was abducted by his Christian nurse from the home of his parents in Bologna, Italy and forcibly baptized as a Christian. Although the case was an isolated one, and was severely criticized in both the European and the American press, the child remained hidden in a convent with the approval of the Archbishop of Bologna and of Pope Pius IX. According to sociologist Chaim I. Waxman's account of the incident, the American Catholic press also supported the abduction.[5]

Although Protestants do not have the same kind of history of aggressive conversion activities of Jews that Catholics have, they nonetheless share with the Catholics the belief that salvation is not possible without the acceptance of Jesus as savior. Therefore, they, too, promote the conversion of non-Christians, Jews in particular, to Christianity. As a matter of fact, according to statistics developed by the sociologist Arthur Ruppin, during the nineteenth century the number of conversions to Protestantism was considerably greater among European Jews than the number of conversions to Roman Catholicism. As reported in *The Universal Jewish Encyclopedia*, the number of Jewish conversions to Christianity during the last century comprised more than 5 percent of the Jewish population in England, Germany, Austro-Hungary, and America. Some of the more illustrious Jewish converts to Christianity include the French actress Sarah Bernhardt, the famous British statesman Benjamin Disraeli, the German poet Heinrich Heine, the philospher Edmund Husserl, and the composer Felix Mendelssohn.[6]

Scholarship on the conversion of Jews tends to support the view that the reasons Jews choose Christianity have changed from ancient to modern times. In the ancient and medieval world, the fear of physical persecution was perhaps the most compelling reason for many Jews to accept Jesus. At the beginning of the modern period, since the end of the eighteenth century, a more compelling reason has been the desire to join the social elite of Christian society. In most recent times in the twentieth century, the most readily apparent reason seems to be a desire for marital harmony. Presumably through all these periods, there were also Jews who converted to Christianity out of basic religious conviction, but these were probably a small minority. It is safe to say that, at least in the United States, the conversion of Jews to Christianity today is lower than in earlier centuries. It is also lower than the rates of conversion of Protestants to Catholicism and Catholics to Protestantism.

As a matter of fact, sociologist Dean R. Hoge, in a 1981 publication of the U. S. Catholic Bishops Conference, pointed out that the number of conversions to Catholicism has declined steadily since the mid-1960s, even as the rate of marriage between Catholics and non-Catholics has increased.[7] Citing a 1969 study of 504 mixed marriages between Catholics and Protestants, Hoge writes "there is reason to believe . . . that Protestants are converting to Catholicism less now than in the past, and Catholics are converting to Protestantism more."[8] The figures may have changed somewhat as a result of the liberalization of Catholic Canon Law regarding marriage with non-Catholics since the mid-1960s.

In addition to these overall patterns of conversion among Protestants, Catholics, and Jews, there is one dramatic development that is of far-reaching importance in understanding the nature and consequences of marriage between Jews and Christians.

Since the early 1950s, when the marriage rate between Jews and Christians began to increase significantly throughout the

United States, the rate of conversions to Judaism also began to increase. The National Jewish Population Study (1972) found that in approximately one-third of all intermarriages, the Christian partner converted to Judaism. Subsequent demographic surveys by Floyd Fowler in Boston (1975), Albert Mayer in Kansas City (1977), and Bruce Phillips in Denver (1982) all show that the rate of increase in conversion of Christians married to Jews has gone hand in hand with increases in intermarriage in general. These studies, along with my own survey of intermarried couples, show that the rate of conversion to Judaism among intermarriages has increased approximately threefold (300 percent) in the last thirty years.[9]

To flesh out the percentages with actual numbers, there is, for example, the research of Rabbi David Eichhorn—published in 1954—in which he estimated that the Reform and Conservative movements were converting approximately 1,500 to 1,750 non-Jews annually. In recent personal conversations, the directors of the Reform movement's Commission on Outreach estimated that this program converted approximately 7,000 to 8,000 persons to Judaism each year. The Orthodox and Conservative branches of Judaism, however, have a more traditional, restrictive attitude toward conversion. Also, there is no systematic information about recent conversions performed by their rabbis. Yet, a survey of Orthodox rabbis in 1965 found that there may have been as much as a 50 percent increase in the number of applicants for conversion coming to the attention of Orthodox rabbis between 1955 and 1965. That same study estimated that Orthodox rabbis converted at least 1,000 Christians to Judaism between 1962 and 1965. Leaders of the Conservative rabbinate estimate that there currently may be between 3,000 and 4,000 conversions taking place within their movement each year.[10]

The weight and direction of these numbers point to at least two conclusions. First, increasing numbers of intermarriages are conversionary rather than mixed marriages, indicating a desire on the part of the marriage partners to eliminate their religious differences by one spouse embracing the heritage of the other. Second, the desire on the part of the intermarried couple to achieve a homogeneous religious heritage within their own nuclear family does not lead them to choose the religion of the majority. Rather, it seems to lead those who choose any religion to choose the religion of the minority, that is, Judaism. Of course, even as we contemplate the significance of the numerical trends outlined above, it must be remembered that only about one-third of the intermarriages between Jews and Christians result in the conversion of the Christian partner to Judaism. About 10 percent of the born-Jewish partners convert either to the religion of their Christian spouse or to another religion, and another 17 percent simply relinquish their identities as Jews. ("I no longer consider myself Jewish." "My parents were Jewish, but I am not.")

The largest proportion of intermarriages (43 percent) remain religious and ethnically mixed marriages, in which neither spouse converts to the religion of the other, nor does the couple convert to another religion.

Nevertheless, the growing number of conversions to Judaism in the past thirty years is a remarkable trend in the light of the historical experience of the past 1600 years. It is witness to the growing stature of the Jewish community and Judaism as a religion in the eyes of Christians, to the religious consequences of an open and egalitarian society, and to the shifting tide of rabbinic policy in the face of modern Jewish family life.

As might be expected, even in the midst of these truly historical developments, there remain pockets of Jewish traditionalism in which conversion in the context of intermarriage is prohibited. As recently as June 1984, for example, the rabbis and lay leaders of fifteen Orthodox congregations and organizations of the Syrian and Near Eastern Jewish Communities of Greater New York and New Jersey (representing between 20,000 to 40,000 Jews) publicly reaffirmed to their community a proclamation that was first made in 1935.

In brief, that proclamation decreed that

> no male or female member of our community has the right to
> intermarry with a non-Jew. . . . We further decree that no future
> Rabbinic Court of the Community should have the right or au-
> thority to convert male or female non-Jews who seek to marry
> into our community.[11]

The 1984 reaffirmation of that proclamation is brief and blunt. Its
four short articles are as follows:

I. Our community will never accept any converts, male or
female, for marriage.
II. The Rabbi will not perform any religious ceremonies for such
couples—i.e., marriages, circumcision, Bar Mitzvahs, etc. In
fact, the Congregation's premises will be banned to them for
use of any religious or social nature.
III. The Mesadrim [deacons] of the Congregation will not accord
any honor to the convert or to one married to a convert. . . .
In addition, the aforesaid person, male or female, will not be
allowed to purchase a seat, permanently or for the Holidays,
in our Congregations.
IV. After death of the said person, he or she is not to be buried in
the Cemetery of our Community, known as Rodfe Zedek,
regardless of financial considerations.

Apparently the latest decree recognizes that in recent times
it has become relatively easy for intermarried couples to find
rabbis who would facilitate the conversion of the non-Jewish
spouse. Therefore, it seeks to assure the community that converts will not be accepted, regardless of who converted them.
The decree also spells out stiff penalties of deprivation of communal rights for any of their members who would intermarry,
even if they married a person who became Jewish.

In a spirit somewhat similar to the draconian principles described above, an association of Orthodox rabbis and lay leaders, calling themselves the Shofar Association of America, used
a full-page advertisement in *The New York Times* (September 21,
1984) to call upon all people to reject conversions to Judaism that
are performed by Conservative or Reform rabbis.

Obviously, these proclamations reflect the views of a relatively small minority in the Jewish community, since otherwise such large numbers of conversions would not be occurring. But the fact that they are expressed at all is a reminder of the depth of feeling that the issue of intermarriage and conversion arouses among those who are most concerned with the social as well as the cultural and religious survival of the Jewish people. Apparently this vocal minority does not see the conversion of Christians to Judaism as a legitimate way of resolving the breach of tradition created by intermarriage. Rather, they see conversions that are entered into as a consequence of intermarriage as a violation of ancient Jewish law and also as a possible cultural and religious dilution of the tradition. Traditionalists fear that converts are more interested in the social harmony of the family than in the integrity of the Jewish faith and tradition.

This view of the meaning of conversion has not been dismissed lightly by people who are genuinely concerned about the integrity of religion, nor can it be dismissed lightly because of its direct political and symbolic consequences in Israel. As recently as January 1985, the religious parties of the Israeli Parliament, which enjoy extraordinary power in a fragile coalition government, introduced legislation that would, in effect, invalidate the Jewishness of all converts who became Jewish under Conservative or Reform auspices. Although such an act would have had very little practical effect on the lives of most Jews, be they converts or not, it would have been symbolically devastating. Even the Prime Minister of Israel Shimon Peres warned his colleagues that if the legislation were passed, it "would destroy the unity of the Jewish people around the world." The move was voted down, but only by a slim margin.

The reason the Orthodox parties insist upon what is now known as the Amendment to the Law of Return is that they believe—as do the traditionalists described above—that most conversions performed under the auspices of Conservative and Reformed rabbis are contrary to the age-old *halachah*, the corpus of traditional Jewish law. Authentic conversions, they argue, require that the convert live according to *all* the laws of the Torah, the Five Books of Moses, and its Talmudic interpretations. According to the Orthodox point of view, Conservative and Reform rabbis take great liberties in the interpretation of those laws, even to the point of dispensing with some of them altogether.

Therefore, they contend, Conservative and Reform rabbis are not faithful bearers of the Torah and cannot be relied upon to perform valid conversions. The amendment proposed by the Orthodox parties would insert language into the important 1950 Israeli Law of Return—the law granting Jews the world over the right to claim citizenship in the State of Israel—to proclaim that only those converts are entitled to the benefits of that law whose conversion was performed "according to halachah." That key phrase, in effect, would render all Conservative and Reform conversions invalid in the eyes of the Israeli government.

This is not the place to expand upon the policies of Jewish and Israeli religious factions, but the furor over the Law of Return is a good indication of just how far a small segment of the Jewish population will go to maintain what they perceive as sacred tradition. It also indicates the far-reaching consequences that such personal matters as intermarriage and conversion can have in the life of a people. But what of the life of the converts themselves? What of their families?

The following letter from a Jewish mother, whose son had intermarried, is a poignant illustration of the sometimes bitter consequences of policies carried to their extreme.

Seven years ago I was an arrogant and cavalier Jewish mother. I was positive that intermarriage would never touch my family. My husband and I provided a traditional home for our children. We kept kosher, observed all the holidays, and insisted that our children join us in synagogue every week. My children attended a Jewish day school, were active in the Jewish community center, and were sent to Jewish camps each summer when they were

young. They were our pride and joy. Our children took pride in
their Jewish heritage and loved the traditions. Everything seemed
so bright and promising for my family.

And then darkness invaded our lives. My son met and fell in
love with a girl who was not born Jewish. We were shocked,
unprepared. We tried reason and threats; but it was to no avail.
We sought help. Our Rabbi supported our anger, but was not
able to help us deal with the problem. When we, in a fit of blind
rage, decided to sever our ties with our son, our Rabbi agreed
with us. We treated it like a scandal, and our friends and relatives
rallied around us. Our son pleaded with us for acceptance. His
future wife had even converted to Judaism, but we were determined to win this battle and not give in.

We did not attend the wedding.

We stopped financing the rest of our son's education.

We told him we no longer considered him our son.

It has been six years since I've seen my son. I am told that I
have two lovely grandchildren that I may never meet.

In the meantime, I find it ironic (painfully), that our Rabbi's
son intermarried three years ago. His wife converted and not
another word was uttered. My friends and relatives have all had
experiences with intermarriage, but only a few eyebrows were
raised. My only other child, a daughter, died three years ago at
age twenty-three from leukemia. I have dissociated myself from
everything. My days are filled with remorse and my nights with
tears. I am so desolate and distraught. I feel very alone.

My husband throws himself into his work and heaps accusa-
tions on me. I lash back at him and the cycle repeats itself. My
entire world revolved around my two beautiful children. I say to
my husband over and over again—what have we done? Will we
ever see our son and his family again? What is a mother to do?

Fortunately for most families, such rigid opposition to intermarriage, particularly when conversion has taken place, is becoming a rarity. In fact, there is a strong sentiment beginning to
prevail in the American-Jewish community (not only the Reform) that, perhaps, it is time to reconsider the traditional opposition to conversion.

In contrast to the traditionalists' fears, one frequently hears
rabbis and others who are active in organized Jewish life re-

marking that "converts are our best Jews." Indeed, there are ancient Talmudic passages attesting to the same assessment.

> The *ger* [proselyte] is dearer to God than Israel was when the nation assembled at the foot of Mount Sinai. For Israel would not have accepted the Torah without seeing the thunders and lightening and the quaking mountain and hearing the sound of the shofar, whereas the proselyte, without a single miracle, consecrates himself to the Holy One. . . . Can anyone be deemed more worthy of God's love?[12]

In yet another passage of the Talmud, Rav, the founder of the academy at Sura, is quoted as saying "whosoever seeks to be converted should be accepted. Do not impugn the motives of *gerim* [proselytes]. Perhaps they come for the sake of Heaven."[13]

There seems to be no shortage of modern day examples of converts who have "made good," so to speak. From presidents of synagogues to rabbis, to heads of chapters in major Jewish organizations, the roster of leadership in American Jewish religious life is dotted, with increasing frequency, by former Christians who converted to Judaism. Invariably, these converts chose to become Jews within the context of intermarriage. Three outstanding contemporary examples of such individuals are Rachel Cowan, Lydia Kukoff, and Kerry Ben David.

Rachel is the descendant of early New England Episcopalians, and is currently the director of education at the Ansche Chesed Synagogue in New York City and a rabbinical student. Rachel married the writer Paul Cowan in 1965. As Paul recalled in his own spiritual autobiography, *An Orphan in History,*

> Rachel and I were married under a butternut tree at her uncle's farm in Williamsburg, Massachusetts. Unlike most interfaith couples, we never focused on the issue of who would officiate. The chaplain of Smith College, a Black minister, a civil rights advocate, and a poker-playing buddy of Rachel's uncle, agreed to perform the ceremony. I think it was Rachel, not I, who insisted that Jesus' name be excised from the service. In the end, we devised our own secular litany. . . . After that, the Reverend Anderson pronounced us husband and wife. I put a glass on the

ground and broke it with my heel—that was the only Jewish
wedding custom I knew—and the minister said "shalom."[14]

Rachel's conversion to Judaism took place late in 1980, some
fifteen years and two adolescent children into her marriage. In
the interim, she had been a social worker, civil rights activist,
photographer, feminist, and mother. She also clearly tracked
Paul's own religious evolution from an assimilated, cosmopolitan Jewish journalist to a devout Jew. Like the biblical Naomi
who returned to the land of her people after the death of her
children and husband, Paul's return to the traditions of his ancestors appears to have been hastened, if not triggered, by the
tragic death of his parents in 1976. One cannot help but extend
the analogy to Rachel, as if she were following in the footsteps
of Ruth, except that her religious evolution was tied to that of
her husband, not to her mother-in-law.

In the aftermath of the Yom Kippur War in 1973, Rachel
became particularly concerned about the meaning of Jewishness, the nature of Jewish identity (especially for her children), and the relationship of Jews to Israel. "Rachel thought
about such questions," writes Paul, "even more seriously than
most of our Jewish friends. Paradoxically, in those days she
cared more about Lisa's and Matt's [their children] Jewish identity than I did." Rachel had earlier started the Purple Circle Day-
Care Center for neighborhood families on the Upper West Side
of Manhattan, many of whom were either Jewish or intermarried. Now stimulated by a desire to impart some of the Jewish
heritage to her own children, she enlisted the help of Jerry Raik,
one of the parents in the Purple Circle, who was an enthralling
storyteller with a strong Jewish education. Together, they began
organizing annual celebrations of Hanukkah and Passover in
the Cowan home. Before long, Rachel and some of the other
parents wanted something more continuous by way of Jewish
education for their children. Through a series of fortuitous links
in the neighborhood, the Havurah School was born. The school,

which included mostly the children of other intermarried families like Paul and Rachel's, also drew many of the adults into
serious discussions about their own identities. Paul recalls that

> By the autumn of 1975, Rachel and Lisa and Matt and I had begun
> to light Shabbos candles almost every Friday night. It was the first
> Jewish ritual we regularly observed as a family. In retrospect, I
> think we adopted it for our own distinct emotional reasons, and
> not for religious ones.[15]

At the end of 1978, Rachel decided to embark on the path
toward becoming Jewish. Paul had just completed an assign-
ment in California and called Rachel to describe his experiences.

> To my astonishment, she told me that she planned to convert.
> That day, she said, she'd talked to Steve Shaw, a Conservative
> rabbi we both knew, to find out how to do so. She said that she
> had been thinking about the idea for months, ever since she
> discovered that worshipping as a Jew released something inside
> her which enabled her to think about God; to feel, at rare mo-
> ments, a faith whose intensity startled her. But she had to take
> the first step toward conversion herself to be sure that it stemmed
> from her own private decision to become a Jew, not from a re-
> sidual wish to please me.[16]

By this time, the Cowans were active, well-known members
of the liberal Jewish community on the Upper West Side. Also
during this time, that area of Manhattan underwent a significant
demographic change: Young urban professionals were replacing
an older population. The demographic shift took a heavy toll on
the Ansche Chesed Synagogue, diminishing its once large
and prosperous membership to a handful of elderly people.
Through the urgings of a friend and mentor, Rabbi Wolfe Kel-
man, the Cowans mobilized their Jewish friends in the area,
who themselves were connected with a number of local *havurah*
groups (loosely structured fellowship groups for Jewish prayer
and study), to help revive Ansche Chesed.

The enterprise of reviving a once august but now decaying
Jewish institution obviously drew Paul and Rachel even closer to

one another, as well as to their local Jewish friends. It was in its sanctuary that Rachel ultimately became a Jew. In her own words, conversion marked both a beginning and a completion.

> When I fell in love with Paul seventeen years ago, I began to identify with the Jewish people. Over time, I have felt that identi-fication broaden from him to his parents, Polly and Lou, to my friends here tonight and to the larger Jewish community; and to the country Israel. It has become increasingly important for me not just to identify with Judaism, but to be a Jew. I have always been proud to be a Yankee from New England. Now I'm proud to be a Jew.[17]

Paul's reaction, as he reports on it in his book, is equally signifi-cant in understanding the consequences, at least, of Rachel's conversion.

> For years I had thought I was completely indifferent to Rachel's religious decisions. She was the wife I loved, no matter what she chose to call herself. But now I knew that I felt stronger because Rachel was one of us.[18]

Inevitably, for Rachel and Paul the spiritual journey to Judaism, to Ansche Chesed, and to the whole West Side *havurah* community was intertwined with a journey toward their own greater emotional closeness. By re-discovering his own Jewish roots, Paul was able to share his heritage with Rachel, but only through Rachel's conversion to Judaism was Paul able to come to share that heritage without reservation or inhibition.

Rachel's choosing to become Jewish after fifteen years of marriage also hints at the abiding tension between love and tradition. It is not a tension that couples encounter at the begin-ning of their relationship and then proceed to settle once and for all. In the lives of many, it remains a source of puzzlement and stress, perhaps even emotional distance, at times insignificant, at times distressing. For Rachel, the decision to convert was clearly related to a set of historical and biographical circum-stances: the Yom Kippur War in 1973, Paul's increasing personal and journalistic involvement with his own Jewish heritage, and the approach of her daughter Lisa's twelfth birthday, at which time it was most likely that Lisa would have a Bat Mitzvah (the rite of passage into young adulthood for Jewish girls, the equivalent of the boys' Bar Mitzvah). When Rachel and Paul first met, fell in love, and married, their differences in tradition were of little concern or consequence. Their mutual interest and activities in the civil rights movement were of much greater concern. "In those years," Paul writes, "the civil rights movement provided each of us with an entirely satisfying secular creed." It also provided an ideological framework in which the two could see themselves as being part of a shared value system. Biographical and historical evolution would erode the adequacy of that shared value system, it seems, in the course of their life together. It took Rachel's conversion and Paul's discovery of his roots to restore it, this time on a religious rather than a secular basis.

Lydia Kukoff is currently a director of the Commission on Reform Jewish Outreach in Los Angeles. This division of the Union of American Hebrew Congregations has as its mission to bring the message of Judaism to Christians, particularly those who are married to Jews, who may wish to examine and embrace it. Lydia is also a convert to Judaism; a Jew with an extraordinary dedication to her self-chosen people.

Lydia grew up in a large, warm, and unusual Italian family. Although both her parents were second-generation children of Italian immigrants, her family were pious Baptists—at least on her father's side. Her mother has been a lifelong Catholic, as were nearly all her neighbors. "When I was a child, my family was active in the Baptist church, and I was a churchgoing, baptized Baptist." Her paternal grandfather's family had converted to Baptism soon after their immigration to America. "During my adolescent years," Lydia writes in her own book, *Choosing Judaism*,

> I underwent a crisis of faith. . . . At that time I began reading about Judaism. My best friend in high school was an observant

Jew, and I was attracted to what I perceived as a whole way of life. One day, I impulsively told my mother that some day I was going to convert to Judaism. She looked at me and said, "Uh huh," used to my outrageous statements at that stage of my life. . . . In college I took many courses in comparative religion and the Bible. I had always loved the Bible, having studied it extensively as a Baptist.[19]

Lydia's drift toward Judaism began long before she met Ben Kukoff. When they did meet, in 1964, both their mutual attraction and her decision to convert to Judaism were almost instantaneous. Lydia moved to New York City from her native Philadelphia soon after graduating from college and was teaching English as a second language at New York University when she met Ben. Ben was the second-generation son of Orthodox Jewish immigrant parents, a native of Brooklyn, and a rising young actor at the time of their meeting. "Almost the minute we met we knew we were going to be married. It seemed almost unreal," Lydia recalled. In fact, they were married within the year of their meeting. For Lydia, to become Jewish came as naturally as marrying Ben.

Most of my friends were Jews. Most of the men I dated were Jews. It became apparent to me that I could never marry anybody who was not Jewish. . . . Becoming a Jew seemed very logical. . . . Then, as I was considering conversion, I met my husband-to-be. I finally decided to end my "fence sitting." This was serious. Even though I had already begun to consider myself "unofficially Jewish," the time had arrived for my formal conversion. We talked about it, to be sure, but there was no debate.[20]

When she went home to tell her parents that she was going to marry Ben and convert to Judaism, "My family was less than thrilled," Lydia recalls. "Why doesn't he convert?" they asked. "Why should he convert to something I don't believe in?" Lydia replied. That exchange seems to have been the sum and substance of any family dispute about the issue. The Marella family was apparently warmly taken with Ben, as was the Kukoff family with Lydia. Her decision to convert prior to marriage was a particular relief to Ben, given his own Orthodox background and his parents' traditionalism.

Lydia and Ben were married within weeks of her conversion to Judaism in 1965. "When I woke up the morning after my conversion," Lydia writes,

> I felt wonderful. I felt sparkling new, excited, charged up. I wanted to start being Jewish. I said to my finance, "What are we going to do now" and he said, "What do you mean? What we're doing is just fine."[21]

In fact, Ben was quite satisfied to know that his wife was Jewish and that they would lead the kind of Jewish life that is typical of young New York Jewish professionals: occasional synagogue attendance and the practice of some of the family rituals around the holidays, but otherwise no significant involvement with Jewish organizational life or the world of Jewish thought, learning, and practice. "In New York, it was really easy to be Jewish, almost by osmosis," Lydia recalled, "without having to do anything about it."

Around 1970, the Kukoffs moved to Los Angeles with one young son, David. Soon thereafter their daughter Naomi was born. It became clear to Lydia as well as to Ben that it takes more to be Jewish in Los Angeles than it does in New York. Also, the need to raise the children in some kind of Jewish context made them both aware of the need for greater involvement with some of the local Jewish institutions or at least with other Jewish families with similar needs. Lydia also became aware of her own personal need to deepen her familiarity with Jewish life and culture so as to be able to better educate her children. She began to take some courses at UCLA in Judaic Studies, much as she had taken comparative religion courses when she was in college, only this time she was taking courses on Jewish subjects as an insider. The family also joined a local *havurah* in which they began to observe holidays together with other young families like theirs.

By that time, Lydia had become aware that although she

was a Jew, she had not been as well prepared to practice being Jewish as a "native-born" might.

> I didn't feel authentic performing rituals and I didn't know where to go for support. In a flash of insight, I understood what should have been clear all along. Conversion was not the "end" of anything! Instead, it marked a beginning![22]

She was also aware that while she was forging a path for herself, there were thousands of others who would be equally adrift in their newly chosen community, with a multitude of unsettled— not to say unsettling—issues of religious practice, conviction, and personal identity. "At that point, I think, I really wanted to become a rabbi who would know both the inside world of Judaism and the inside world of the convert," Lydia recalled, but the practical demands of raising a young family precluded that career choice. Instead, Lydia embarked on a three-year Masters' program in Judaic Studies at the local Hebrew Union College, from which she received her degree in 1978.

She knew, of course, how unique she was as a graduate student in Judaica. But she was also aware of the widespread need for a sympathetic introduction to Judaism for Christians and converts who were married to Jews. She also knew that because of the age-old diffidence about conversion in the Jewish community, no such program of introduction was available. Many rabbis performed conversions, particularly in the Reform movement in which she was educated, but the focus of those programs was on formal education, not socialization into a culture and community. Nor was there any follow-up with converts after they became Jews. Her memory of her own "post-conversion depression"–"I was Jewish but I didn't know how to practice Judaism"[22]—focused her own career plan. She wanted to apply her growing professional expertise as a Jew to guiding others who found themselves in similar circumstances.

In her case, as in Rachel's, history had a way of combining with biography in an unexpected way. In the same year that Lydia received her Masters' degree from Hebrew Union Col-

lege, Rabbi Alexander Schindler, President of the Reform movement's synagogue body, the Union of American Hebrew Congregations, gave a historical address at its annual meeting. In
that address, he called upon his movement to welcome converts. In situations of intermarriage, he proposed, "the conversion of the non-Jewish partner-to-be is clearly the first desideratum and we make a reasonable effort to attain it." "But,"
he went on to say,

> We do not help them make a Jewish home, to rear their children
> Jewishly, to grapple with their peculiar problems. More serious
> still, we do not really embrace them, enable them to feel a close
> kinship with our people.[23]

After exploring the various problems that converts had with
the Jewish community and that the Jewish community had with
intermarriage and conversion, Rabbi Schindler proposed that
his movement "launch a carefully conceived Outreach Program" primarily aimed at Christians who are married to or are
planning marriage to Jews. Moreover, he felt that his program
should also be made available to "all Americans who are unchurched and who are seeking roots in religion."

The plan was enthusiastically endorsed by the Board of
Trustees of the Union, but its implementation would require an
unusual combination of skills and experiences that was not
readily available among America's Jews, much less the American rabbinate. Rabbis have difficulty enough reaching Jews. The
prospect of reaching Christians was almost unthinkable. Following Schindler's address, a number of faculty members at the
Hebrew Union College recognized that their newly minted Masters' student, Lydia Kukoff, would be ideally suited to spear-
head the program proposed. And so it came to be. Having
chosen Judaism, Lydia was now chosen by one of its major
branches to pioneer a program of outreach to Christians. Her
own mission of clarifying, for herself and other converts, the
meaning of Judaism in life just happened to coincide with the
needs of the Reform movement, indeed, with the needs of large

segments of American Jewry in general. The convergence of her own exceptional personal qualities with the historical necessities of American Jewish life has enabled Lydia to advance the cause of modern Judaism in ways that would have been surely unthinkable as recently as three or four decades ago. They were certainly not thinkable by her as she was first making her decision to become Jewish.

Kerry McDevitt, the descendant of an illustrious Catholic family from Philadelphia, was on his way to an operatic career as a baritone when he met Batya Godfrey, an alto who was raised as an observant Conservative Jew. Despite their differences in religion, Batya's parents were accepting of Kerry, and the young couple's marriage was performed by a rabbi even though Kerry had not converted at the time. There was no question that Kerry and Batya's children would be raised as Jews, but once the children started to attend a Jewish day school, Kerry began to realize that "things were developing in the family that I was not part of. I felt," he says, "as though a ship were slowly leaving the dock and I wasn't on board."[24]

A need to feel fully part of the culture and tempo of his own family led Kerry to the Jewish Center of White Plains, a Reform temple, where he began to take courses in Judaism with Rabbi Maurice Davis. After two years of study and self-examination, Kerry converted to Judaism. Unfortunately, as an only child with his mother and grandmother as his sole living relatives, his conversion did result in some distancing from them. His mother, a devout Catholic, did not accept his conversion to Judaism, and he simply did not have the heart to inform his grandmother of it.

In 1981, Kerry's change of religion triggered a change in his career as well. He enrolled in the school of sacred music of the Hebrew Union College and began to prepare for a new career as a cantor. In the fall of 1984, he took his first post at the Scarsdale Synagogue. A year earlier, he had changed his surname from McDevitt to Ben David.

When I worked as a cantor at Westchester Reform Temple in Scarsdale, I felt the name was distracting people, was making me a novelty, a curiosity on the *bimah* [podium], and creating a certain distraction from prayer. Also, I wanted to identify as totally as possible with being a Jew. As a convert, I was McDevitt, but as you get deeper into the process, and the veneer, the paint, stroke after stroke, layer after layer, keeps covering up and changing the product, you're suddenly at the point where you're not a McDevitt anymore. . . . That's why this name change has been so pleasant. I've enjoyed it so much because I can forget! Every time I pick up the telephone I am not reminded. Every time I write my name, or see a piece of stationery, or write a check, I am not constantly reminded of this jarring aspect of a name that was very non-Jewish and an identity that's trying to be Jewish.[25]

The Bishop McDevitt High School in Philadelphia was named after one of Kerry's great-uncles. Naturally, helping his children avoid any confusion about their Jewish identity was an added motivation to change McDevitt to Ben David. Etymologically, the Irish "Mc" means "son of." "Ben" is its Hebrew equivalent, as is "David" the equivalent of "Devitt."

Years of marriage had to unfold for Kerry, as they had had to for Rachel, before he would choose Judaism as his faith and the Jews as his people. For both, too, the solidifying of bonds with their spouses and children seems to have been a significant cause as well as an inextricable consequence of their conversion.

Rachel, Lydia, and Kerry are exemplars to the American-Jewish community as Jews and as converts. As Jews, they exemplify the vitality and meaning that the Jewish tradition in a variety of its forms can bring to individuals and their families. As converts, they illustrate the profound effects that conversion to Judaism can have on people even when it occurs after many years of marriage, as in the case of Rachel and Kerry. They also illustrate, by example, some of the diversity and some of the uniformity of the conversion experience.

Rachel's and Lydia's conversions were apparently rather easily accepted by their parents. Kerry's was not. All three made a significant career for themselves within the organized Jewish community: Rachel and Lydia building specifically on their experiences as converts, Kerry refocusing his artistic talent as a singer to become a cantor. For each one, too, conversion played a significant role in helping to harmonize their relationship with their spouses and children, although for Lydia, it was a foregone conclusion that she would become Jewish even before she met Ben.

Such obviously favorable examples of converts inevitably raise questions about the majority of converts. Who are they? How are they affected by conversion? Why did they choose Judaism when, in fact, most Christians who are married to Jews do not?

The question of why some Christians convert to Judaism when most do not, and why so many Christians convert to Judaism when so few Jews convert to the religion of their Christian mates, draws our attention to the social characteristics of the individuals involved. By learning a little more about who they are sociologically, we may be better able to determine the reason for their choices in resolving the cultural difference between themselves and their Christian spouses. Again, we turn our attention to the available survey data.

Perhaps the most striking fact about conversions to Judaism is that, to a very large extent, they are entered into by women. The National Jewish Population Study found that in intermarriages where the husband was born Jewish and the wife was not, the rate of conversion to Judaism was 27 percent. In the marriages in which the wife was born Jewish, the rate of conversion was only about 3 percent. Although other studies have not found such a glaring discrepancy in the rate of conversion to Judaism between men and women, they, too, have found that it is disproportionately Christian women who convert to Judaism. For example, studies by Rabbi Sanford Seltzer (1984) and by one of his former graduate students, Steven Huberman (1979), found that the overwhelming majority of students enrolled in the Reform movement's "Introduction to Judaism" courses were women—according to Huberman, 66 percent, to Seltzer, 75 percent.[26]

My own study of intermarrieds found that there also appear to be differences in the incidence of conversion to Judaism among Christians from different religious backgrounds, as shown below. As these figures indicate, those coming from a Catholic background are the least likely to convert to Judaism, followed by those who come from a family in which there was no identification with any religion. Christian women who came from families in which there had been a family history of inter-marriage (e.g., between Protestants and Catholics), as in Lydia Kukoff's case, were the most likely to choose Jewish identifica-tion. Perhaps the hunger for a consistency of religious tradition in the family stems not only from one's own intermarriage, but from that of one's parents or grandparents as well.

Statistically, converts were also somewhat more likely to come from families that did not belong to a church, or were not active participants in a church, and intermarriages were more apt to result in the conversion of the Christian spouse if the Jewish spouse came from a more traditional family. The table below shows that conversions were most frequent in inter-marriages in which the born-Jewish partner came from an Orthodox background.

Percentage of Conversions by Religious Background of the Christian Partner

Did Christian spouse convert?	Background			
	Catholic	Protestant	Other	None
Yes	14	26	37	15
No	86	74	63	85
Total	100	100	100	100

Percentage of Conversions among Intermarrieds By Religious Family
Background of Born Jews

Did Christian spouse convert?	Religious background of born Jews			
	Orthodox	Conservative	Reform	None
Yes	31	19	28	15
No	69	81	72	85
Total	100	100	100	100

Assuming that the greater the attachment of a Jewish
spouse to his heritage, the more likely he is to influence his
fiancée or spouse to convert, one might have expected that
those from Conservative Jewish backgrounds would have outpaced the Reform in their rate of conversions, but such is not the
case. Jewish intermarriers from Reform families follow close
upon the heels of their brethren from Orthodox backgrounds in
inspiring their mates to become Jews. Apparently, certain forms
of traditionalism and religious liberalism, which are associated
with the Orthodox and the Reform, respectively, may have similar effects on the identity resolutions of intermarriers, at least as
far as the conversion of Christian spouses is concerned. The
reason for the relatively much lower rate of conversions in intermarriages in which the Jewish partner was from a Conservative
Jewish background remains a mystery.

One additional insight about conversions to Judaism has to
do with its timing. My survey of intermarrieds suggests that it
occurs at distinct, and possibly predictable points along the family's life cycle, as shown below.

The largest proportion of conversions occur right before
marriage. Often the marriage follows within a matter of days or
weeks after the conversion, and the conversion is timed to enable the couple to have a traditional Jewish wedding. In a small
number of cases, the conversion occurs before the convert even

meets the spouse. Invariably, these cases involve the remarriage of a convert who was previously married to a Jew. Most striking is the fact that 44 percent of the conversions we found occurred *after* the marriage, with more than 20 percent occurring *after* the birth of the first child. These conversions are obviously not entered into "for the sake of marriage," in the conventional sense of that phrase. As we have seen in the examples of Rachel Cowan and Kerry Ben David, they have much to do with the quality of family life, but they are not conversions for the sake of marriage. Interviews with those who become Jewish after the birth of their first child disclosed that most often such conversions took place before the Bar or Bat Mitzvah of the first child, the impending marriage of the first child, or in the planning of one's interment with one's Jewish spouse.

Although an openness to the spiritual message of Judaism is clearly present among most of the converts I interviewed, the salient motives for choosing to become Jewish by way of the formal conversion ceremony were the desire to share a common faith and religious life-style with one's spouse and to provide the convert's children with a coherent religious tradition. Apparently for many, these needs or desires are not aroused before marriage, but come up later in life.

It would seem that whenever conversions occur, they are

Percentage of Conversions Occurring at
Various Points along the Family Life Cycle

Stage in family life cycle	Percentage of conversions
Before meeting spouse	15
Before marriage	40
Before first child	23
Other	22
Total	100

not likely to stem from an epiphany or some deep spiritual experience. Rather, they grow out of a desire to remake one's self, one's social identity, so that it is more congruent with that of one's spouse and children. The fact that those Christians who choose to become Jewish are disproportionately women, disproportionately from backgrounds in which there is no distinct or exclusive religious tradition, and disproportionately people who themselves were unidentified with a religion before marriage, all suggest that the need for conversion may be felt more keenly by those whose identity is less well grounded in a religious or ethnic tradition than that of their husband or wife. As we saw in earlier chapters, this formula appears to favor the Jewish mate in most intermarriages.

The timing of conversion also points to its complex linkage to momentous occasions in life. As we have seen, nearly all conversions to Judaism took place just before certain points of transition in the life course of the family (e.g., marriage, birth, rites of passage). In most families, those transitions evoke all over again feelings about one's own heritage and about the heritage of one's spouse. Those transitions, because of their linkage to larger family and community networks, lead the non-Jewish partner to reexamine the competing claims of love, sense of self, and heritage. When a family's life-style is even tangentially connected to the Jewish tradition, it is likely that transitions will evoke and emphasize that connection.

A baby-naming ceremony, a circumcision, Hebrew school, a Bar or Bat Mitzvah, will all affirm some sort of tie to the Jewish heritage. Later in life, planning for burial will confront couples, once again, with the issue of identification and tradition. According to traditional Jewish law, non-Jews may not be buried in a Jewish cemetery, nor does Jewish law and custom permit Jews to be buried in a non-Jewish cemetery. Therefore, even late in life, the conversations concerning funeral planning can lead to considerable tension in a mixed marriage.

Various life transition points all have the potential for making the Christian partner in a mixed marriage feel that she is somehow separate from or alien to her Jewish spouse and children. Very likely, it is just that feeling that exerts pressure to become Jewish, and accounts for the high proportion of conversions occurring after marriage.

This pressure or psychological need is, of course, not equally felt by all. As we have seen, most intermarriages do not involve conversion to Judaism or to any other faith. Perhaps others feel such needs less keenly or find other ways than conversion to meet them. However this question might be resolved by future research, the available evidence and experience suggests that a substantial number of intermarrieds do feel the need to integrate their love for one another with a unified heritage. That need impels the great majority of conversions.

Why the forces that impel conversions to Judaism among intermarrieds do not seem to stimulate a larger number of conversions to Christianity on the part of Jewish spouses, is a mystery. Perhaps a great many more actually take place than our methods of research have been able to detect. Certainly there are as many Christian families in which the joint participation in church life and religious activity is as deeply bound up with family life as there are Jewish families. Also, when Catholics seek dispensation to marry non-Catholics, they are expected to declare to the Church that they will do all in their power to share their faith with their children by having them baptized and raised as Catholics. Such a vow, if it is taken, is bound to place a considerable amount of pressure on Jewish marriage partners either to avoid having children or to consider conversion to Catholicism.

In Chapter Seven, we did see, in the examples of Paul and Maxine (he became an Episcopalian) and Mildred and Tony (she attended Catholic Church with his family), that some Jewish intermarriers will become Christians. In both cases, there had been a total break with the Jewish family long before the conversion itself. Paul's parents had died before he ever met Maxine.

Mildred's parents had practically disowned her when she married Tony. Also in both cases, there was strong pressure by the Christian family to induce the Jewish mate to join their community.

Rabbi Roy Rosenberg of the Temple of Universal Judaism in New York City, whose congregation is made up almost exclusively of unconverted intermarried couples, points out that because Christianity emphasizes the personal faith of the individual as the basis of salvation, there is much less of an emphasis on the communal and familial aspects of the Christian life. Hence, he reasons, there is much less familial pressure for the Jew to convert. Also, none of the major Christian denominations makes the conversion of the non-Christian spouse a precondition for marriage or for the celebration of any other life cycle event within their churches. Consequently, the incidence of Jews converting to Christianity remains very low and is not likely to be stimulated by the same identity needs as are conversions to Judaism. Theology and social psychology converge, it seems, in fostering conversions to Judaism among intermarrieds. It is probably this same kind of convergence that accounts for the persistence of Jewishness we observed in Chapter Six.

But does conversion really eliminate the differences of heritage and tradition between husband and wife in an intermarriage? And is conversion necessary to eliminate those differences?

In many respects, it is easier to answer the second question than the first. Conversion is necessary for those who plan to live their lives within a Jewish community, who want to participate in the Jewish community at those points in their lives when they seek its institutions. There is considerable debate within the organized Jewish community over the status of Christians and other non-Jews who are married to Jews. Should they be permitted to join and participate in synagogue life? Particularly in intermarriages in which the wife is not Jewish, traditional Jewish law does not regard the children as Jews. As recently as March

1983, the Central Conference of American Rabbis, the Reform
rabbinate, felt it necessary to adopt a resolution to the effect that

> the child of one Jewish parent is under the presumption of Jewish
> descent. This presumption of the Jewish status of the offspring of
> any mixed marriage is to be established through appropriate and
> timely public and formal acts of identification with the Jewish
> faith and people.

However, this resolution has met with uniform and vigorous
opposition from Conservative and Orthodox Jews. At this point,
these vexing communal issues probably make it impossible for
mixed married couples to resolve the differences in their heritage as long as they maintain any substantial contact with the
Jewish community.

Therefore, the conversion of the Christian spouse becomes
a social as well as an emotional necessity if the intermarried
couple is to become an integrated part of the Jewish community.
Of course, more liberal congregations, be they Reform or Conservative, will make great efforts to accommodate the needs of
mixed couples, permitting membership and participation in
congregational life, accepting the children of Christian mothers
into Hebrew schools, and permitting such children to go
through a Bar or a Bat Mitzvah. But a great many will not,
particularly among the Conservative and the Orthodox Jews.
Also, given the long history of fear that Jews have had of Christians, conversion becomes the ultimate statement of love and
acceptance for both the individual Jew and for his people. Perhaps because most intermarrying Jews do not have such long
historical memories or have lost their culturally bred insecurity,
they do not convey the expectation of such a profound spiritual
statement of love and acceptance to their Christian husbands or
wives, but it is quite clear that, in most instances, when the
Christian partner does convert to Judaism, her Jewish husband,
or his Jewish wife, reads that act as an expression of deep family
loyalty as much as a profession of faith. Very likely, when a

Jewish partner converts to the Christianity of his spouse, the Christian partner will feel the same way. But perhaps far fewer Christian intermarriers need that kind of assurance and acceptance from Jews. After all, they are members of the majority, unless they are Catholic.

On the other hand, our survey indicates that even without conversion, a minority of couples maintain a distinctly Jewish family life-style. About 18 percent of such couples belong to synagogues, although invariably it is only the Jewish spouse who enjoys full membership privileges. More than one-third of such couples gave their children a specifically Jewish name like David or Miriam or Benjamin or Sarah. About 25 percent regularly celebrate the Passover in their own homes, and nearly 30 percent attend High Holy Day services together. About 30 percent contribute to Jewish philanthropic causes, and about 20 percent provide their children with a formal Jewish education.

As might be expected, of course, the level of Jewish observance and participation is far greater among the conversionary families. In my survey, nearly 70 percent of converted families are affiliated with a synagogue, most usually Reform. Over 70 percent attend synagogue services regularly on the High Holy Days and about the same percentage celebrate Passover regularly.

In order to determine whether there were any systematic differences in the level of Jewish observance in mixed and conversionary marriages, a variety of observances were combined to create a scale of Jewish observance. The scale included seven items: regular participation in services, individual prayer at home, having only kosher meat in the home, lighting candles on Friday evening to usher in the Sabbath, making *kiddush* [a traditional blessing over wine] on the Sabbath and holidays, fasting on Yom Kippur, and lighting candles on the eight days of Hanukkah. Some might say that this is an almost arbitrary selection of observances, because an active Jewish life-style would include a multitude of other observances as well, but although one can

quibble with the selection of these seven observances as indicators of Jewish behavior, they were, in fact, sufficient to provide
an overall portrait of Jewish observance among conversionary
and mixed marriages.

The regular performance of each of the seven observances
gained respondents one point for each observance. Thus, the
maximum observance score was "7," and the minimum observance score "0." The average score of the entire sample of intermarried couples was 2.9, meaning that the typical intermarried
family observed about three out of the seven observances.
When we compared the mixed marriages with the conversionary marriages, however, we found substantial differences between them. The average observance score for mixed marriages
was 1.7, but for conversionary marriages, it ranged from 4.5 for
those converts who became Jewish under Reform auspices, to 7
for those who became Jewish under Conservative or Orthodox
auspices.

In other words, these findings suggest that there is a clear
association between conversion and higher levels of Jewish observance. Converts were also much more likely to have had
their sons circumcised according to Jewish tradition—72 versus
43 percent for mixed couples. They were also far more likely to
have had their children go through a Bar or Bat Mitzvah than
mixed couples—71 versus 30 percent. They were more than
twice as likely than the latter to have given their children a
Hebrew name—82 versus 36 percent. And about 60 percent of
the conversionary families were providing their children with
some type of formal Jewish education, or were planning to do
so, in contrast to 20 percent of the mixed couples.

Of course, comparing the relative levels of Jewish observance among conversionary and mixed marriages does not tell
us anything about how converts and their families would compare to typical American Jews. Such comparisons have not been
made as yet. However, based on a variety of general surveys of
American Jewish religious behavior, it appears that converts

and their families are every bit as observant as typical American Jews. Based on their religious behavior, converts are virtually indistinguisable from Jews born into the fold.

But religious observance constitutes only a part, perhaps only a small part, of what typical American Jews understand by Jewishness. Numerous studies of contemporary Jewish life have shown that the world view of most of America's Jews is far more secular than religious, far more a skein of attitudes than a set of observances. The bonds that tie Jews together into a community, quite apart from shared religious observances, are the fear of anti-Semitism, a profound concern for the security of the State of Israel, a desire to live among and to associate with fellow Jews, and a sense of responsibility for Jews the world over. These values or beliefs might be thought of as the social ethic or the civil religion of American Jews. They are the cultural fabric of a people as opposed to their faith.

It is far more difficult to determine the extent to which converts share in the social ethos of Jewry than the extent of their Jewish observance. A number of our interviews suggested, however, that it was far easier to learn to behave as Jews than to feel and think like them. In his study of converts to Judaism in Boston, Steven Huberman asked respondents why their friendship pattern was not more exclusively Jewish. Typical American Jews tend to have mostly Jewish friends, according to most Jewish population surveys.

> Many converts indicated that they did not necessarily feel more comfortable with born Jews than with non-Jews . . . particularly young ones indicated that they felt somewhat inhibited and self-conscious with born Jews . . . they did not feel completely detached from their own ethnic backgrounds . . . they do not abandon their non-Jewish friends easily.[27]

Huberman concludes that

> converts as a group define their Judaism in religious rather than communal or ethnic terms. To converts, Judaism is basically a religion like their former faith.[28]

For the masses of born Jews, it seems to be quite a different matter.

It should be emphasized that the discrepancy between the Jewishness of converts and of born Jews cannot and must not be attributed to a lack of sincerity on the part of either. Rather, I believe, the nature of the conversion process itself and the social expectations of the Jewish community place a greater emphasis on how converts act than on how they think and feel. Ironically, it is precisely the desire to *feel* more unified with one's spouse and children that has led a great many converts to become Jewish in the first place. The task of forging that sense of unity will probably remain a lifelong challenge for them, as indeed it must for mixed couples, and perhaps for most modern families.

The accretion of collective memories and sensibilities that comprise the traditions of families and communities is probably as difficult to acquire by choice as it is to schuck off. Love and social psychological need may drive one person to adopt the faith of the other. Religious institutions may sanction the choice and validate it, but it remains the work of lifelong learning and communication for two people from different traditions to form a homogeneous family heritage of their own. And, at times, even the most sincere effort at harmonizing family traditions simply will not work, as the following painful letter makes clear.

> I converted to Judaism for marriage and to appease my husband's grandparents. The entire conversion experience was cold and meaningless. My in-laws and husband dropped any kind of Jewish practice immediately after the conversion. There was not much practice to begin with, and they had pretended mostly for the sake of the grandparents. When they retired to Florida all religious practice stopped. At first, I did not care. However, his grandparents had been adoring, wonderful people. They treated me with love and respect, and cared about my two little girls. Because of them, I became more drawn to Judaism for myself, and later for the sake of my little girls.
>
> This might have been a happy story. But I was ridiculed and shunned by my husband's family for my Jewish practices. I became "too Jewish" for them. We were ignored completely.

I had strained relations with my family from the beginning, because of the marriage and the conversion. His grandparents were now too far away, but we managed frequent visits to Florida. When I learned that my husband was stealing funds from his company, I filed for divorce. You cannot believe how alone and desperate I was feeling. My family would only take me back if I renounced my Judaism. My Jewish family would not let me practice it.

When everyone had turned their backs on me and things had hit rock bottom, I found a friend and a savior. Through a newspaper column in the *Jewish Exponent* (a Philadelphia Jewish paper), I contacted a group called "Jewish Converts Network." This pro-converts group had a wonderful leader. She met with me at different times to accommodate my schedule. She wrote to me or called me every week when we couldn't make arrangements to meet. Her relentless patience and tolerance strengthened my resolve to continue to be a Jew, no matter what. At times I had cursed all Jews for my feelings of rejection. But she never rejected me. She knew what I was feeling, because she herself was a convert.

I am fine now. I have a job. My children attend a Jewish day school, and I am finally dating a nice Jewish man. But I worry about others like myself. There must be many others who are shunned and lost.

Chapter Nine

CHILDREN OF INTERMARRIAGE

Children of
Intermarriage

How well men and women succeed at the task of reconciling the twin pressures of their love for one another and the claims of their respective traditions will determine, in large measure, how satisfying their marriage will be. But perhaps an even greater challenge than that of achieving a satisfactory relationship with one another, is the challenge intermarried couples face in raising their children. Indeed, as we have seen in earlier chapters, the ideals of child rearing that each person brings to a marriage are often one of the key issues of marital negotiation in an intermarriage.

Although voluntary childlessness is certainly an option in modern family life, having and raising children remains one of the goals of the vast majority of families. Included in child rearing is the intimate and complex process of socialization—the minute and relentless flow of interaction between parents and children through which the older generation shapes the world of its young in conformity with its own values, hopes, and strengths, as well as its weaknesses. Parents need not be ideologically committed to making their children conformists. In fact, most modern parents are committed to allowing their children to discover and cultivate their own unique potentials. But the nature of parent–child communication inevitably leads children to acquire from parents their initial views of the world, of other people, and of the cosmos and their values in general. It is also from their parents that children derive their initial definitions of themselves, their identity and location within the larger society. To the extent that children think at all contemplatively about themselves, their first inner "gut reaction" to the question "Who am I?" is likely to be "My mother's and father's little girl" or "little boy."

The questions, as well as the answers, become more sophisticated with maturity, but the foundation of the more abstract answers will remain embedded in one's ties to his parents and, by extension, to his ancestors. Even an attempt to reject those ties will leave one's consciousness enmeshed within them.

Intermarried couples, as all husbands and wives, are well aware that their own upbringing, their heritage, and memories with respect to even such universal questions as "Daddy, how did the world begin?" or "Mommy, what does it mean to pray?" will filter into how they raise their own children. Whether for the sake of the child or for their own peace of mind, parents generally try to provide answers to those global questions in a way that is consistent with their own innermost thoughts, as well as with the sensibilities of their spouse. As might be expected, intermarried couples usually have to try harder to reconcile their dual heritage. Particularly in mixed marriages, neither parent wants to inject "too much" Jewishness or Christianity into the children's upbringing, lest they become confused by their own family circumstances or actually biased against one of their parents. Often the net effect of such caution is to deny children substantial access to either tradition beyond the occasional celebration of important religious holidays.

However, the best efforts of intermarried parents to shield themselves and their children from the disturbing question of the family's dual heritage will frequently be frustrated by outsiders or by the children's friends.

More than thirty years ago, the English–Jewish writer Emanuel Litvinoff expressed the hopes and frustrations of many an intermarried parent. He was writing of his own two "Children of Two Inheritances" in *Commentary* magazine (1953).

> When I first met Irene I was a young army lieutenant and she was an even younger army dispatch rider. . . . As the daughter of a

regular soldier, and having spent most of her childhood in military stations abroad, Irene at nineteen was largely unaware of a "Jewish problem. . . ." She was, indeed, a person with a large innocence of social distinctions at that time. . . . Nominally Presbyterian, Irene [also English] had been alienated from church going because of the fear and repression which had been an important element in the teaching and practice of her religion. . . . One thing that particularly horrified her, she told me, was her parents' view that if an unbaptized child should die, it would be refused admission into heaven.[1]

Irene wanted to protect her own children from doctrines like that. Litvinoff recalls that he had no special doctrines from which he would either want to safeguard his children from or which he thought he would want to pass on to them, at least none that had any specific religious component. His own family's Jewish convictions were more ceremonial than doctrinal, and they were nominal at that. As Irene spent more time with the Litvinoff family, she began to understand something of the complexity of the Jewish relationship to the larger society.

She was at first not a little bewildered and defensive, for although she had been received cordially and my mother made great efforts to put her at ease, my mother had also, both consciously and unwittingly, emphasized that the Jews were an exclusive and superior people, that they were cleaner, more moral, kinder to children, and their cooking was the best in the world. Irene was at this time pregnant and began seriously to think of "the problem" as it affected her children. One day she told me that she thought she ought to adopt the Jewish religion "so the children will be accepted and will know where they belong." I discouraged the idea.

I felt that most Jewish parents overemphasized the differences between their children and those of non-Jews. There was a kind of "anti-*goy*ism" in the Jewish environment, a tendency to stress Jewish intellectual and moral superiority that I wanted to keep from my children. I believed that organized religion in the 20th-century society was a retrogressive agent. . . . I wanted my children to grow up in the tradition of humanism . . . their education should emphasize the common elements among peo-

248

CHAPTER NINE

ples rather than the differences. Yet I also held that this was not incompatible with bringing them up in full consciousness of their Jewish inheritance. The Jewish sense of history, the Jewish quality of endurance, the Jewish fellowship and unity are too valuable to discard. . . . I wanted the Jewish and English elements in my children's heritage to be harmoniously combined, so that within them there would be no conflict between Moses and Shakespeare, Maimonides and John Locke, and I wanted Israel to be as much a part of their familiar landscape as the Ridings of Yorkshire. Irene was in agreement with all this.[2]

Sounds familiar? Although the context is English and the period is the early 1950s, the feelings and aspirations are easily recognizable on the contemporary American scene. The sentiments expressed by Emanuel Litvinoff were spoken almost verbatim by one of our survey respondents, Larry Newman, a journalist in Los Angeles. At age 35, he is married to Susan, a graduate student who is a lapsed Catholic. They have no children and are unsure about whether they will have any, but Larry is clear about one thing. He is not interested in having his children go through the same kind of Hebrew school education that he suffered through for three years. "The Bar Mitzvah was not worth the effort." At the same time, Larry finds Jewish history and Jewish folk culture fascinating. "He is always explaining one thing or another about Judaism to me," Susan interjected in the course of our interview. Like Litvinoff, Larry Newman expected that his hypothetical children would be well-balanced, eclectic Americans with an intellectual and aesthetic appreciation of their Jewish heritage, but "without Jewish hang-ups" about anti-Semitism or exclusiveness or any special sense of choseness.

As always, it is a lot easier to raise hypothetical children than flesh-and-blood real ones. Litvinoff came to this sobering realization as soon as his children began to attend school.

Vida, our eldest child, attended a nursery school from the age of three or four, and then a kindergarten of a progressive school. . . . But one day—in the course of a torrent of recitations about pussy cats, Miss Muffets, sing a song of sixpence—Vida began to sing:

> Away in the manger,
> No crib for his bed,
> The Little Lord Jesus
> Laid down his sweet head, etc.

This development was quite unanticipated. What did one do about Jesus in the nursery, the gentle Jesus meek and mild? Looking back on my own childhood, I could not recall any time when the name "Jesus Christ" did not arouse fear, clearly an emotion communicated by my parents and badly tangled up with pogrom reminiscences. . . . Quite recently Vida, now nine, was told by a girl at school that "the Jews killed Jesus," but replied with strict composure that that was very silly, "Jesus was just a story."

It was not until we moved to a new district, when Vida was six and Julian three, that the anticipated occurred. On arriving home after the first day of the term, Vida said "Daddy, my teacher says I must ask you if I'm Christian or Jewish." My theory that she would have acquired sufficient awareness to answer the question on her own had obviously been wrong.[3]

Teachers today are not likely to press children with such questions, at least not in America, but other children or their parents will. Even for Litvinoff, "more trouble arose when a lady came down our street canvassing for children to attend Sunday school classes at the local Anglican church." His children were terribly disappointed that they couldn't go when some of their close friends on the block went. Other problems that struck home for the Litvinoff children were the anti-Semitism of some of the Christian neighbors (Julian was startled to learn that Mrs. Clark didn't like him. "Brian told me his mother doesn't like you because you're Jewish") and the admonishments of their Jewish neighbor ("Mr. Goldstein says Jews should never eat bacon"; "Mr. Goldstein says we're to come over on Seder night"; "Mr. Goldstein says all Jewish boys and girls must go to synagogue").

Ultimately, the Mr. Goldsteins and the Mrs. Clarks in the neighborhood wreck the best-laid plans of intermarrieds. The idealistic plans for transmitting a harmonious view of the family's dual heritage founder on the prejudices of the people next door. Or perhaps, the people next door merely articulate some of the unspoken fears that lurk in the hearts of the couple themselves, at least as far as observances go. Whatever the case, it is clear, from both the Litvinoff story and from my own numerous interviews, that the prospect of raising children with a consistently humanistic philosophy that will neither bias them toward others nor leave them the object of others' prejudices is well nigh impossible. Although Litvinoff himself stuck close to his early philosophy of raising children without an exclusivist sense of group identity, he reluctantly acknowledged his children's apparent affinity for Jewishness and cultivated it by taking his children to Israel for occasional visits with friends and relatives. From his account, it appears that the Litvinoff children made a successful adjustment, becoming very much the ideal secular Jews that their father himself had wished to be. But of course, we only have the report of the father. The children have not spoken.

In an effort to get at other children's sides of the intermarriage experience, I conducted a survey between 1981 and 1983 of the offspring of the intermarried couples who are participated in my original survey of 1976. By their nature, written surveys— conducted through the mail—can never achieve the depth and color of the personal accounts we obtained in the original study of intermarrieds. But the survey did enable us to focus on several important "outcome" questions, that is, questions concerning the outcome of being raised in an intermarriage. One of the aims of the survey was to determine how children of intermarriages learn to view themselves: As Jews? As Christians? As something else? Do they identify more with their fathers or their mothers? We also wanted to find out what aspects of their respective heritages they incorporated in their own lives, particularly with respect to religion.

A second goal of the study was to find out what effect, if

any, intermarrige had on the relationships of children with their parents. Finally, we wanted to determine whether children who grow up in an intermarried family experience any significant insecurity about themselves—a feeling, perhaps, that they do not quite belong anywhere.

In 1937, the sociologist Everett Stonequist coined the term "marginal man" to describe the type of person who lives on the edge of two cultures, equally at home in both, but not fully belonging to either.[4] Stonequist relied heavily upon case histories of people born of intermarriages. Such individuals, Stonequist suggested, might have a broader cultural vision and achieve greater mobility between different heritages than most people, but they were likely to experience intolerance and non-acceptance from the two primary groups in which they moved. Stonequist's "marginals" paid a high price for their tenuous social position in the form of insecurity, anxiety, and discomfort. I wondered, too, whether the children of the intermarried couples I had encountered still paid such a steep price for their dual heritage.

In 1981, letters were sent to all the couples who took part in the 1976 study, asking them for the addresses of their children, aged 16 or older, who might be invited to participate in a follow-up study. According to our earlier data, the couples had a total of 792 children, 491 of them eligible by age for inclusion in the present survey. However, the inquiries to parents yielded usable mailing addresses for only 394.

During the first six months of 1982, a pretested questionnaire was sent to all the reachable offspring; and by September, 117 completed questionnaires had been received, representing children from 70 different families—a response rate of 29.6 percent.

Fifty-five respondents (47 percent) were men; 62 respondents (53 percent) were women. The group ranged in age from 16 to 46 years, but most were in their mid-twenties and 55 percent came from families with annual incomes of $50,000 or more. Thirty-seven (32 percent) were married, 80 (68 percent) were not.

The major portion of the study compared the responses of two subgroups—the offspring of conversionary marriages and those of mixed marriages. Forty-two respondents (36 percent) reported that their Christian-born parents had converted to Judaism; seventy-five (64 percent) stated that their Christian parents had not. Three-quarters of the respondents had Christian-born mothers and Jewish-born fathers—a proportion somewhat different from the 65/35 percent reported in previous intermarriage studies, including the 1976 AJC-sponsored study cited earlier. Another difference between the current sample and the 1976 sample is that, in the original survey, only 21 percent consisted of conversionary families, whereas 36 percent of the respondents of the current study come from such families. Thus, the present sample includes a disproportionately large number of children from conversionary marriages.

Like the earlier sample, this group of 117 respondents is somewhat skewed in its regional distribution and in income and education levels. Since this is the first study of such a population, there are no known general characteristics of the children of intermarriage against which this sample might be measured, and it is possible that children of intermarried couples from smaller communities, or less affluent backgrounds, might respond quite differently to some of the questions.

It should be noted that, with a sample this size, differences of 15 percent or more between the responses of children of conversionary marriages and those of mixed marriages are generally statistically significant. In terms of the study's objectives, however, the virtual absence of differences in some of the responses of the two groups is perhaps of equal interest.

The first and most direct questions about the effect of being raised in an intermarriage have to do with how the children identify themselves in terms of group or religious identity.

These are necessarily subtle and complex questions that do not readily lend themselves to survey questionnaires. But overt group identification can be investigated in this way, and it is one of the issues addressed by this study.

Jewish group identity is generally defined in terms of both religion and ethnic background. Among the questions the respondents were asked were what religion their parents had designated for them when they were born, and what religious group they most closely identified with at the time of the survey.

Children of conversionary marriages were more than three times as likely to identify as Jews than were children of mixed marriages. The overwhelming majority of the children of conversionary marriages were identified as Jewish at birth, and virtually all continued to identify themselves as Jewish at the time of the survey. Sixteen percent said they did not identify with any religion; none said they considered themselves Christians. By contrast, only 14 percent of the offspring of mixed marriages were identified as Jewish at birth, and 24 percent—a 10 percent increase—considered themselves Jewish at the time of the sur-

Religious Group Identity of Children at Birth and
Affirmed Now

Religious identity	Conversionary families		Mixed marriages	
	Birth (%)	Now (%)	Birth (%)	Now (%)
Jewish	86	84	14	24
Protestant	8	—	16	13
Catholic	—	—	16	13
Other	3	—	16	16
None	3	16	38	34

Children's Identification with Parents' Ethnic Ancestry

Identification	Mother converted (%)[a]	Mother not converted (%)[a]	Father converted (%)[b]	Father not converted (%)[b]
With father's ethnicity	48	30	50	19
With mother's ethnicity	8	26	—	19
With ethnicity of both	18	16	50	38
With ethnicity of neither	26	28	—	24

[a]Mother born Christian, father born Jewish.
[b]Mother born Jewish, father born Christian

vey. About one-third of this group identified with no religious group at all, and the rest considered themselves Christians or members of some other religious community.

The findings suggest that conversionary families, with their greater likelihood of identifying their children as Jewish at birth, tend to ensure a high probability of Jewish identification among the offspring, whereas mixed marriages are likely to result in a dramatic decline in Jewish identification in the subsequent generation.

The questionnaire also probed the respondents' ethnic identification. Do children of intermarriage identify more closely with their mother's ethnic heritage or their father's?

A sizable difference in percentage is revealed between those respondents who identified exclusively with the ethnic ancestry of their Jewish-born father when their Christian mother did not convert (30 percent) and those who identified exclusively with their non-converted Christian father when their mother was Jewish (19 percent). When the Christian parent did not convert, identification with the ethnic ancestry of both parents was more than double if the mother was Jewish (38 percent) than if the father was Jewish (16 percent).

The figures suggest that the children of conversionary marriages are more prone to see their ethnic identity, but not their religious identity, as an amalgam of two heritages. Thus, although the overwhelming majority (84 percent) of the respondents whose Christian parent had converted to Judaism affirmed their current religious identity as Jewish, far fewer (only about one-half) identified exclusively with the ethnic ancestry of their Jewish-born parent.

From these figures, it would appear that Jewish fathers are more likely than Jewish mothers to have children whose ethnic identification is exclusively Jewish. Christian fathers seem to have less of an effect on the ethnic identity of their children than Jewish fathers.

Having established whether the children of our intermarried families considered themselves to be Jews, I was curious to learn what some of the specific socializing experiences that might have led to their form of identification were. Was any formal religious instruction given? Did they belong to a church or synagogue? Did they go through any of the formal rites of passage associated with Judaism or Christianity? Or did they acquire their sense of religious and ethnic identity only through the natural flow of family attitudes and activities?

None of the children who came from conversionary families had been baptized. None had had a church Confirmation. On the other hand, all the boys from such backgrounds were circumcised, and all but nine of both the boys and the girls had had a Bar or Bat Mitzvah or had been confirmed in a synagogue. In about one-third of the cases, they had gone through both a Bar or Bat Mitzvah and a confirmation ceremony in the synagogue.

Of the seventy-five respondents who were the offspring of mixed marriages, 28 percent had been baptized and 20 percent had gone through a church Confirmation. Of this same seventy-five, about 14 percent had gone through a Bar or Bat Mitzvah or a Jewish Confirmation. As these numbers suggest, the majority had none of the customary Christian or Jewish formal rites of passage.

Three-quarters of the children of conversionary marriages were receiving or had received some type of formal Jewish education. About 10 percent had also received some type of formal education about Christianity in a Sunday school prior to the time the converting parent became Jewish. Among the children of mixed marriages, nearly one-half had received some type of Christian instruction, usually a brief stint at Sunday school in early childhood. About 20 percent also received some type of formal Jewish instruction; often at a local Hebrew Sunday school, also in early childhood. Children of conversionary marriages, it seems, are significantly more likely to receive formal religious instruction than are the children of mixed marriages, and, of course, they are vastly more likely to receive such instruction in Judaism, not Christianity.

One of the obvious consequences of religious socialization is membership in a synagogue or church, and our respondents were no exception. Of those who were from conversionary families, 90 percent had parents who belonged to a synagogue, and 45 percent reported themselves as belonging to a synagogue as well. None reported belonging to a church. Of those who were from mixed marriages, 20 percent had parents who belonged to a synagogue and 33 percent had parents who belonged to a church. In but a handful of cases, they came from families in which one parent belonged to a synagogue and one to a church. Of these respondents themselves, 25 percent reported belonging to a church and 5 percent reported belonging to a synagogue.

These faceless numbers suggest a variety of conclusions about how the offspring of intermarriages handle their religious identities. Those who come from conversionary families clearly have a stronger grounding in institutional religious life. They are more likely to have been given formal religious instruction,

Frequency of Synagogue and Church Attendance by Children of
Intermarriers

	In conversionary families		In mixed marriages	
	Teens (%)	Adults (%)	Teens (%)	Adults (%)
Synagogue attendance				
Never	15	42	81	93
High holidays	36	50	15	5
4 to 5 times a year	15	4	4	2
6 to 10 times a year	12	4	—	—
More than 10 times a year	22	—	—	—
Church attendance				
Never	64	96	36	47
1 to 2 times a year	31	4	19	18
3 to 4 times a year	—	—	7	13
5 to 10 times a year	—	—	—	5
More than 10 times a year	5	—	38	17

more likely to have had parents who belonged to a synagogue, and are more likely to belong to a synagogue themselves. In short, they are far more likely to have roots in institutionalized Judaism than are children of mixed marriages. The children of mixed marriages are not only far less likely to be linked to institutionalized Judaism through rites of passage, Jewish education, or synagogue membership, they are also significantly less likely to be linked to any kind of institutionalized religion. Interestingly, although there may be a more formal affiliation among the children of conversionary families than among those from mixed marriages, attendance at religious services seems to

be somewhat more prevalent among the offspring of mixed marriages, at least in church, as the following table indicates.

It is also interesting to note that nearly one-third of the
offspring of conversionary families attended church a couple of
times a year, at least when they were children or teenagers, but
not as adults. This finding underscores the fact that conversion
does not eliminate the ties that many such families continue to
maintain with their Christian relatives; ties that will draw at
least some of them into occasional participation in Christian
services with their families. Presumably these ties affect children
more than adults, since children are more apt to be left in the
care of their grandparents.

Membership and participation in institutionalized religion
may, at times, reflect social conventions rather than personal
conviction or preference, but holiday celebrations, particularly
in one's home, express more directly a person's heartfelt choices
with respect to his ancestral or chosen heritage. Therefore, I
asked respondents which major holidays they celebrated and
how they celebrated them. The tables below are numerical sum-
maries of their replies. Adults were asked to recollect which

Which Holidays Did You Celebrate?

	Adult Children of		Teenagers of	
Holidays	Conversionary families (%)	Mixed marriages (%)	Conversionary families (%)	Mixed marriages (%)
Christmas	70	95	65	95
Easter	19	53	19	80
Hanukkah	76	30	92	33
Passover	79	35	100	37
Rosh Hashanah	66	22	88	21
Yom Kippur	66	18	88	20
Shabbat	21	4	50	6

Have You Done Any of the Following in the Past Year?

| | Children of | |
| | Conversionary families (%) | Mixed marriages (%) |
Religious activity		
Decorated a Christmas tree	22	81
Gave Christmas presents	59	93
Lit candles on Hanukkah	69	24
Made a Seder on Passover	69	24
Fasted on Yom Kippur	44	6

holidays were observed in their parents' home when they were teenagers. All respondents were asked to indicate whether they themselves had marked five particular holidays in specific ways the previous year.

The findings show that although children of conversionary marriages observed Jewish holidays far more than did children of mixed marriages, they were less observant than their parents had been. As many as 70 percent of the offspring of conversionary marriages also celebrated Christmas—a figure considerably higher than the percentage of mixed marriage offspring who celebrated Passover and Hanukkah, the two most popular holidays among American Jews. Although observance of Hanukkah is widely believed to have evolved as a kind of "Jewish equivalent" to Christmas, the cultural preference in intermarried families seems to be largely in favor of Christmas. A great many respondents from conversionary families who reported celebrating Hanukkah also said they celebrated Christmas, and only a relatively small proportion of those from mixed marriages who celebrated Christmas also reported celebrating Hanukkah.

It should, however, be added that the observance of Christmas in the homes of most conversionary families focused on its most secular and contemporary dimension—the giving of presents. The percentage of children of mixed marriages who lit Hanukkah candles in their homes (24 percent) was approximately the same as the percentages of children of conversionary marriages who decorated a Christmas tree (22 percent).

Both tables show that a large majority of the respondents from conversionary marriages observed the major Jewish holidays of Rosh Hashanah, Yom Kippur, and Passover.

In 1981, sociologist Steven M. Cohen surveyed a random sample of American Jewish adults.[5] He found that approximately 77 percent attended a Passover Seder, 67 percent lit candles on Hanukkah, and 54 percent fasted on Yom Kippur. It appears that children of conversionary marriages who identify as Jews tend to behave in these matters much as the broader Jewish community does, except for their additional observance of the secular aspects of Christmas.

These statistics on holiday observances suggest, as did the earlier data on the more institutional forms of religious identification, that most children are not evenhandedly exposed to an amalgam of traditions. Rather, they are more likely to be exposed to either predominantly Jewish or predominantly Christian traditions. The one and only notable exception to that pattern is Christmas and Hanukkah. Their coincidence on the calendar probably contributes to both being celebrated in some of the intermarried families. Yet, even with these two popular holidays, only about 20 percent of those from mixed marriages—nearly all of whom celebrate Christmas—celebrate Hanukkah. Also, only about 20 percent of those from conversionary marriages—nearly all of whom celebrate Hanukkah—celebrate Christmas with a tree in the house.

Perhaps the artifacts and concrete expressions of each tradition—its symbols, its texts, its tunes, and its emotional evocations—do not blend easily. Perhaps intermarried parents feel that they cannot transmit both traditions with equal sensitivity, or they do not want to expose themselves and their children to potentially disturbing theological and existential questions.

Whatever the reason, the ideals of cultural pluralism, in

which intermarriage itself is embedded, do *not* translate into a true blending of traditions in the raising of children. For the most part, children of intermarriages are reared either as Jews or Christians, not as both, and in perhaps as many as one-third of the cases, they are reared as *neither*.

In the latter case, there is an apparent desire on the part of intermarried families to avoid the "ethnic" traits of either side. They want to present a home to their children, as well as to themselves, that is indifferent to any potentially disturbing incongruities. Writing of such families in 1960, the Harvard senior Philip Rosten—himself a product of a mixed marriage— observed that the parents

> lean towards gentile mannerisms not from purpose but from inevitability. What is "Jewish" can usually be labeled, while what is gentile is so entwined with the American culture that differentiating features are impossible.[6]

Further, he quotes one of his interview subjects on the same theme:

> There was no attempt to make any culture dominant. Nobody in our family ever thinks in Jewish or gentile terms. Our home is sort of a cultureless thing—I guess you'd say our culture is liberalism rather than any national or religious culture.[7]

Of course, what is imparted by families to their children and what is felt by the children as the recipients of their parents' teachings is not quite the same thing. Although children may be raised as Christians or Jews, the awareness of their dual heritage affects their upbringing in ways that are not likely to be found in the single-heritage Jewish or Christian home. A child raised as a Jew might be reminded by a friend or a neighbor, "You're not really Jewish, are you?" A child raised as a Christian, but being aware that one of his parents is Jewish, may have the following type of rude awakening:

> I was young—seven or eight. There was a little girl who came over to play with me and we were running on the hillside and she said "Let's pretend we're Nazis trying to kill Jews." Well here I

was and I knew my mother was Jewish, but I didn't know what a
Jew was.[8]

Such brief and almost impersonal encounters cast a disturbing shadow over whatever form of heritage children are being
raised in at home and makes them realize that they really are not
quite like all other Jews or Christians. Nor do they have the
option of a unique self-definition all their own because, by and
large, society is already divided into ethnic and religious groupings with which the great majority have learned to identify.
Depending on how the offspring of intermarriage becomes
aware of their particular social identity, Rosten observed, they
may become either *conflicted* about their identity, or perhaps
more *self-aware*, or they may become *detached* altogether from
both their heritages, seeking out environments in which the
issue will be ignored. Those who are conflicted are never quite
sure with which group they ought to identify, which group will
accept them for its own. The self-aware feel that they have a
unique ability to look at beliefs and customs in a much broader,
almost scholarly analytic perspective ("I've been forced to view
things from two different sides and I've been accustomed to
looking at just about everything in more than one way"). Those
who are detached take the position,

I don't want to be thought of as a half-breed Jew or gentile. I want
to be taken as an individual without any binding ethnic ties, to
choose my own religion, my own culture, and have people accept
that instead of putting me with Jews or gentiles.[9]

Rosten's "mischlings," as he called them, were a very small
and special group: fifteen undergraduates at Harvard and
Radcliffe in 1954. By virtue of their clearly elite circumstances,
they were surely more apt to feel marginal, and particularly
uneasy about their Jewishness than a larger and more representative cross section of offspring of intermarriage. Nevertheless,
the psychodynamics of marginality, the mixed feelings of inner
conflict, the deeper sense of self-awareness and detachment, are

likely to be found to a greater or lesser degree among most of this population.

But what effect do those psychological states have upon the attitudes that these children harbor toward their two heritages? How do those feelings affect their relationships with their immediate families? And, ultimately, how do those feelings play themselves out in these children's sense of self?

In a somewhat clumsy attempt to gauge attitudes toward their respective heritages, my survey asked respondents "How would you rate your attitude. . . ?" toward Judaism, Jews as people, Christianity, Christians as people, synagogue activities, church activities, and religion in general. Their replies were scored as "favorable," "neutral," or "unfavorable." The table below describes how the offspring of conversionary and mixed marriages compare on these attitudes.

The terms used in the table were intentionally nebulous to permit each person to attach to them whatever meaning he or she wished. Such terms as "What is your attitude toward . . . ?" generally permit people to take their emotional pulse, as it were, without feeling inhibited, intellectually.

Looking at the numbers, one is immediately struck by the fact that most of the children of both types of intermarriages are generally favorably disposed toward Jews and Christians alike. When it comes to the religions themselves, the differences between the two groups become more apparent. First, both groups are far less inclined to have favorable attitudes toward religion in general than they have toward Jews and Christians, or toward Judaism or Christianity. Also, those who are from mixed marriages are significantly more likely to have an unfavorable attitude toward religion than are those who are from conversionary families.

The children of mixed marriages are about equally as likely to be favorable in their attitudes toward both Judaism and Christianity. The children of conversionary marriages (the conversion

Percentage of Respondents with Varying Attitudes on Seven Items Pertaining to Groups

Items	Attitude	Children of Conversionary families	Children of Mixed marriages
Religion in general	Favorable	58	39
	Neutral	14	19
	Unfavorable	28	42
		100	100
Judaism	Favorable	75	63
	Neutral	19	21
	Unfavorable	6	16
		100	100
Jews as people	Favorable	83	65
	Neutral	11	26
	Unfavorable	6	9
		100	100
Christianity	Favorable	47	61
	Neutral	22	20
	Unfavorable	31	19
		100	100
Christians as people	Favorable	86	86
	Neutral	8	14
	Unfavorable	6	—
		100	100
Synagogue	Favorable	33	15
	Neutral	25	40
	Unfavorable	42	45
		100	100
Church	Favorable	3	34
	Neutral	26	26
	Unfavorable	71	40
		100	100

being to Judaism), on the other hand, are more likely to be more favorably disposed toward Judaism than they are toward Christianity. Yet when it comes to their attitude towards Jews-as-people and Christians-as-people, the children of conversionary marriages were about equally as likely to feel favorably disposed toward both, whereas the children of mixed marriages were significantly more likely to be more favorably disposed toward Christians than toward Jews.

Finally, the numbers demonstrate that neither group is likely to be favorably disposed toward the institutional forms of either Judaism or Christianity. Only a minority of either group expressed a favorable attitude toward synagogue or church activities.

Looking at these percentages in the light of the earlier figures on religious and holiday observances, one sees a pattern emerge. The children of conversionary families participated in Jewish religious observance much more than did the children of mixed marriages. This same group also tend to have more favorable attitudes toward religion in general, and Judaism in particular, and toward Jews as people than those who were raised in mixed marriages. Yet, their obviously greater sense of Jewishness notwithstanding, they seem to be as favorably disposed towards Christians-as-people as they are toward Jews. By contrast, the children of mixed marriages, who had evidenced much less religious participation, particularly in Judaism, are about equally favorably disposed to both religions, but are more likely to be favorably disposed toward Christians-as-people than toward Jews-as-people.

In short, what these numerical patterns suggest is that although the children of conversionary marriages might be more observant as Jews, their attitudes are as appreciative of Christians as they are of Jews. The children of mixed marriages, on the other hand, are far less likely to observe Jewish traditions, but they are also less likely to be equally appreciative in their attitudes toward Jews and Christians. They are more likely to lean toward the latter. Put another way, the children of conversionary marriages behave and socialize much more like typical American Jews than their counterparts from mixed marriages, but they feel an apparently equal "at homeness" with Christians. The children of mixed marriages, for the most part, neither participate in the rites of Jews, nor do they feel as favorably disposed toward Jews as they do toward Christians.

In fact, other items in our survey indicated that the great majority of offspring from both types of intermarriages are likely to have a mixed group of Jewish and Christian friends (whereas most typical American Jews tend to have a primarily Jewish circle of friends), and the great majority of both groups *rejected* the typically particularistic notion that Jews have a greater responsibility to help other Jews in need than they have to help all people in need equally. To the extent that the children of conversionary marriages reject any of the common expressions of Jewish particularism (the notion of exclusive group membership and exclusive group loyalty), they are likely to experience a sense of marginality within the Jewish community. On the other hand, to the extent the children of mixed marriages participate in the practices and institutions of Jewish life and feel a sense of attachment to the Jewish people, they are likely to feel marginal either to some members of their own family or to the Jewish community. Probably that is one important reason why the offspring of mixed marriages do not gravitate toward identification with or participation in the Jewish community.

It might be argued that one of the chief reasons for the differences between the children of conversionary marriages and the children of mixed marriages is that, according to traditional Jewish law, children who are born to a Christian mother are not Jewish unless they convert, even though children born to a Jewish mother and a Christian father are presumed to be Jewish under that law. Since most intermarriages are, in fact, between Jewish men and Christian women, the resulting off spring of those marriages are simply not Jewish. The philosophical inequities inherent in that law, and its possible demographic consequences in writing off large numbers of children as not Jewish by definition, have led the Reform movement as recently as in 1983 to issue a resolution on "patrilineal descent."[10] That resolution declared that, at least according to the Reform rabbinate in America, "the child of one Jewish parent is under the presumption of Jewish descent" regardless of whether that one parent is the father or the mother. "This presumption of the Jewish status," the resolution continues, "is to be established through appropriate and timely public and formal acts of identification with the Jewish faith and people." The resolution was immediately rejected and vociferously criticized by both the Conservative and the Orthodox Jewish leadership as a gross violation of the *halachah* and a potential threat to the unity and viability of the future of the Jewish community.

Fortunately or unfortunately, depending on one's perspective, there is nothing in the reported experiences of the children of intermarriage that would lend much social scientific support to either side of the issue. There are isolated instances in which children of Jewish fathers and Christian mothers, who have been raised as Jews, are denied the institutional privileges of Jewishness, such as Bar or Bat Mitzvah, because of the *halachah*. The Reform resolution certainly corrects that injustice and the emotional strains that might be created thereby. However, as we have seen, such children tend to be a rather small minority. Most children who are raised in a mixed marriage of that type are minimally exposed to their Jewish heritage. They are not likely to seek the benefits of the Reform resolution. It remains an open question as to whether the resolution itself might stimulate more of such families to raise their children as Jews in the first place. We have also seen in Chapter Eight that a great many conversions are sought precisely to enable the family to forge a more homogeneous heritage for their children. The Reform resolution on "patrilineal descent" could possibly undermine that

268 CHAPTER NINE

particular motivation for conversion. Therefore, in the present
state of our understanding the process of identification among
the children of intermarriages, that resolution remains of du-
bious value. It certainly does not advance the cause of Jewish
family unity the same way as the conversion of the mother does.

However children of intermarriages ultimately think of
themselves in terms of religion and ethnic identity, they invariably have to come to terms with the fact that their parents have
different backgrounds, that they may have both Jewish and
Christian relatives, and that they may feel, at times, an emotional pressure to view themselves as belonging to one branch of
the family more than the other.

As Stonequist's marginal man concept underscores, it has
long been believed that children of intermarriage belong, in
some sense, to two cultures, without feeling fully at home in
either. To probe for evidence of such discomfort, the questionnaire asked the respondents to react to eleven statements describing different emotional states, and to indicate how frequently they experienced these feelings.

Individual replies were scored on a scale from "1" to "7." A
score of "1" meant that the respondent experienced the particular feeling rarely or never. A score of "7" meant that he or she
had the particular feeling often. All of our respondents' scores
were added to arrive at a group average for each item.

For the first seven items, a high average score suggests a
high degree of comfort about relationships with others, as well
as a feeling of comfort about themselves. For the last four items,
a low average score suggests a high degree of comfort. Thus, the
scores on the items in the table can be read as indicating higher
or lower degrees of what Stonequist called marginality. More
discomfort suggests greater marginality.

Among the first seven items, the respondents demonstrated their highest degree of marginality on Items 3, 4, and 7
("having a sense of close fellowship with a group," "being at

Indicators of Comfort with One's Identity

Indicator	Average frequency
1. Being well liked by those I really care about	6.0
2. Finding family occasions a source of warmth	5.4
3. Having a sense of close fellowship with a group	4.7
4. Being at peace	4.6
5. Being confident about my future	5.1
6. Knowing my own mind and what I want out of life	5.0
7. Some Higher Being caring about me	3.2
8. No one really understanding me	3.2
9. Wishing I could be born again as someone else	1.8
10. Lacking historic roots	2.2
11. Wishing I knew what my parents expect of me	2.4

peace," "some Higher Being caring about me"). Among the last four items, their marginality was highest on Item 8 ("no one really understanding me").

On the other hand, apparently very few respondents felt their marginality keenly enough to want to be born again as someone else (Item 9), nor did they seem to connect their feelings of marginality, if they had any, with a lack of historic roots (Item 10).

The fact that the majority felt well liked by those they really cared about (Item 1) and found their families to be a source of warmth (Item 2) suggests that respondents did not experience a significant sense of discomfort concerning their identity—and probably could not be said to experience much marginality. It should be emphasized that these scores remain only exploratory and speculative estimates of the degree of marginality among children of intermarriage. However, in the absence of more reliable data, and given the widespread concern about possible emotional consequences of child rearing in intermarriage, it is useful to have some benchmark measurements. For the present, it may be hypothesized that marginality, in the sense described by Stonequist, is not a problem for the great majority of such children.

It is worth pondering that respondents from mixed marriages felt no greater lack of historical roots (Item 10) than children of conversionary marriages; neither did they indicate a greater sense of conflict about what their parents expected of them (Item 11). In fact, if the responses are representative of a broader pattern, children of conversionary marriages appeared to be somewhat more prone to symptoms of marginality. There could even be a slight psychological disadvantage to being the child of such a marriage.

For example, when the replies from the same survey to the question "How much personal stress have you experienced in choosing your ethnic identity?" were rated on a scale from "1" ("very little or none") to "8" ("a great deal"), the average score for all the respondents was 2.2. The children of conversionary marriages whose mothers converted scored 2.4, and the children of mixed marriages whose mothers did not convert scored 2.0—again, differences that are not statistically significant, but consistent enough to be suggestive. It is possible that since in conversionary families religion is of greater significance than in mixed marriages, children of the former are somewhat more prone to experience symptoms of marginality than are children of the latter. This hypothesis remains to be tested by more controlled research.

Do children of intermarried families feel a conflict of loyalties relative to their parents? Are they drawn more to one parent than to the other? Do the children of conversionary marriages differ in this matter from children of mixed marriages?

To measure the emotional closeness of the respondents to parents and relatives, they were asked to imagine themselves at the center of five concentric rings.

Ring 1, nearest to the center, represents the closest relationship, with each consecutively numbered ring representing

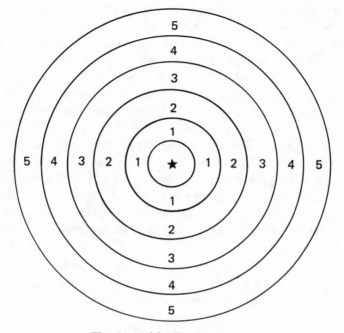

The rings of family closeness.

relationships of progressively greater emotional distance. The respondents were asked which of those circles best represented how close they felt to their mothers, fathers, and grandparents.

On the average, the children of conversionary families had an overall parental closeness score (a summary value measuring their closeness to both parents) of 1.5; they were equally close to both their parents.

The overall parental closeness score for the children of mixed marriages was 1.7. These respondents were closer to Jewish-born mothers (1.2) than to Jewish-born fathers (1.9). Those with Christian fathers in this group were even closer to their Jewish mothers (1.2) than were children of conversionary marriages with Jewish fathers and mothers who became Jewish

(1.5). But children of typical conversionary marriages (Christian mother converted) were slightly closer to their Jewish fathers (1.5) than children of typical mixed marriages in which their Jewish fathers were married to non-Jewish mothers (1.9). The closeness score for Christian fathers was 1.8.

In my 1976 survey of intermarried couples, men and women were asked how frequently they visited their parents and spoke to them on the telephone. About 55 percent of the Jewish-born respondents said they saw their parents at least a few times a month; 77 percent spoke to them on the telephone at least once a week. Only about 30 percent of their Christian-born mates visited their own parents as often, and only 55 percent called them as frequently. In the present survey of their children, those who no longer lived at home were asked how often

Frequency of Children Spending at Least One Hour with Parent

| | Families converted to Judaism | Mixed marriages | |
| | Christian-born mother[a] (%) | Christian mother (%) | Christian father (%) |
Frequency			
With mother			
At least once a week	55	37	20
At least once a month	15	19	30
Less than once a month	30	44	50
With father			
At least once a week	50	40	20
At least once a month	20	14	20
Less than once a month	30	46	60

[a]Since there were so few examples, the category of Christian-born father was omitted.

Frequency of Children Talking to Parents on Telephone

Frequency	Families converted to Judaism	Mixed marriages	
	Christian-born mother[a] (%)	Christian mother (%)	Christian father (%)
With mother			
At least once a week	70	48	74
At least once a month	30	52	26
Less than once a month	—	—	—
With father			
At least once a week	70	44	45
At least once a month	30	47	44
Less than once a month	—	9	11

[a]Since there were so few examples, the category of Christian-born father was omitted.

they spent at least one hour with their parents and how often they spoke with them by telephone.

The children of conversionary marriages were more likely to see and call their parents than the children of mixed marriages. Children of mixed marriages were far less likely to see their parents on a weekly or even a monthly basis. However, children of Jewish mothers married to non-converted Christian fathers called their mothers most often. This finding is in keeping with the "closeness score" of 1.2, established earlier.

In sum, the children of conversionary marriages seemed to follow the characteristically Jewish pattern of frequent visiting and phoning, and the children of mixed marriages seemed to follow the more characteristically Christian pattern of less frequent visiting and phoning (except for the frequent telephone contact with their Jewish mothers). This finding is consistent with a number of sociopsychological theories of cognitive and affective balance. Such theories postulate that people confronted by very difficult or impossible choices often withdraw from both alternatives. Perhaps one way that children of mixed marriages resolve having to "choose" between the heritages of their parents is to distance themselves from both parents, at least in terms of contact if not in feelings. Since the children of conversionary marriages are not faced with such a choice, they may be more likely to feel equally close to both of their parents and closer to their parents altogether than the children of mixed marriages.

Placements on the consecutively numbered concentric rings make it clear that the respondents felt less close to their grandparents than to their parents. Interestingly, although children of conversionary marriages were slightly closer to their parents than children of mixed marriages, the pattern was reversed in relations with their grandparents. The children of conversionary marriages had an average closeness score of 3.0 *vis-à-vis* their grandparents, and the children of mixed marriages had an average score of 2.7. It should be recalled that the higher the numerical score, the greater the implied emotional distance.

Children of conversionary marriages were found to be slightly closer to their Jewish grandparents (average score, 3.0) than to their Christian grandparents (3.4), whereas respondents from mixed marriages were somewhat closer to their Christian grandparents (average score, 2.6) than to their Jewish grandparents (2.8).

Why children of conversionary marriages seem more distant from their grandparents on both sides is open to conjecture. It is possible that the conversion to Judaism by the Christian spouse creates an emotional distance between the conversionary couple and their Christian in-laws, which carries over to the children. Paradoxically, the conversion may also lead to distancing from Jewish in-laws who, in many cases, urged that step on the younger couple. Having satisfied their Jewish parents, some conversionary couples may express their residual resentment by distancing themselves and their children from the parents.

The adult respondents were asked whether they and their family had lived "close by" (within an hour's drive) their grandparents as children or teenagers.

More respondents in all categories had lived closer to their Jewish grandparents as children than to their Christian grandparents. Even more children of mixed marriages had lived near their Jewish grandparents than those of conversionary marriages; in fact, 69 percent of the children of unconverted Christian fathers—more than any other group—had done so. A closer scrutiny of the data revealed that in this last category of respondents, 38 percent, the highest percentage of all, had lived within walking distance of their Jewish grandparents. Children of typical conversionary marriages, on the other hand, had the highest percentage (46) living more than a five-hour drive away from their Jewish grandparents.

Obviously physical proximity to one's grandparents is not

Children's Residential Proximity to Grandparents[a]

Proximity to	Families converted to Judaism	Mixed marriages	
	Christian-born mother[b]	Christian mother	Christian father
Maternal grandparents[c]	38% (C)	47% (C)	69% (J)
Paternal grandparents[c]	54% (J)	68% (J)	40% (C)

[a]Columns do not add up to 100% because figures were omitted for those living farther than one hour by car.
[b]Since there were so few examples, the category of Christian-born father was omitted.
[c]Christian (C) or Jewish (J) grandparents.

necessarily either a cause or a consequence of particular attitudes or behavior, but the findings underscore that there is no simple association between the conversion of the Christian partner and the closeness of extended Jewish family ties.

Social research has found that grandchildren are generally closer to their maternal than to their paternal grandparents. This is even more likely when the maternal grandparents are Jewish. In this study, too, when the respondents were asked how much they enjoyed spending time with their grandparents, all seemed more favorably disposed toward their maternal than toward their paternal grandparents.

Fifty-eight percent of the children of conversionary marriages, and 36 percent of those of mixed marriages, reported that they enjoyed the company of their maternal grandparents "a lot." In this case, however, the maternal grandparents were Christian. In contrast, 45 percent of the conversionary offspring and 33 percent of the mixed marriage offspring felt the same way toward their paternal—Jewish—grandparents.

Enjoy the Company of Grandparents

| | Children of | |
	Converted Jewish families, Christian-born mother (%)	Mixed marriages, Christian mother (%)
Of maternal grandparents		
A lot	58	36
Somewhat	34	48
Not at all	8	16
Of paternal grandparents		
A lot	45	33
Somewhat	33	56
Not at all	22	11

Since the analysis in this table was limited to children of Christian-born mothers, it is not known whether the preference for the Christian grandparents was due to maternal influence or religious–ethnic variables or both.

These academic numbers seem rather remote from the concrete experience of the people whose lives we have been examining, yet they do add up to an overall impression that the children of intermarriages do not feel any keen pangs of conflict or confusion about themselves, nor do they have fractured relationships with their parents and families. Marginality and all its associated psychological perils undoubtedly plague some, but most are unperturbed by their dual heritage.

The increasing incidence of intermarriage, and the declining significance of ethnic and religious differences between Jews and Christians, in general, have probably lessened the emotional consequences of being raised in an intermarried home; the Mrs. Clarks and the Mr. Goldsteins of this world notwithstanding.

Although the emotional and family consequences of being raised in an intermarriage may not be as painful or as difficult as we might have thought on the basis of research on earlier generations, its social consequences for Jewish and Christian communities could be. To a very great extent, the survey evidence we have seen in this chapter points to a pervasive "anti-institutionalism" as far as religious and ethnic identity is concerned. This attitude undermines institutions, of course, but in the long run, it could also leave the majority of the children of intermarriage bereft of any institutional support for whatever conception of religion or ethnicity they might have.

Chapter Ten

LIVING WITH PARTIAL ANSWERS

Living with Partial
Answers

All happy families resemble one another, Tolstoi wrote in *Anna Karenina*; every unhappy family is unhappy in its own fashion. From the glimpses we have had into the lives of a number of men and women, it should be evident that intermarriage belies that generalization. Happy or not, intermarriages differ among themselves, as well as from other marriages, in a number of ways. Among themselves, intermarriages differ according to whether one spouse will embrace and join the religion of the other, whether both spouses will retain their attachments to their respective religious and ethnic backgrounds, or whether they will both reject their own heritages—possibly even embracing a new one. Each of these strategies has worked for large numbers of intermarrieds, with many happy marriages the result. Each has also produced many instances of great struggles within individual hearts as well as between married people and their respective parents.

Intermarriages differ from marriages between people of the same religious and ethnic background, to a greater or lesser extent, depending on how much importance the partners attach to their respective traditions. Were such traditions of little concern or consequence, intermarried couples and their families would be not much different from all other families. The fact is that over 90 percent of Americans classify themselves as being of one religion or another when asked in public opinion polls, "What is your religious preference?" Even if they are not particularly religious in their personal lives, or members of a church or synagogue, the overwhelming majority see themselves as being part of and having roots in some ways linked to a distinct religious heritage. As that linkage, however minimal, is usually through one's parents and ancestors, some religious heritage is likely to be part of most American's inner sense of self, or identity. Consequently, intermarriages differ from others. Couples who come from different religious and ethnic backgrounds will have to bridge cultural, historical, ritual, belief, or value systems that, in fact, are separate in the world around them. What most intermarried couples affirm by the very nature of their relationship is disconfirmed by the group structure of society at large. Given the overall tolerant social climate of modern America, fortunately the discrepancy between the affirmations of intermarrieds and the social reality of group differences and even hostilities need not lead to any personal hardships. Yet, as we have seen repeatedly, those differences will not go away. One way or another, virtually all intermarried couples grapple with the differences in their heritages in an emotional as well as a practical effort to reconcile their love for one another with whatever attachments they may have to their traditions.

The chief purpose of this book has been to explore the variety of ways in which couples engage in that reconciliation, to examine the various forces around them that further or hinder that effort, and to comprehend what consequences intermarriage brings on the marriage partners and their children.

We have found that marriages between Jews and Christians fall into four broad categories. They are the *conversionist,* the *assimilationist,* the *integrationist,* and the *rejectionist.* The conversionist marriage—which constitutes about 33 percent of intermarriages—overcomes differences in religion by having the Christian partner convert to Judaism. The assimilationist marriage—constituting approximately 10 percent of intermarriages—tries to eliminate the differences in background by having the Jewish partner convert to Christianity. The largest proportion, about 43 percent, represent what I call the integrationist marriage. Neither spouse converts to the religion of the other or to any other religion. They maintain some linkage with their respective traditions, which they attempt to combine into a blended family heritage of their own making. The remaining approximately 15 percent of intermarriages are composed of couples who decided to relinquish any involvement with their respective traditions and to reject all forms of religious or ethnic group identification.

Which of the four strategies couples will choose, and with what specific ingredients of mind and heart they will forge a harmonious life together, depends on a host of factors: the extent of their own religious training and commitment; the quality of their relationships with their parents during childhood and at the time of marriage; the relative social status of the marriage partners; and the social climate of their communities and personal networks, that is, its tolerance for diversity.

Regardless of the ways in which these forces work themselves out in the lives of particular couples, the great majority of the intermarriages we have seen—the conversionist and the integrationist types—fly in the face of long-prevailing conventional wisdom regarding marriages between Jews and Christians. Both happy and unhappy intermarriages point to the powerful tensions between love and tradition. They point to the persistence of subtle meanings, symbols, and values from a dimly understood past in each human heart, even as it tries to express and define itself in its longings of the present. This is of particular significance for the Jewish community, which has long feared that intermarriage on a large scale could spell its doom.

There are two commonly held views about the intermarriage of Jews. One is that it leads to their eventual disappearance through assimilation. The other is that it leads to a cultural blending that is beneficial both to the minority culture and to the majority Christian culture. Some look on intermarriage with great favor and hopeful anticipation, while others openly deplore it. Generally speaking, the people who have been the most enthusiastic champions of intermarriage, themselves often in such marriages, have subscribed to Zangwill's image of America as a "melting pot." They tend to view their intermarriage as he viewed such marriages: a testimonial to the power of love over age-old social divisions, a testimonial to the creative power of the open society. They see intermarriage as the most intimate human context in which once-divided cultures are melded together to yield a new and enriched heritage.

The alternate view, which sees intermarriage as leading to the eventual assimilation and ultimate disappearance of Jews, has its roots in a somewhat different image of American society. According to this image, America is composed of a majority culture, predominantly Christian, and a number of minority groups, including Jews, who do not identify completely with the majority. Although, in principle, American society endorses the value of cultural pluralism—the notion that all minority cultures ought to flourish harmoniously in the body politic—the relatively higher status of the majority culture leads to the adoption of the values and habits of the majority by the minority. And, in the case of intermarriage, it leads to the assimilation of the minority member into the majority group. This particular perspective has led a great many Jewish parents, as well as Jewish communal leaders, to be alarmed by the increasing incidence of marriage between Jews and Christians. They fear that Jews might eventually be swallowed up by the majority.

Although both perspectives embrace the essentially multifarious character of American society, they also both see that character as somehow inherently unstable, at least by implication. They both see social and cultural diversity as a condition that will inexorably give way to homogeneity, and they both see in intermarriage the path to that outcome. The difference between the two perspectives is that out of the Zangwillian "melting pot" there would emerge a new cultural amalgam, with only a few traces of the diverse cultural ingredients that went into it. From the other perspective, assimilated minorities would disappear into the majority, leaving no trace of their distinctive culture.

Of course neither of the two perspectives is monolithic. Many subscribe to variations of each. For example, the "melting pot" image has two variants: one secular, the other religious. The secular variant regards all religions as basically irrational and divisive. According to this variant, intermarriage enables people to overcome religion in general, thus bringing society closer to an age of universal harmony based on human emotions and reason. The religious variant regards the differences among the various faiths as largely misguided human inventions that have distorted underlying divine principles upon which all religions, in fact, are based. From this latter variant, intermarriage actually hastens the melting away of the superficial husk of most religions to reveal a pure religion untainted by age-old social prejudices. Loving men and women will distill and combine the essential kernels of truth from their respective faiths and blend them into a new harmonious heritage in their homes.

Not surprisingly, those who subscribe to a "melting pot" image of society, in any of its variant forms, are the most accepting of intermarriage. And those who intermarry are likely to find that image most congenial. A careful examination of the living reality of intermarriages, however, offers little support for any form of the "melting pot" idea. With but rare exceptions, the couples who are most ready to blend their heritages, the group I have called the integrationists, are generally less familiar with their own or with the other's traditions than are couples in the other categories. They wear their Jewishness and Christianity very lightly, attending to them with minimal holiday observances that will give pleasure to the children and not inconvenience the adults. In most cases, their blend of heritages is not a search for a true religion nor is it the realization that humanist–rationalist values have overcome the need for the trappings of any religion. Rather, in the vast majority of cases, intermarriage involves a negotiated détente of habits, observances, and tastes. "I'll go with you to church at Easter time if you come with me to the synagogue on Rosh Hashana," or the more popular "You can put up the Christmas tree, and I'll light the *menorah.*'' In these and many other similar examples, couples are not so much forging a blended cultural heritage as they are recognizing each other's need for a continued, albeit limited attachment to their respective religious traditions. Their love for one another leads them to grant each other limited territorial rights for their respective heritages within a jointly shared home. In turn, each is present for and partakes in the customs and observances of the other as a kind of goodwill ambassador of a foreign culture.

The view of intermarriage as a stage in the long-term trend toward the assimilation of minorities into the dominant majority also has a least two variants: one external, the other internal. One side envisions the absorption of the intermarried Jew into the Christian society. The other side envisions the transformation of the Jewish family and culture by incorporating Christians into its folds. Those who hold these views, be they parents of intermarrieds or others, generally tend to take a dim view of intermarriage for either personal or ideological reasons, and often for both. They fear, as Lewis Benjamin wrote in his book, *The Passing of an English Jew* (1907): "What centuries of persecution had been powerless to do, will have been effected in a score of years by friendly intercourse."[1] If the observances of children of mixed marriages are any indicators of the long-term effect of intermarriage, Lewis Benjamin may be proved correct.

But as we look back upon much of our data and a great many of the couples we encountered on these pages, it seems fairly clear that intermarriage itself rarely leads to assimilation. Particularly in those instances in which the Jewish partner converted to the religion of his Christian mate, or where both husband and wife relinquished their ancestral identification, it is quite clear that assimilation preceded rather than followed intermarriage. Yet in from 20 to 40 percent of the mixed marriages, which mainly fall into what I have called the integrationist type, there were all kinds of life-styles that perpetuated the Jewish as well as the Christian heritage (e.g., celebration of Hanukkah and Passover, synagogue attendance on the High Holy Days, Christmas and Easter celebrations, and objects in the home that reflected the dual family heritage). Although these families may be on the road to assimilation in the long run, they appear to be very much at the beginning of that road and not at its end. Therefore, it is unlikely that they consciously wish to have the Jewish elements of the family disappear in the majority culture. Should the assimilation of the descendants of such families, in fact, come to pass after a generation or two, it will have to be explained in more complex terms than simply as a result of their parents' or grandparents' intermarriage. It will have to be explained also in terms of the larger social pressures brought to bear on them and, most specifically, in terms of the responses of the Jewish and Christian communities to them.

The large and increasing number of conversions to Judaism also strongly challenges the notion that intermarriage makes assimilation inevitable. As we have seen, when one Jewish partner had a strong commitment to his religion, and the Christian partner a relatively weaker commitment, there was a strong probability that the latter would convert. Indeed, it was generally the spouse with the stronger commitment and the greater power in the relationship who determined how family heritages would be articulated in the family's life-style.

These facts would dictate against the popular sociological view that, in intermarriages between minority and majority members (i.e., Jews and Christians), the minority group member will seek to assimilate into the culture and social world of the majority group member. They also leave us with a question about the causes and consequences of modern intermarriage between Jews and Christians.

Neither the cultural blender of the "melting pot" nor the expected workings of minority–majority group relations would seem to account satisfactorily for what we have observed in the lives of most of our intermarried couples. The détente of heritages among most of the mixed marrieds, the persistence of

Judaism or Christianity among a significant number, the large and growing numbers of conversions into the minority religion coupled with some of the lingering attachments of converts to Judaism (e.g., the Bar Mitzvah with the Vietnamese flavor), all force us to abandon the conventional wisdom. We are moved to ask again, How do we explain that love does not conquer all other feelings of attachment or commitment, particularly those to one's ancestral tradition? And by the same token, How do we explain the persistence of tradition in the lives of couples who, by their very choice of marriage partners, have indicated that they can live beyond if not without tradition in significant areas of their lives? Perhaps the answer may be found in the uniquely modern understanding of love and tradition.

Historian Morton Hunt has described the unique meanings that different ages have attributed to the human emotions they have called love. The ancients, like Lucretius, saw love as a dangerous emotion that "causes frenzied and irrational actions, and consumes the lover's strength and wastes his substance." Others saw it as an inflicted condition flung upon men and women by cupid. Some, perhaps more lighthearted, saw love merely as a game. With the rise of Christianity, love was sanitized, sublimated, transfigured into devotion, and made the principal civilizer of otherwise brutish hearts. Knights and troubadours of the eleventh century elevated that Christianized sentiment in the art form and life-style of courtly love. "One of the most original contributions of courtly love," Hunt writes, "was its attribution of character improvement and ethical value to the condition of loving. The theme appears in every incarnation of romantic love." Additional refinements by such Neoplatonists as Dante and Petrarch, by such Puritans as Milton, by hosts of Victorian writers, and most lately by psychologists of various persuasions have transformed love into a life-building force, an existential necessity. Writes Hunt,

> The contemporary ideal of marriage is distinctly romantic since it definitely allies love to ethical goals; modern men and women are

overwhelmingly convinced that without married love, life is bar-
ren, selfish, ungenerous, and pointless. The very critics of romantic love agree on this ethical value of married love. Psychia-
trists view the ability to love givingly and generously as a sign of
maturity, and maturity is agreed to be good. Anthropologists
grant to love a life-preserving value since it meets two creatures'
emotional needs and in the process continues the species and
society.[2]

Through its various historical transformations, love has
emerged as that quality of emotion that drives men and women
to self-discovery, self-expression, and self-improvement. To the
Socratic commandment, "Know thyself," the modern mind has
added, "Love thyself," or better, "Complete thyself" through
loving and being loved by another. The high place accorded to
love among the gamut of human emotions, finally, places the
felt experience of the individual at the center of social life. In a
most profound way, it marks the realization of one of the cardinal modern freedoms: the pursuit of happiness.

From the vantage point of the modern love ethic, nothing
could be more natural than the marriage of men and women
across all kinds of social barriers. If those barriers stand in the
way of individual happiness, they must be eliminated, at least in
the lives of these couples. After all, love is the principal avenue
to the completion of the self, or so the romantic ideals of the
modern age have taught us. But were this view of love and its
relationship to self all encompassing, why would intermarried
couples struggle to come to terms with the differences in their
heritage? Why do they all not simply toss their divisive traditions to the wind—as some of them, in fact, have done?

Attachment to parents, kin, and community may be part of
the answer. But, it seems to me, there is more to it than simple
psychological dependency. Love itself, with its modern focus on
the inner world of the individual, may foster a sense of isolation
on the part of all married couples who, for all kinds of reasons,
deeply value privacy. The world created by love is very small. It

is highly fragile, and necessarily transitory, as life is transitory. Moreover, the needs of the self for completeness and security are not entirely met by sexual and emotional bonding alone. There is general agreement among social scientists that human beings also have an inescapable need for meaning, a kind of cosmic order. In his treatise on tradition, sociologist Edward Shils writes,

> Human beings do not fare well in a disordered world. They need to live within a framework of a world of which they possess a chart. They need categories and rules . . . criteria of judgment. They cannot construct these for themselves. This is one of the limits of the ideal of total emancipation and self-regulation. . . . Human beings need the help of their ancestors . . . biological ancestors as well as ancestors of communities and institutions. . . . The loss of contact with the accomplishments of ancestors deprives subsequent generations of the guiding charts which all human beings, even geniuses and prophets, need.[3]

Without the moral, aesthetic, and evaluative charts that are the products of a live tradition, the world is bound to be experienced as chaotic and meaningless. It is not an experience conducive to personal happiness.

Yet many people cannot be completely enthusiastic about the great religious traditions that have given meaning and cosmic order to the world through the centuries. As these great systems evolved, they hardened into intellectual and institutional orthodoxies in which average men and women, in fact, have found less and less meaning and comfort. Communal and institutional ancestors came to be perceived by some as pedants, rather than reliable sympathetic guides. Instead of dispelling chaos and meaninglessness, they came to add to them, for some, through the imposition of rules and restrictions that had lost their meaning over time, but were still enforced. Perhaps that is the tragic flaw of great traditions: Their capacity to change and remain relevant lags behind the shifting conditions of human life that beg for meaning.

Since the mid-eighteenth century, the pace of change in Western societies has quickened so that the life charts provided by Christianity and Judaism have become less and less meaningful to an increasing number of people. Religion was replaced by the material and intellectual promises of science, or by a domestic happiness to be forged out of sexually-based love. Modern marriage and consciousness, in general, and intermarriage, in particular, are themselves products of this great transformation.

However, by the late twentieth century, science and sexual love have also been disqualified in the minds and hearts of large numbers of people as dependable sources of meaning or order, much less salvation. The threat of human self-annihilation through the application of scientific discoveries and the persistence and even the increase of dangers linked to the political exploitation of the environment have led masses of thoughtful men and women to abandon their earlier expectations of science as a cure for all ills.

The increasing divorce rate, the conflict over sex roles, and the persistence of difficulties along the path to a sexual and emotional utopia through marriage have also led to a scaling down of expectations about the redemptive power of love.

The reappraisal of science and love as bases for a secular salvation has given age-old traditions, once doomed to oblivion, a new lease on life. Since the mid-1970s, America has witnessed a religious revival that has brought millions of men and women back to ancestral traditions despite a powerful secular trend that had prevailed for nearly a hundred years. Although few of the intermarried couples we have encountered on these pages have been touched by this revival directly, they have not been immune to the need it reflects. Their needs include a persistent thirst for meaning that transcends the vagaries of the present moment, a quest for community, and the desire to feel connected to the past and the future as well as to live in the present.

The willingness of modern men and women to acknowledge and meet these needs inevitably leads them to look upon tradition with more curiosity, or even sympathy, than they might have fifty or one hundred years ago. At the same time, they have made it clear that they are not prepared to abandon the great sense of personal fulfillment that is to be had from love. In the final analysis, then, intermarriers differ from other couples only in that they stand at the cutting edge of the universal dilemma of modern consciousness: how to resolve the legitimate claims of love and tradition. Their lives, as presented on these pages, represent the partial answers to that question. But perhaps that question can only be partially answered.

NOTES

Preface

1. Oscar Handlin, *The Uprooted* (New York: Grosset & Dunlap, 1951), p. 3.
2. Egon Mayer and Carl Sheingold, *Intermarriage and the Jewish Future* (New York: American Jewish Committee, 1979).
3. Egon Mayer, *Children of Intermarriage* (New York: American Jewish Committee, 1983).

Chapter 1

1. Francesco Alberoni, *Falling in Love* (New York: Random House, 1983), p. 6.
2. Ibid., p. 17.
3. John B. Halsted, *Romanticism: Definition, Explanation, and Evaluation* (Lexington, MA: D. C. Heath and Company, 1965).
4. Edward Shorter, *The Making of the Modern Family* (New York: Basic Books, Inc., 1975); Ellen K. Rothman, *Hands and Hearts: A History of Courtship in America* (New York: Basic Books, Inc., 1984).
5. Morton M. Hunt, *The Natural History of Love* (New York: Alfred A. Knopf, Inc./Minerva Press, 1959, 1967).
6. Ibid., p. 26.
7. Joseph Stein, *Fiddler on the Roof.* Broadway musical.
8. Hunt, *The Natural History of Love*, p. 25.
9. William M. Kephart, *The Family, Society, and the Individual*, 3d Ed. (New York: Houghton Mifflin Company, 1972), p. 137.
10. Shorter, *The Making of the Modern Family*, p. 148.
11. Selma Stern, *Court Jew* (Philadelphia, PA: Jewish Publication Society, 1951).
12. Rothman, *Hands and Hearts*, pp. 28–29.
13. Jan Lewis, *The Pursuit of Happiness: Family and Values in Jefferson's Virginia* (New York: Cambridge University Press, 1983).
14. Shorter, *The Making of the Modern Family*, pp. 121–122.

15. Ibid., p. 148.
16. J. Hector St. John Crevecoeur, *Letters of an American Farmer* (New York: Dolphin Books, n.d.), pp. 49–50.
17. Israel Zangwill, *The Melting Pot* (New York: Macmillan Company, 1908).
18. Arthur Mann, *The One and the Many* (Chicago: Chicago University Press, 1979), p. 100.
19. Ibid., pp. 75–76.
20. Ibid., p. 111.
21. Ibid., p. 117.
22. Heinrich Graetz, *History of the Jews* (Philadelphia, PA: The Jewish Publication Society, 1956), v. 5, p. 697.
23. Malcolm H. Stern, "Jewish Marriage and Intermarriage in the Federal Period, 1776–1840," *American Jewish Archives* (November 1967), pp. 142–143.
24. Milton L. Barron, "The Incidence of Jewish Intermarriage in Europe and America," *American Sociological Review* 11:1 (February 1946), pp. 6–13.
25. Moshe Davis, "Mixed Marriage in Western Jewry," *Jewish Journal of Sociology* 10:2 (December 1968) pp. 177–210.
26. Ande Manners, *Poor Cousins* (Greenwich, CT: Fawcett Publications, 1972), p. 25.
27. Arthur Ruppin, *The Jews in the Modern World* (New York: Arno Press, 1973), pp. 318–321.
28. Chaim I. Waxman, *America's Jews in Transition* (Philadelphia, PA: Temple University Press, 1983), pp. 29–31.
29. National Jewish Population Study, "Intermarriage" (New York: Council of Jewish Federations, 1971). Mimeograph.
30. Isaac Metzker, *A Bintle Brief* (New York: Ballantine Books, 1971), pp. 76–77.
31. Ibid., pp. 91–92.
32. Julius Drachsler, *Democracy and Assimilation* (New York: Macmillan Company, 1920), p. 126.
33. Milton M. Gordon, *Assimilation in American Life* (New York: Oxford University Press, 1964), p. 80.
34. Elihu Bergman, "The American Jewish Population Erosion," *Midstream* 23:8 (October 1977).
35. Andrew M. Greeley, *Crisis in the Church* (Chicago: Thomas More Press, 1979), p. 150.
36. Richard D. Alba, "Social Assimilation among American Catholic

National Origin Groups," *American Sociological Review* 41:6 (1976), pp. 1030–1046.

37. Konrad Bercovici, *Crimes of Charity* (1917).
38. Michael Novak, *The Rise of the Unmeltable Ethnics* (New York: Macmillan Publishing Company, 1971).
39. Herbert J. Gans, *The Levittowners* (New York: Vintage Books, 1969); Michael Parenti, "Ethnic Politics and the Persistence of Ethnic Identification," *American Political Science Review* 61 (September 1967), pp. 717–726.
40. Bill R. Lindner, *How to Trace Your Family History* (New York: Dodd Mead Company, 1978); Arthur Kurzweil, *From Generation to Generation: How to Trace Your Jewish Geneology* (New York: Morrow, 1980).
41. United Jewish Appeal, *Book of Songs and Blessings* (New York: United Jewish Appeal, 1980), p. 25.
42. Floyd J. Fowler, *1975 Community Survey: A Study of the Jewish Population of Greater Boston* (Boston: Combined Jewish Philanthropies, 1977); Albert Mayer, *The Jewish Population Study of the Greater Kansas City Area* (Kansas City: Jewish Federation, 1977); Bruce A. Phillips, *Denver Jewish Population Study* (Denver: Allied Jewish Federation, 1982).
43. David M. Eichhorn, *Conversion to Judaism* (New York; Ktav Publishing House, Inc., 1965), p. 213.
44. Slogan from a popular bill board advertisement in the New York area for Levy's Real Jewish Rye Bread.

Chapter 2

1. Peter L. Berger and Hansfried Kellner, "Marriage and the Construction of Reality," *Diogenes* 4 (1964), p. 8.
2. Emile Durkheim, *The Division of Labor in Society* (New York: The Free Press, 1964), pp. 79–81.
3. Shorter, *The Making of the Modern Family*, p. 71.
4. Ibid., pp. 258–259.
5. Rothman, *Hands and Hearts*.
6. Berger and Kellner, "Marriage and the Construction of Reality," p. 9.
7. Ibid.
8. Ibid.
9. Ibid., p. 5.
10. Ibid., p. 13.
11. Alberoni, *Falling in Love*, p. 35.

12. Ibid., p. 25.

13. Lewis Benjamin, *The Passing of an English Jew* (1907).

Chapter 3

1. Moshe Weissman, *The Midrash Says* (Brooklyn, NY: Benei Yaakov Publications, 1980), p. 218.

2. Isaac M. Fein, *The Making of an American Jewish Community: The History of Baltimore Jewry* (Philadelphia, PA: The Jewish Publication Society, 1971), p. 7.

3. *The Universal Jewish Encyclopedia* (New York: The Universal Jewish Encyclopedia, Inc.) 1941 Ed., s.v. "Goldwater," pp. 41–42.

4. Max Vorspan and Lloyd P. Gartner, *History of the Jews of Los Angeles* (San Marino, CA: The Huntington Library, 1970), p. 8.

5. Ibid., p. 24.

6. Ibid., pp. 95–96.

7. Ibid., p. 97.

8. Jacob Rader Marcus, *American Jewry Documents Eighteenth Century* (Cincinnati, OH: The Hebrew Union College Press, 1959), p. 188.

9. Ibid., pp. 137–138.

10. Ibid., pp. 30–31.

11. Stephen Birminghan, *Our Crowd: The Great German Jewish Families of New York* (New York: Harper & Row, 1967).

12. Marvin and Bernard Kalb, *Kissinger* (New York: Little, Brown, and Co., 1974).

13. Kephart, *The Family*, pp. 323–329.

14. Erich Rosenthal, "Studies of Jewish Intermarriage in the United States," *American Jewish Year Book* 64 (1963), pp. 41–43.

15. Rela Geffen Monson, *Jewish Campus Life* (New York: American Jewish Committee, 1984), p. 23.

Chapter 4

1. Louis A. Berman, *Jews and Intermarriage: A Study in Personality and Culture* (New York: Thomas Yoseloff, 1968).

2. Karl Abraham, *Clinical Papers and Essays on Psychoanalysis* (New York: Basic Books, 1955), v. II, pp. 48–50.

3. Robert K. Merton, "Intermarriage and the Social Structure," *Psychiatry* 4:3 (August 1941), pp. 361–374.

4. Monson, *Jewish Campus Life*, pp. 32–35.

5. Marshall Sklare, *America's Jews* (New York: Random House, 1971); Charles Liebman, *The Ambivalent American Jew* (Philadelphia, PA:

The Jewish Publication Society, 1973); Steven M. Cohen, *American Modernity and Jewish Identity* (New York: Tavistock Publications, 1983).

6. Gallup Report, "Survey Finds Greater Acceptance of Interracial, Interfaith Marriages" (Princeton: The Gallup Organization, June 1983).

7. John E. Mayer, *Jewish-Gentile Courtship* (New York: Free Press, 1961), p. 62.

8. Ibid., p. 70.

9. Ibid., p. 90.

10. Michelle Green and Linda Marx, "Twice-Divorced Mary Tyler Moore, 45, Heads for the Altar Again," *People Magazine* (December 5, 1984), pp. 152–153.

11. Robert Windeler, "Diana Ross 'Mahogany' Star & Bob Silberstein Have a Marriage That's Ok," *People Magazine* (January 26, 1976), pp. 23–26.

12. Ira L. Reiss, *The Family System in America* (New York: Holt, Rinehart, and Winston, Inc., 1971), pp. 90–95.

13. Mayer, *Jewish-Gentile Courtship*, p. 89.

14. Ibid., p. 90.

15. Ibid., p. 91.

16. Philip Blumstein and Pepper Schwartz, *American Couples* (New York: William Morrow and Company, 1983), p. 307.

17. Alberoni, *Falling in Love*, p. 30.

Chapter 5

1. Andrew M. Greeley, *Why Can't They Be Like Us?* (New York: E. P. Dutton & Company, 1971).

2. Evelyn Kaye, *Crosscurrents: Children, Families and Religion* (New York: Clarkson N. Potter, Inc., 1980), pp. 15–30.

3. Ibid., p. 18.

4. Ibid., p. 19.

5. Ibid., p. 20.

6. Ibid., p. 24.

7. Ibid., p. 27.

8. Ibid., p. 28.

9. Harold T. Christensen and Kenneth E. Barber, "Interfaith versus Intrafaith Marriages in Indiana," *Journal of Marriage and the Family* 29:3 (August 1967), pp. 461–469.

10. Alberoni, *Falling in Love*, p. 35.

11. Edward Shils, *Tradition* (Chicago: University of Chicago Press, 1981), p. 34.
12. Ibid., p. 96.

Chapter 6

1. Gordon, *Assimilation in American Life*, p. 80.
2. Will Herberg, *Protestant–Catholic–Jew* (New York: Doubleday and Company, Inc., 1955).

Chapter 7

1. Alberoni, *Falling in Love*, p. 97.
2. Letha D. Scanzoni and John Scanzoni, *Men, Women, and Change* (New York: McGraw-Hill, Inc., 1981), pp. 437–463.
3. Ibid., p. 453.
4. Kephart, *The Family*, p. 399.
5. Jerold S. Heiss, "Premarital Characteristics of the Religiously Intermarried in an Urban Area," *American Sociological Review* 25:1 (February 1960).
6. David Caplovitz and Fred Sherrow, *The Religious Drop-Outs: Apostasy among College Graduates* (Beverly Hills, CA: Sage Publications, Inc., 1977).

Chapter 8

1. *The Holy Scriptures*, "The Book of Ruth" (Philadelphia, PA: The Jewish Publication Society, 1955), p. 1087.
2. Eichhorn, *Conversion to Judaism*, pp. 63–65.
3. *Universal Jewish Encyclopedia*, s.v. "Proselytes."
4. Shlomo Eidelberg, *The Jews and the Crusaders* (Madison, WI: The University of Wisconsin Press, 1977), p. 37.
5. Waxman, *America's Jews in Transition*, pp. 19–20.
6. *Universal Jewish Encyclopedia*, s.v. "Converts."
7. Dean R. Hoge et al., *Converts, Dropouts, and Returnees* (New York: The Pilgrim Press, 1981), pp. 28–30.
8. Dean R. Hoge and Kathleen M. Ferry, *Empirical Research on Interfaith Marriage in America* (Washington, DC: United States Catholic Conference, 1981), pp. 18–21.
9. Egon Mayer, "Jews By Choice," *Proceedings of the Rabbinical Assembly* (New York: Jewish Theological Seminary, 1983).
10. Ibid., p. 59.
11. Mimeographed leaflet circulated within the community.

12. Sydney B. Hoenig, "Conversion during the Talmudic Period," in Eichhorn, *Conversion to Judaism*, p. 59.
13. Ibid., p. 64.
14. Paul Cowan, *An Orphan in History* (New York: Doubleday and Company, 1982), p. 132.
15. Ibid., p. 172.
16. Ibid., p. 217.
17. Ibid., p. 231.
18. Ibid., p. 231.
19. Lydia Kukoff, *Choosing Judaism* (New York: Union of American Hebrew Congregations, 1981), pp. 11–12.
20. Ibid., p. 14.
21. Ibid., p. 17.
22. Ibid., p. 18.
23. Alexander M. Schindler, "Address to the Board of Trustees of the Union of American Hebrew Congregations," (Houston, TX: December 2, 1978). Mimeograph.
24. Naomi Godfrey, "Ben-David," *The Jewish Week* (October 19, 1984), p. 4.
25. Ibid.
26. Steven Huberman, *New Jews: The Dynamics of Religious Conversion* (New York: Union of American Hebrew Congregations, 1979); Sanford Seltzer, "Who Enrolls in the Introduction to Judaism Program? A Report From Four American Cities," *Horizon Institute Report* (New York: Union of American Hebrew Congregations, 1984).
27. Huberman, *New Jews*, p. 25.
28. Ibid., p. 26.

Chapter 9

1. Emanuel Litvinoff, "Children of Two Inheritances: How It Worked Itself Out," *Commentary Magazine* 15:3 (March 1953), p. 273.
2. Ibid., p. 274.
3. Ibid., p. 275.
4. Everett V. Stonequist, *The Marginal Man: A Study in Personality and Cultural Conflicts* (New York: Charles Scribner and Sons, 1937).
5. Steven M. Cohen, "National Survey of American Jews, 1981," American Jewish Committee. Mimeograph.
6. Philip Rosten, *The Mischling: Child of the Jewish-Gentile Marriage* (Cambridge, MA: Harvard University, 1960). Undergraduate Honors Thesis, p. 48.

7. Ibid.
8. Ibid., p. 53.
9. Ibid., p. 56.
10. Central Conference of American Rabbis, "Resolution on the Status of Children of Mixed Marriages." Adopted on March 15, 1983. Mimeograph.

Chapter 10

1. Benjamin, *The Passing of an English Jew.*
2. Hunt, *The Natural History of Love*, p. 370.
3. Shils, *Tradition*, p. 326.

SELECTED BIBLIOGRAPHY ON INTERMARRIAGE

Barron, Milton L. *The Blending American: Patterns of Intermarriage.* Chicago: Quadrangle Books, 1972.

Bensimon, Doris and Francoise Lautman. *Un Mariage. Deux Traditions: Chretiens et Juifs.* Brussels, Belgium: Editions de l'Universite de Bruxelles, 1977.

Berman, Louis A. *Jews and Intermarraige: A Study in Personality and Culture.* New York: Thomas Yoseloff, 1968.

Besanceney, Paul H. *Interfaith Marriages: Who and Why.* New Haven: College & University Press. 1970.

Bossard, James H. and Eleanor S. Boll. *One Marriage, Two Faiths: Guidance on Interfaith Marriage.* New York: Ronald Press. 1957.

Cahnman, Werner J. *Intermarriage and Jewish Life in America.* New York: Herzl Press, 1963.

Caplovitz, David and Harry Levy. *Interreligious Dating among College Students.* New York: Bureau of Applied Social Research, 1965.

Drachsler, Julius. *Intermarriage in New York City: A Statistical Study of the Amalgamation of European Peoples.* New York: Columbia University Press, 1921.

Eichhorn, David M. *Conversion to Judaism: A History and Analysis.* New York: Ktav Publishing House, 1966.

Eichhorn, David M. *Jewish Intermarriages.* Satellite Beach, FL: Satellite Books, 1974.

Epstein, Louis M. *Marriage Laws in the Bible and the Talmud.* Cambridge, MA: Harvard University Press, 1942.

Gordon, Albert I. *Intermarriage: Interfaith, Interracial, Interethnic.* Boston: Beacon Press, 1964.

Hathorn, Raban *et al. Marriage: An Interfaith Guide for All Couples.* New York: Association Press, 1970.

Hoge, Dean R. *Converts, Dropouts, and Returnees.* Washington, DC, U.S. Catholic Bishops Conference, 1981.

Kaye, Evelyn. *Crosscurrents: Children, Families and Religion.* New York: Clarkson N. Potter, 1980.

Luka, Ronald. *When a Christian and a Jew Marry.* New York: Paulist Press, 1973.

Marcson, Simon. *The Prediction of Intermarriage.* Chicago, University of Chicago, 1950. Ph.D. Dissertation.

Mayer, John E. *Jewish-Gentile Courtships.* New York: The Free Press, 1961.

Porterfield, Ernest. *Black and White Mixed Marriages.* Chicago: Nelson-Hall, 1978.

Rosten, Philip. *The Mischling: Child of the Jewish-Gentile Marriage.* Cambridge, MA, Harvard University, 1960. Unpublished Honors Thesis.

Sherrow, Fred S. *Patterns of Religious Intermarriage among American College Graduates.* New York, Columbia University, 1971. Unpublished Ph.D. Dissertation.

AFTERWORD

How families evolve throughout life as they tackle the challenges of love and tradition cannot be summed up adequately by anyone. Each family ultimately writes its own book. My hope is that by faithfully recording and transmitting aspects of other people's lives I have helped you in the inevitable task of deepening your own self-understanding. But as long as life continues to unfold, that task does not end for either you or me. I would hope that you might take a little time to reflect on those features of the book that have been the most meaningful to you, or perhaps, comment on some aspects of your own personal experience with love and tradition and drop me a note. I will make a sincere effort to respond to your communications and to keep you informed of my continued thinking and research in this area. You may reach me by writing to

Dr. Egon Mayer
Department of Sociology
Brooklyn College
Brooklyn, N.Y. 11210

NAME INDEX

305

SUBJECT INDEX